CREATING
Catholics

CREATING
Catholics

Catechism and Primary Education
in Early Modern France

KAREN E. CARTER

University of Notre Dame Press
Notre Dame, Indiana

Library of Congress Cataloging-in-Publication Data

Carter, Karen E., 1951–
    Creating Catholics : catechism and primary education in early modern France /
Karen E. Carter.
        p.   cm.
    Includes bibliographical references and index.
    ISBN-13: 978-0-268-02304-1 (pbk. : alk. paper)
    ISBN-10: 0-268-02304-2 (pbk. : alk. paper)
    1. Catholic Church—Education—France—History—17th century.
2. Catholic Church—Education—France—History—18th century.
3. Education, Primary—France—History—17th century.   4. Education,
Primary—France—History—18th century.   5. Baltimore catechism—Study
and teaching (Primary)—France.   6. Counter-Reformation—France.   I. Title.
    LC506.F7b C25   2010
    268'.8244—dc22
                                                                2010037735

∞ *The paper in this book meets the guidelines for permanence and durability of
the Committee on Production Guidelines for Book Longevity of the Council on
Library Resources.*

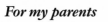
For my parents

Contents

Tables

Acknowledgments

Financial support for my research was provided by the Cultural Services Division of the French Embassy in Washington, D.C., in the form of a Chateaubriand fellowship for the 2003–2004 academic year. I owe a great debt to the staff of the departmental archives in Auxerre, Reims, and Châlons-en-Champagne, for their patience with a green American researcher. I may have gotten a lot of inquisitive looks, but my questions were always answered with professionalism and kindness. I must also thank the Georgetown University Department of History for a Davis fellowship in 2005–2006, which gave me a free semester to write, and the College of Family, Home and Social Sciences at Brigham Young University for a research grant that allowed one last trip to the archives. Previous versions of some portions of the book have appeared in *French Historical Studies* (published by Duke University Press) and the *Catholic Historical Review* (published by the Catholic University of America Press); I thank those institutions for granting me permission to draw upon this material again here. I am also grateful to the two anonymous readers who read the manuscript and provided many useful suggestions, as well as to the editorial staff at the University of Notre Dame Press for indispensable help in putting the final version of the book together.

I began working on the topic of catechisms and education twelve years ago, so my debts are many. At Georgetown, special thanks must go to my mentor, Jim Collins. He may have been baffled by my lack of interest in French wines—perhaps an unforgivable failing for a French historian—but his support for my work never suffered for it. Amy Leonard's considerable efforts on my behalf are also much appreciated. Other friends, colleagues, and faculty members who lent support during my Georgetown years include Roxie France-Nuriddin, Alison Games, Doris Goldstein, Harriet Gray, Deborah Hirschi, John McNeill, Jo Ann Moran Cruz, Anita Nolen, Felicia Roşu, and Richard Stites. I also thank Keith Luria, of North Carolina State, for his insightful comments and suggestions during the dissertation phase of this project.

My colleagues at Brigham Young have become tremendous friends, and I cannot thank them enough for their personal and academic support. My greatest debt is to Craig Harline, who suggested that I study catechisms in the first place; without his support over the last twelve years, this project would never have reached completion. Lunches with Craig, Kendall Brown, Eric Dursteler, Don Harreld, Chris Hodson, Shawn Miller, Susan Rugh, and other "lunch van" regulars sustained me through the writing process and provided much-needed diversions. Rebecca de Schweinitz, Amy Harris, Aaron Skabelund, and I all arrived in the department together as junior faculty and created an instant support group for each other—thanks go to each of them for all of the conversations and gripe sessions in the hallways and over meals. Members of history department and campus-wide writing groups read several portions of the manuscript and gave me useful insights about my research and writing.

Last but not least—my family. I don't think any of my siblings ever really wanted to know much about catechisms, but they have listened to me anyway, and some of them even read chapters. I am grateful to them for putting up with me year after year. My nieces and nephews are too young to understand anything about what I do, but I have their pictures surrounding me whenever I sit down to write, and their little faces have made me smile and urged me forward on many an occasion. My parents, Mary and Steven Carter, deserve much, much more than a simple thank you, even if it is in print. This book is as much yours as it is mine. *Merci infiniment.*

Introduction

One of the most interesting questions in the study of religion centers around belief: why do adherents of a particular religious confession believe what they believe? For the early modern period in France, this question has often led historians to matters of religious conversion. The Protestant Reformation in France was primarily an urban event, and by the time the religious wars began most towns and cities counted at least a few Huguenots among their numbers. Because the inhabitants of so many of France's urban areas experienced violent conflicts over religious issues during the second half of the sixteenth century, a number of historians have attempted to uncover the reasons for this division by examining whether factors like gender, profession, location, and class might account for confessional preference.[1] These historians ultimately discovered that the reasons behind religious conversion defy simple explanations, but in their attempts to understand religious motivations and sensibilities they uncovered the fulcrum upon which the whole Reformation hinged: the ordinary lives and religious beliefs of France's urban artisans, printers, and magistrates.

On the other hand, the focus on urban Protestantism leaves out the masses of French peasants who remained Catholic through the upheavals of the religious wars and beyond. While that crucial moment of decision for a Huguenot or a member of the Catholic League makes for a dramatic symbol of the changes that the Reformation brought about in the second half of the sixteenth century, the long-term commitment of the French countryside to Catholicism stands out as an even more tantalizing—and axiomatic—characteristic of the early modern period. My initial question about the nature of religious belief, when placed in a rural context, leads to many additional questions that encompass not only belief itself but also the dissemination of religious knowledge and practices over time and space. Why did the peasant farmer attend Mass every Sunday and take communion at least once a year? Why did he insist on baptizing his children, and why did he and his wife dedicate even a small portion of their scant resources to the Catholic Church? Why did they believe in Catholicism, and why did their children and their children's children continue to believe?

There are, I believe, two elements of early modern Catholicism that can significantly advance the historian's understanding of these particular questions: catechism and rural primary schools (*petites écoles*). Although no historical document can fully explain why any individual or society chose to believe in and follow a given religion, the surviving documents surrounding catechisms and schools do provide unique details that allow us to contemplate the framework within which French Catholics constructed and understood religious belief and religious education. This framework was not always entirely orthodox, nor did it remain uniform from individual to individual. As a key element of early modern religious education, however, catechisms were an important step in a standardization process that could strengthen that framework and give it more stability. Reform-minded clergymen envisioned a comprehensive program of religious education that would unify and systematize Catholic practices at both the parish and diocesan levels. They saw themselves as using catechisms and schools to create Catholics through the orthodox instructions provided for each new generation of believers.

The bishops' primary motivation for aiming their educational efforts at children rather than adults resulted from their conviction that the type of religious education children received would have a tremendous influence on what they believed—and how they demonstrated that belief—as adults. The archbishop of Reims, Alexandre-Angélique de Talleyrand-Périgord (uncle of the Revolutionary churchman-turned-diplomat Talleyrand), emphasized in his late eighteenth-century rules for schoolteachers that the right sort of education could indeed make all the difference in ensuring the dissemination of orthodox Catholicism:

> Children are the most precious part of Christianity, the resources of the church and the state; it is in the cultivation of these young plants that a pastor can begin the renewal of his parish, and without attention to the children, the pastor will never complete this work. Scripture and experience confirm this truth, and teach us that the first impressions are the most lasting that a man has; he does not stray from the path that he entered in his youth even in old age. When he has received from his earliest years the principles of integrity and religion, he usually conserves them for all his life. Thus, nothing merits our attention, and the attention of the curés, more than the establishment and the conduct of schoolmasters, who are charged in part with the education of children.[2]

What better way, then, to examine questions of belief than to focus on children's education? Catechism classes and primary schools—the gathering of parents and clergy in homes, schools, and churches to teach doctrine and behavior to the next generation of believers—were meaningful social and religious practices that allow the historian to investigate the creation and transmission of Catholic belief. It is around these two institutions, and the Catholic Reformation movement to which they owed their origins, that this book is organized. It argues that children's religious education was the centerpiece of Catholic reform in the seventeenth and eighteenth centuries, and as a result Catholic believers—especially in rural areas—knew more about the doctrines and behaviors of their religion than they ever had in the past. At the same time, the bishops' program of religious education was implemented by curés, parents, and village notables at the parish level, and these local authorities adapted the program to suit their own needs. Thus, the Catholic Reformation can be seen as a result of interaction and compromise between the clergy and the laity, rather than a top-down process of institutional reform.

Catechism and the Foundations of Orthodoxy and Orthopraxy

The core of all primary and religious education in the early modern period was the catechism. On Sundays and feast days in parishes all over France during the seventeenth and eighteenth centuries, curés opened the doors of their churches and rang the bells, calling the children to catechism class. By listening to and memorizing a series of questions and answers, children between the ages of seven and fourteen learned the basic doctrines of Catholicism—everything they would need to know for their salvation. Even children who could not read learned the catechism, since every child who wanted to take first communion had to demonstrate that he or she had successfully memorized the text.

Catechisms written by a number of different authors were used throughout France in the early modern period, but most contained similar elements. Catechisms usually began with the Apostles' Creed—a twelve-article statement of fundamental Christian beliefs. In the process of memorizing the Creed, children learned orthodox doctrines about God, Jesus Christ, and the mysteries of the Incarnation and the Redemption. Sections on the Decalogue offered lessons on the Ten Commandments as well as the commandments of the church. The sacraments received the greatest amount of attention in most catechisms; children memorized more responses to questions on baptism, confession, and communion than any other topic. Finally, children learned a number of prayers by heart (in both Latin and French, in many cases).

Catechisms taught much more than theology, however. In fact, the catechisms that bishops published often downplayed even the most basic and fundamental aspects of Catholic doctrine in order to empha-size the more outward and visible elements of Catholicism—primarily the moral and ethical code of behavior prescribed by the Decalogue and the public, ritualistic characteristics of the sacraments. Bishops be-lieved that the regulation of the laity's behavior would lead to belief, rather than the other way around, so they limited the amount of the-ology in their texts and instead included material that taught children how to properly perform their Christian duties.

The catechetical method itself emphasized behavior rather than doctrine as well, first by requiring children to memorize and publicly recite the texts (usually immediately before or during the increasingly significant first communion ritual), and second by teaching proper re-ligious behavior in both word and deed during catechism classes. Dur-ing the Sunday afternoon hours that children spent with their curés responding to questions about the Trinity and the Beatitudes, they also learned how to sit still in church, pray, respect the church and its priests, give a proper confession, take communion, and obey those in authority over them. These societal expectations and behaviors could last a lifetime, even if children eventually forgot the exact words of the catechism itself.

Although the catechism has substantial potential as a historical source, children's religious education is a topic that has been curiously neglected by historians of the Catholic Reformation in France. For ex-ample, when Victor Carrière published his three-volume *Introduction aux études d'histoire ecclésiastique locale* in the 1930s, with the intent to es-tablish the parameters for future inquiries into French religious history, he did not include catechisms in his list of source materials available for the early modern period.[3] More recent historians have also over-looked the importance of the religious education of children in the Catholic Reformation period. Most acknowledge the church's involve-ment in catechetical instruction but then move on to other Catholic Reformation topics—such as Jansenism, the reform of the religious orders, and the secular clergy. The laity's involvement is often studied through their role in confraternities, missions, the cult of the saints, charity, poor relief, and the persistence of popular religious practices after the Council of Trent.[4] But the church's primary means of replac-ing popular beliefs and practices with orthodoxy and orthopraxy—the catechism—is rarely discussed in depth in these studies. The education of new generations of believers, as perhaps the most crucial aspect of any lasting cultural or religious change, deserves a more extensive treatment.

The catechism is also a key text for understanding rural religion. Urban Catholics had access to a variety of religious practices, provided by lay- or clerical-run confraternities and the religious orders, in addition to their parish churches. Peasants in rural areas had fewer opportunities to experience their religion in an official setting, however, because they lived far from religious orders and from any chapels or churches other than their own parish church. Bishops believed that by emphasizing the catechism, they could compensate for the lack of religious education in rural areas by making the simple truths contained in the text available to all Catholic believers. If rural parents could not prepare their children for first communion by sending them to charity schools run by the religious orders (a common practice in urban areas), they could send them to their parish priest as well as their local lay schoolmaster, who both taught catechism on a regular basis.

I have decided to use catechisms to investigate rural, rather than urban, religion primarily because historians have already used a variety of other sources—like records from confraternities—to examine religious practices in cities and towns.[5] Rural religious practices have left so few traces in the historical record that it makes sense to use the catechism—a text we know a majority of peasants had access to—to study rural religion. And, although most of the urban children from the middle and upper levels of society would have learned their catechism in schools and churches just like rural peasant children, the urban poor often slipped through the cracks and never received any sort of religious education in their early years. Rural peasants received more attention from their curés than their urban counterparts and thus were more likely to learn the catechism.[6] As Châtellier argued in *La religion des pauvres,* missions had some of their greatest successes in rural parishes in the eighteenth century, leading to a significant shift in the importance of rural areas within the church as a whole. Catechism can help us to understand this shift, since the texts were taught not only during the occasional mission but on a weekly or even daily basis in rural churches and schools.[7]

Furthermore, catechisms crossed gender lines in rural areas. Seventeenth- and eighteenth-century educational theorists, as well as church leaders, generally insisted that boys and girls should receive separate educations and study subjects that would be most useful to them in their adult lives.[8] One justification for separate treatment of boys and girls in educational matters was that girls did not need to be exposed to complicated (and thus potentially dangerous) theories or doctrines. Even Fénelon, famous for insisting that girls needed a better education than what most governesses or nunneries provided, pointed out the dangers of turning girls into "les savantes ridicules."[9] Consequently, we might expect to find that the church produced one catechetical text for boys and another for girls. However, because the doctrines in the catechism had already been simplified (by the very fact of their inclusion in the text), bishops had little reason to further differentiate between male and female religious education. As a result, bishops did not publish sex-specific catechisms, and boys and girls memorized the same text. Furthermore, the behaviors learned in catechism class—prayer, participation in the sacraments, and, most importantly, preparation for first communion—were necessary for children of both sexes. Both boys and girls needed instruction in these matters in order to participate in parish life as adults, so both had to learn the catechism.

In rural parishes boys and girls not only learned the same catechism, they attended the same catechism classes and primary schools. Small villages did not have enough resources to teach more than one class, and in most cases boys and girls learned the same things from the same teachers. The classroom was inevitably a gendered space, and at times both the text of the catechism and the way it was taught reinforced certain patriarchal gender roles; for example, girls learned that as children they were subject to their parents and as wives they would be subject to their husbands. At the same time, because girls learned the same Catholic doctrines and behaviors as their brothers did, they may have discovered a certain fluidity in the church's prescribed gender roles. The catechism emphasizes the uniformity of doctrine. Each person residing within the jurisdiction of a particular bishop learned the same catechism: orthodox doctrines and behaviors—at least as they were decreed by the church—did not change depending on age, social status, or gender. According to the catechism, men and women were equal in the eyes of God, and this knowledge could have had a powerful effect on the way that women understood their own religious beliefs and their role within the church structure.

Finally, the study of catechisms provides insight into religious practices at the very end of the early modern era, a time period often neglected by historians of both religion and education. Between 1650 and 1700 French bishops published at least 57 different catechisms in 48 dioceses in France as they attempted to establish uniformity within their own dioceses. The number of diocesan catechisms increased significantly in the eighteenth century, and by 1800 the total stood at 181 catechisms published in 102 dioceses.[10] Thus, the years between 1650 and the French Revolution represent the period when catechisms were the most widely available and when parish priests could ensure that the children in their care memorized Catholic doctrines and learned appropriate religious behaviors and practices. Catechisms were a critical component of the church's reform program, and catechetical education was to be the first—and the most important—exposure to Catholicism for generations of believers.

Pastoral Visits and the Growth of Religious Education in Three French Dioceses

The catechisms themselves can only provide part of the story, however; other sources are needed to fully understand how the Catholic Reformation affected the laity at the parish level. Fortunately, the implementation of another Tridentine reform resulted in a category of documents that provide a variety of details about parish life: visitation records. The Council of Trent required bishops to visit each parish in their dioceses once a year, or, in the larger dioceses, once every two years.[11] During their visits, bishops inspected church property, questioned curés, and met with village notables to make sure that everything in their parishes was running smoothly. Visits provided an opportunity for bishops to find out what was really going on in their dioceses, and the records they left offer a similar opportunity for the historian.[12] Like catechisms, visitation records can illustrate how the clergy and the laity interacted, and they can explain something about belief. The questions that bishops asked, and the responses that the curés and the laity gave, provide an interesting insight into what it meant to be an early modern Catholic believer.

In part 2 of the book I use visitation records from three dioceses in northern France—Auxerre, Châlons-sur-Marne, and Reims—to examine religious and primary education at the parish level. I chose these particular dioceses because each had bishops who left detailed visitation records and because of the differences in prosperity and prestige between the regions.[13] Both Reims and Châlons are in the province of Champagne in northeastern France; today, they make up the departments of the Marne and the Ardennes. As an average-sized diocese, Châlons included four hundred parishes and annexes (or subparishes) within its borders. Reims was one of the largest dioceses in France, with over seven hundred parishes and annexes.[14] Both dioceses were wealthy, with generous ecclesiastical revenues and a relatively prosperous population, and the Champagne region had significantly higher literacy rates than other parts of France, suggesting that educational opportunities—either religious or secular—were more widespread.[15] Auxerre, on the other hand, was a small diocese (just over two hundred parishes and annexes) in Burgundy, about halfway between Paris and Dijon; most of the diocese is now part of the department of the Yonne. Auxerre was considerably less wealthy than either Reims or Châlons, and the ratio of curés to parishioners was much smaller; the bishops of Auxerre would certainly have had fewer resources at their disposal to try to implement programs of religious reform, and an economically challenged people might have been less willing to support those reforms.[16] Literacy rates in Auxerre were significantly lower than in Champagne, although it is statistically an average diocese when compared to France as a whole.

The most useful and most abundant visitation records in these three dioceses begin in the 1650s. Records previous to this date demonstrate that early seventeenth-century visitors were concerned primarily with the property of the church rather than the morals or education of the laity. Bishops conducting these early visits certainly did not take care to inquire about the availability of parish education, religious or otherwise.[17] By the second half of the seventeenth century, however, the content of Reims's visitation records had changed dramatically. Beginning with the episcopate of Archbishop Antoine Barberin (1657–1671), visitors began to make inquiries about attendance at Mass, Easter communion, pilgrimages, confraternities, and, finally, catechism and schools. From this point on, visitors in Reims always made notes about the status of religious and secular education in their parishes. Only a handful of early seventeenth-century visitation records from Châlons-sur-Marne and Auxerre exist,[18] but the situation in other northern French dioceses seems to have been much the same as in Reims. In Rouen, for example, there are a number of visitation records dating from 1445 until the Revolution, but not until the 1650s did visitors begin recording information about schools and catechism. Details about education were included routinely thereafter.[19] Clearly, regulation of the moral and religious behavior of the laity, as well as the education of children, had become one of the bishops' primary concerns by the end of the seventeenth century.

Of course, like any historical document, there are some difficulties with the use of visitation records.[20] Despite the fact that pastoral visits involved the bishop, the curé, and the laity, the task of actually producing the records fell to bishops' secretaries. While the curé's voice is heard in some of the documents, it is filtered through both the bishop and the record-keeper, making it difficult to see his side of the story. Visits were also high-pressure situations for curés; it is entirely possible that a curé might decide to leave out certain details or omit the fact that he was less than diligent at teaching catechism. Because bishops often interviewed curés and their parishioners at the same time, however, it would have been rather difficult for a curé to say that he taught catechism on a regular basis if the village notables standing next to him knew that he had been negligent. Even if the curé and the laity teamed up to try to mislead the bishop, they knew that their deception could easily be uncovered when the bishop asked to hear the children of the parish recite their catechism. Bishops seemed to have a way of exposing what was really going on in a parish, and visitation records often reflect this.

On the other hand, if the children's ignorance was due to the negligence of the parents to send them to catechism class, the curé might have been reluctant to share this with the bishop while in the presence of the parents. Fortunately, other sources from the curés themselves allow a more direct look at the state of education at the parish level. For example, letters written to bishops by curés and by village notables give a good sense of their concerns. In addition, bishops also acquired information about their parishes through questionnaires that they sent to their curés to be filled out and returned. At the end of the seventeenth century, Charles de Caylus asked his curés to send him a report (*état*) on the state of their parishes each year. In Châlons bishops sent out questionnaires in the weeks before a visit, providing an opportunity for curés to report things that they may have been reluctant to share during the public visit. By far the most valuable questionnaires are those sent out by Archbishop Talleyrand-Périgord in an *enquête* of January of 1774 to every parish and annex in Reims. Nearly seven hundred of these thirteen-page questionnaires have survived, and they are filled with details about parish life, including the quality and availability of primary education in the parish. This set of documents is perhaps the largest and most comprehensive source for details about eighteenth-century rural religion anywhere in France, and it provides a window into children's education from the point of view of the curé, who was, after all, primarily responsible for providing that education.[21]

Used in combination, then, visitation records, letters, and questionnaires can provide the viewpoints of both the bishops and the curés and their insights into the progress of religious and primary education in their parishes. Bishops asked their curés to provide information about specific topics, but the priests also took the opportunity to both complain about their parishioners and praise them. Judging by their responses, curés apparently felt quite free to express their feelings in these documents, so we are able to see their concerns as well as their successes. They indicated whether or not their parishioners attended Mass and participated in the sacraments, and how often the taverns were full and the churches empty. They reported the charitable activities their parishioners engaged in but also their tendency to work on Sundays and feast days after Mass. Most importantly, curés told their bishops that they taught catechism on a regular basis and that parents generally made sure that their children attended. To bishops, this meant that the reform of their parishes was well under way.

The Village School: Religious and Primary Education

Bishops did not, however, rely only upon curés to teach the catechism; the clergy expected that children would receive a great deal of their religious instruction by attending local primary schools. In seventeenth- and eighteenth-century France, a *petite école* generally consisted of a lay schoolmaster who taught reading, writing, and catechism for several months of the year. Financial support for these schools came from the community itself, although most schoolmasters' salaries were low and facilities generally lacking. Schoolmasters held classes in their stables or kitchens, and their students sat on benches with their books on their knees. By modern standards the *petites écoles* might seem rather primitive, but the fact that a majority of children in rural areas had the opportunity to obtain a basic education in reading, writing, and religion should not be overlooked. As my analysis of visitation records and other sources will show, the number of schools in operation was much higher than previous historians have recognized: at least 89 percent of all of the parishes in Reims, Châlons-sur-Marne, and Auxerre had established their own schools by the time of the Revolution.

Historians have long recognized the existence of the *petites écoles* in the early modern period, but too often they are relegated to the margins of educational history. Instead of examining the importance and impact of the *petites écoles* from the perspective of the initial founders and supporters of the schools — seventeenth- and eighteenth-century clergy, parents, and village notables — most historians have instead preferred to analyze the types of education that would become more important in the modern world, namely, reading and writing.[22] One of the most obvious signs of this is the fact that historians of French education and literacy overwhelmingly focus on the nineteenth century — the point when, in the standard view, the state began the process of taking over control of primary schooling from the church. These historians implicitly argue that the only schools worth studying are those that the state built and administered.[23]

For example, Raymond Grew and Patrick Harrigan demonstrate the existence of 36,000 schools in France by 1829 and about twice that many by 1906. They rightly point to this as an enormous growth in the availability of schooling but say very little about the thousands of schools that existed before 1829. According to their analysis, primary schools grew most rapidly in the 1830s (55,300 schools were in operation in 1840, a 54 percent increase from 1829).[24] Some areas of France, however, may have experienced this type of growth more than a hundred years earlier, at the end of the seventeenth century and the beginning of the eighteenth. In Auxerre the number of parishes with schools increased from 38 percent in 1700 to 89 percent at the time of the Revolution. Yet because most of these *ancien régime* schools were held in schoolmasters' homes rather than in public school buildings, and because they often favored the teaching of religion and catechism over reading and writing, historians of nineteenth-century education often fail to consider them as schools at all.[25]

Even those historians who do concentrate on the early modern period still analyze the village school in terms of its potential to increase literacy rather than as a multilayered social and religious institution in its own right. Historians who study the *petites écoles* in the early modern period generally agree on two fundamental issues: that local communities hired lay schoolmasters and administered the schools themselves, and that religion was one of the most important subjects taught there, along with reading, writing, and perhaps a bit of arithmetic.[26] Yet in their analysis of these schools, their focus is usually on the so-called profane subjects and the growth of literacy rather than the results of religious instruction. Currently, literacy and other harbingers of modernization are the only metrics available for those who wish to measure the influence of the *petites écoles,* despite the fact that the people who paid for the schools wanted their children to learn both their letters and the catechism.

The need that the *petites écoles* fulfilled was primarily religious and social. In the eighteenth century few parents believed that being able to write would bring great advantages to their children; thus, parents did not pay school fees with learning this skill in mind.[27] Although schools taught some children to write, we may never know exactly how many, and the number was certainly much smaller than those who learned only reading and catechism. Instruction in religion was something that everyone needed, however, and for this reason parents were willing to send their children to the *petites écoles* and pay their fees. In school children learned to read but primarily for religious purposes.

They read their prayers, the catechism, and other religious texts. They also learned to recite their catechism, enabling them to visibly prove their dedication to Catholicism and become a part of the Catholic community by receiving their first communion.

This type of education might seem backward and pedantic to the modern mind, but in the early modern world instruction in religion and morals was indispensable to both individual and community formation. The people of a small hamlet in the diocese of Reims understood this well when they wrote to their archbishop and explained to him that in their community there were "many children of an age to learn to know and serve their creator and to attend the Holy Sacrifice of the Mass, who do not attend at all; but they could attend if there was a Mass and some instructions on feast days and Sundays in the village, and then they would not have to live in ignorance, like the animals, as they do now."[28] Learning the principles of Catholicism was an essential rite of passage for early modern children, and parents expected that schools would provide at least part of the instruction they needed. Memorizing the catechism was just as important as learning to read or write. Thus, the three "R's" of early modern education—read, write, and recite— became inextricably linked in the seventeenth- and eighteenth-century *petites écoles*.

The Catholic Reformation and Confessionalization

Both catechisms and primary schools must be placed within the context of the Catholic Reformation. Beginning in the sixteenth century, the Catholic Church experienced unprecedented changes at all levels of society, as bishops and other clergymen attempted to make the ideal model of Catholicism that their predecessors had envisioned at the Council of Trent a reality in French dioceses and parishes. Of course, reform meant different things to different individuals. The movement for Catholic reform was never fully unified, even within a single diocese,[29] but this diversity has provided fertile ground for historians, who have produced important studies analyzing the interpretation and application of Tridentine Catholicism throughout Europe. Many of these works concentrate on the battle against Protestantism, the institutional church, and the religious orders,[30] while others examine the processes of religious and cultural change in the everyday lives of ordinary Catholic believers.[31] Together, these studies demonstrate the importance of the reform movement and the ways in which members of both clerical and lay populations interpreted the meaning and practice of their religion.

The cooperation of state and church authorities to impose confessional norms of belief and behavior on a largely ignorant population—or the confessionalization process—recently has become an important avenue of research for Catholic Reformation historians. Confessionalization studies began to take shape with a series of articles published by German historians Wolfgang Reinhard and Heinz Schilling beginning in the 1980s.[32] Schilling and Reinhard argued that by the mid-seventeenth century in the Holy Roman Empire, the once-fluid boundaries between the three major religious confessions (the Catholic, Lutheran, and Reformed versions of Christianity) had hardened, and each group defined itself not only in terms of their own specific doctrines but against the doctrines of the other confessions. Furthermore, the process of creating the boundaries between the confessions was carried out by the state in deliberate cooperation with religious authorities. Thus, the early modern state used religious belief to regulate the behavior of its subjects in order to ensure domestic tranquility and to centralize its own power. The bureaucratic institutions built up by the churches became instruments by which state power was wielded, and the clergy became agents of the state. The clergy did not have to be forced into this process, for they found that it enabled them to use the state's power to reinforce their own reform programs. Thus, both church and state worked together to standardize the beliefs and behavior of the laity in early modern Europe.

The confessionalization model has been applied successfully, albeit with some reservations, by historians of numerous European states.[33] For France, Philip Benedict argues that there are essentially two forms of confessionalization: the strong model, in which the state actively supports the confessionalization of its subjects, and the weak model, which deemphasizes the role of the state in favor of the processes of rivalry between the confessions that created consolidated notions of orthodoxy and orthopraxy. Benedict sees little promise in applying the strong model to France and points out the dangers in trying to tie every development of the early modern era to the growth of the state. But

Benedict does see the weak model as holding more promise for French religious history, suggesting that his research into Catholic and Protestant relations in Montpellier supports this theory.[34]

The discussion of primary education in this volume will add to current research on both the Catholic Reformation and confessionalization in several ways. First, in order to fully understand the reform movement, historians need to examine the implementation of that reform in the eighteenth century. The traditional time period for Catholic Reformation studies is often limited to the first 100–150 years or so after the Council of Trent since so many important changes occurred in the French church during that period.[35] Likewise, with the advent of the Enlightenment and the Scientific Revolution, the eighteenth century is often viewed as the beginning of secularization and dechristianization in France. Yet it is also the century when the use of the catechism to teach religious doctrines and behaviors became more regular and widespread than it ever had been in the past. Most curés did not begin teaching catechism with regularity until the end of the seventeenth century, and most villages did not establish schools until that time. Here I follow the example of historians like Philip Hoffman, Timothy Tackett, and Philippe Goujard, who insist on the importance of the eighteenth century for the Catholic Reformation.[36] The programs of the Catholic Reformation could not be implemented with any sort of effectiveness until the eighteenth century, when schools and catechism classes became a regular part of parish life. Thus, religious belief in the eighteenth century—after the church had been able to implement its reforms and after the laity had been given the chance to either accept, reject, or reach some sort of compromise with those reforms—warrants further investigation.

Second, like Benedict, I argue that what he calls the strong confessionalization model, which emphasizes direct influence of the state in the standardization of religious belief, does not apply for much of Catholic France, and it certainly does not apply in the dioceses of Auxerre, Châlons-sur-Marne, and Reims. At the diocesan and parish level, the state had very little interest in church affairs unless there were large groups of Protestants involved. If the church wanted to make any changes, or institute any reforms in Catholic areas, they had to do it themselves, through bishops, parish priests, and their influence on local authorities. State officials had little to do with local schools either; the Crown issued edicts requiring communities to open *petites écoles,* but no official provisions for ensuring that the edict was followed were established. Thus, it was again up to local authorities to hire schoolmasters and encourage children to attend.[37]

Finally, the history of catechisms and the *petites écoles* is critical to understanding interactions between the laity and the clergy at the local level. Historians such as Keith Luria, Marie-Hélène Froeschlé-Chopard, and Wietse de Boer[38] represent an important trend in the history of the Catholic Reformation: the idea that what "reform" meant in the early modern period was not simply the implementation of a completely new form of Tridentine Catholicism by the clergy on an often stubborn and reactionary laity but rather a process of compromise and adaptation by both clergy and laity. Bishops and curés routinely tried to impose their ideas about religious education on their parishes, but if parents and village notables had not hired schoolmasters, paid their fees, and made sure that their children attended schools and catechism classes, the clergy's words would have had little effect. Laity and clergy worked together to implement reform in their dioceses, and thus both groups are responsible for the shape of the Catholic Reformation.

In confessionalization studies the interaction between the laity and either church or state authorities is usually examined in terms of social discipline. Confessionalization historians were heavily influenced by the larger theories of social discipline emphasized so vigorously by scholars like Michel Foucault and Norbert Elias, so a great deal of research has been carried out in order to understand how religious, moral, and civic ideals were implemented and internalized within various states and communities.[39] But recent studies have suggested that historians should avoid portraying the state as the most important force for change in ideas about public behavior. For example, Marc Forster argues that religious change in southwest Germany was instigated by the popular classes and reform from below was much more effective than anything promoted by the elites. Forster also emphasizes that the strong clericalism of the region was popularly motivated.[40] In France an interesting commentary on social discipline comes from Sara Beam's work on farce in the seventeenth century. She argues that a new code of morals and civic behavior did indeed emerge in seventeenth-century France, but it was not due to the influence of Louis XIV's court, as Elias and others have suggested. Instead, the impetus for the change came from the urban bourgeois who were trying to create their own identity and distinguish themselves from the lower classes.[41]

Catechisms might also be seen as a tool used by authorities in their attempt to impose discipline on the parish, but in reality local notables and even ordinary parents were just as responsible for creating and enforcing the code of social behavior found in the catechism as the authorities. Indeed, catechisms defined orthodoxy in a way that had never been done before, yet they also illustrate the existence of a certain amount of dialogue between clergy and laity: bishops had to adapt their catechisms to the needs of the souls in their care or the texts would be discarded and forgotten. An overly long catechism, or a text that focused too narrowly on theology, was of little use to most Catholics, who in turn demanded a more appropriate text. In addition, many parents recognized the benefits that could come from catechism classes, which would enable their children to participate in parish activities and to conform to their own ideas about belief and behavior. A study of catechisms demonstrates that the laity's goals merged with those of both church and secular authorities, and the texts can reveal a great deal about the beliefs shared by a wide segment of the population. They are one of the few sources available that can help to identify the intersection of clerical and lay ideas about Catholic doctrines and practices and, thus, allow a richer and more nuanced view of the Catholic Reformation.

✿— The book is organized as follows: Part 1 examines the diocesan catechisms themselves—their content, organization, and method. Catechisms were intended to provide a very specific type of education, and this is demonstrated by the bishops' overall goals for their catechetical program and by the material in the texts. Bishops and curés expected the children who memorized the catechism to learn both doctrines and behaviors, but they placed the most emphasis on the more practical and outward aspects of Catholicism: prayer, the Ten Commandments, and the sacraments. Part 2 looks more closely at how the bishops' program of religious education was actually implemented at the ground level in Auxerre, Châlons-sur-Marne, and Reims. Chapter 3 deals with the curés—their background, education, and dedication to religious education. Chapters 4 and 5 focus on schoolteachers, their schools, and their participation in religious education.

The final chapter concludes with an evaluation of the effectiveness of both the *petites écoles* and primary education in general. Due to a significant amount of cooperation between the clergy and the laity, a system of primary education involving both village schools and church catechism classes was firmly in place in all three of these dioceses by the time of the French Revolution. The Catholic Reformation achieved its greatest success in rural villages in the eighteenth century, where believers went to Mass every week, confessed their sins and took communion at Easter, and passed along knowledge of Catholic doctrines and practices to the next generation through catechism and primary schools. As a result of this education, Catholic worship and practice, at least in their outward manifestations, were as uniform and regulated as they had ever been in France. Although we may never know if conformity in doctrine and practice led to sincere religious belief, the bishops of the church believed that it would:

Always ask the same questions, in the same terms. So that your children always give the same responses in the same words, choose those which are the most natural, the most simple, and the most customary, and do not change them in any way; by this method the children will respond with boldness, ease, promptness, and pleasure. They will order their ideas; they will become accustomed to doctrinal language, and as they grow up their knowledge will be arranged and retained; it will grow and expand through Sermons, readings and reflection; they will find within themselves what once came from without.[42]

PART ONE

Diocesan Catechisms in Seventeenth- and Eighteenth-Century France

CHAPTER ONE

The Science of Salvation
Catechisms and Catholic Reform

Of all the sciences which should be the object of your application, this is the most useful. It alone teaches us the true destiny of man, the ardor with which he must desire it, and what he must do to obtain it. . . . All the knowledge to which the world attaches handsome names and grand ideas—is it worthy to be compared to this? Alas, what good is a knowledge of all the rest, if the only necessary science is ignored?

—Bishop Scipion Jérôme Bégon

Bishop Bégon of the diocese of Toul was just one of several early modern French bishops to refer to a knowledge of Christian truths as a science. For example, a bishop of Saint-Claude described his newly revised catechism as the "science of salvation" and emphasized that any child who neglected to learn this science would find himself on the path of ignorance, superstition, and vice rather than virtue and obedience. A bishop of Laon urged parents to use his 1698 catechism to teach their children the "science of religion," while the bishop of Soissons argued that his catechism contained "the science of the holy, the science of salvation."[1]

What did these bishops mean by "science"? During the early modern period, the word "science" evolved from being synonymous with "knowledge" to its more modern definition of a systematically organized body of knowledge on a given subject.[2] For seventeenth- and eighteenth-century bishops, the "science of salvation" was a science in the latter sense. Just as the philosophers and scientists of the period claimed that a knowledge of the science of physics would enable one to understand the movement of the planets or the laws governing motion in the physical world, bishops claimed that a knowledge of the science of salvation—conveniently found in the catechisms they issued for their dioceses—would lead to an understanding of God's involvement in the world and provide the tools needed to gain salvation in the next life.

The bishops' emphasis on catechism and the science of salvation was part of the larger Catholic Reformation movement taking place in the seventeenth and eighteenth centuries. Catholic efforts to reform both clergy and laity had begun with the Council of Trent (1545–1563), but it took several decades for the church to effect significant change. By the end of the seventeenth century, bishops had taken a number of important steps toward reform: they established seminaries to train their parish priests, issued dozens of ordinances and regulations governing clerical behavior, and held regular synods to establish and maintain clerical discipline and order.[3] The bishops' next major task in the reform process was to educate the laity in orthodox Catholic doctrines and practices, and for this they needed a consistent method of instruction: the catechism.[4]

Yet the catechism has received very little attention from historians, who often either overlook or take for granted the importance of children's religious education in the Catholic Reformation period.[5] In fact, modern historians often mistakenly classify the catechism as an ineffective method of instruction. Because the basic catechetical method—the often tedious process of memorization and repeated recitation—is entirely antithetical to modern methods of education, the institution of weekly catechism classes by elite reforming bishops is misunderstood as mere pedantry. Previous studies have emphasized that because religious education centered on memorizing the catechism, children quickly became bored and usually forgot everything they learned. Some historians argue that the results of catechetical education therefore reversed the reformers' actual intentions by instilling in children an aversion to religious education and everything associated with it; however, we cannot allow modern attitudes to distort our understanding of early modern educational methods.[6] Bishops, parish priests, and parents believed that memorizing doctrines through the questions and answers of the catechism was the most appropriate way to instill Catholicism into young children and even ignorant adults, as the large numbers of catechisms printed in early modern France attest.[7]

Despite the seemingly obtuse nature of the catechetical method, a closer examination of the history of catechisms in early modern France demonstrates the ways in which the bishops adapted their catechisms to meet the needs of their parishioners. The institution of weekly catechism classes by elite reforming bishops was not a top-down process of indoctrination of the masses; instead, it was a way for bishops to work with the laity and the parish clergy in order to develop a program of religious education that would satisfy the needs of both parties. In suggesting that the laity influenced the content and methods of the catechisms published by theologians and clergymen I borrow from Peter Brown, who argued against a two-tiered model of orthodox and popular belief in his work on the cult of the saints in the early medieval period. Brown sees the cult of the saints as a point where the clergy and the laity met and mingled, and I see catechism in the same way. Similarly, John Arnold has pointed out the limitations of the idea that religious tenets expounded on by the clergy could be disseminated with little modification directly to the laity, and he urges historians of medieval religion to avoid the two-cultures model of high/low or literate/oral. A recent study by Wietse de Boer shows that this applies equally well to the early modern period, as he demonstrates how Archbishop Charles Borromeo's ideas about confession were modified by the parish clergy who applied his teachings in the diocese of Milan. These authors provide evidence of a dialectic between the clergy and the laity that was part of the regulation of religious belief and practice, and this same interaction appears in the history of the French catechism as well.[8]

After several decades of trial and error with different types of catechisms, the laity, the parish clergy, and the bishops reached a compromise about catechetical education in France. Both clergy and parents realized that catechism classes should teach children proper Catholic behavior rather than complicated theology or doctrines. The clergymen and theologians who wrote these catechisms meant them to be comprehensive, step-by-step instructions for children to follow in their daily lives regarding what to believe and what to do in order to live as true Catholics. As children learned to obey the Ten Commandments and participate in the sacraments, their curés and parents taught them a moral and ethical code that they could follow throughout their lives. Even if they did not fully understand the complexity of Catholic doctrines, these children could still perform Catholic rites and behave like Catholics in their everyday lives—a result that both the laity and the bishops found entirely acceptable.

The Origins of the Catechism and the Catechetical Method

Early modern proponents of the catechetical method often emphasized the fact that the catechism and the catechetical method had been associated with Christianity from its very beginnings. They noted that catechists were still using the same simple texts and doctrines that the apostles had used in the first century after Christ's death. Pierre-Modeste Hézard, a nineteenth-century curé who published a history of French catechisms in the year 1900, provides as evidence of this a long list of New Testament passages that deal with topics that would later become the standard subjects of early modern catechisms: baptism, the Lord's Supper, prayer, faith, grace, sins, virtues, and, of course, Christ's birth, life, and sacrifice.[9]

Despite these similarities between scripture and catechism, however, we should not imagine that the same catechetical method employed by the apostles continued to be used throughout the Roman era and the Middle Ages and into the early modern period; it is much more likely that there are similarities because the theologians who wrote catechisms used the apostles' accounts as examples for their own texts. The catechetical method of the early modern period was in fact quite different from that used in the early church, primarily due to the timing of the instruction. Most of the growth of the early church resulted from missionary work, with adults learning basic doctrines before their baptism and conversion to the faith. As missionaries tried to make their message acceptable to the people of the Mediterranean world, they emphasized Christian rituals as replacements for Roman sacrifices and ceremonies. The most important of these rituals was baptism, and as Christianity spread during the second and third centuries, baptism became a community affair, performed in the presence of an assembly of the faithful. In order to undergo such a public rite, leaders had to prepare the convert for drastic changes in faith and lifestyle—hence the practice of catechizing the inductee in the basic tenets of the Christian faith.[10] Hézard argues that catechizing took place year-round but was intensified during the two-week period of Easter; once a potential Christian had been catechized during three Easter seasons, he or she could be baptized.[11]

As the church grew, and adult baptism became more and more rare, the practice of catechizing at baptism began to disappear. Parents had their children baptized soon after birth, and infants were hardly in a position to learn the catechism; instead, parents chose godparents, who then accepted the responsibility for the child's religious education. Because the catechizing process was no longer tied to a significant Catholic ritual, the practice of regular catechization of either children or adults, using any sort of standardized process or text, largely disappeared until the early modern period, when learning the catechism before first communion would become an important step in the religious life of children and young adults.

Medieval catechisms—at least those meant for children—were therefore quite rare. Hézard lists a number of medieval texts that he classifies as catechisms, written by such important church figures as Origen, Chrysostom, Augustine, Ambrose, and Abelard, but these authors included a great deal of sophisticated theology in their texts and wrote them with a clerical rather than a lay audience in mind.[12] The one exception is the *Oeuvre tripartite*, written by Jean Gerson in the early fifteenth century. Gerson meant for his three-part manual dealing with the Decalogue, confession, and the "science of dying well" to be used by curés in their instructions, and he also wrote a companion text, *L'ABC des simples gens,* for children learning to read. But Gerson did not use the question-and-answer format in his texts, and the *Oeuvre tripartite* did not find an extensive audience until the sixteenth century.[13]

The use of catechisms to teach Christian doctrines was thus not an entirely new practice in the early modern period. Yet because no standardized text or method of instruction existed, and because the education and dedication of medieval priests were often questionable, religious education for the laity in the Middle Ages was usually perfunctory, haphazard, and incomplete. Medieval French clergymen who wished to instruct the people of their parishes would have had them memorize a few prayers as well as the Decalogue, but any other instruction came at the discretion of the parish priest. Some priests may have had a manuscript copy of Gerson's text to use in their teaching, or perhaps written instructions that had been passed on informally from curé to curé. In some cases the diocesan handbook, or *rituel,* may have contained some material that could be used for instruction.[14] Since the vast majority of the laity could not read, however, all of the curé's teaching would have been done orally, thus further decreasing the likelihood of standardization.

With the Protestant Reformation came an attempt to standardize religious education for children, and during the Reformation era the catechism began to take on its modern form. The laity's ignorance of fundamental Christian truths ranked high among the myriad problems reformers like Luther and Calvin found with the Catholic Church in the early sixteenth century; with the help of the printing press and an exploding market for the printed word, Protestant reformers turned the catechism into a tool that would not only alleviate some of this ignorance but create a new generation of young people who would know and practice reformed versions of Christianity. While Protestants did not invent the catechetical method, they can certainly claim credit for transforming the catechism into an inexpensive and portable text that was easy to teach and read. Protestants were also the first to combine both the written and oral aspects of religious education by producing printed texts designed to be not only read and internalized but also memorized and recited.

Both Luther and Calvin produced their own catechisms intended for children and those ignorant of Protestant theology. Luther published two catechisms in 1529, a small and a large; while the large version was 140 pages long and much too complex for most of the laity, the small version contained only 30 pages written in dialogue form and could be used to teach even very young children the basics of the Christian religion.[15] Although a French translation of Luther's small catechism appeared in 1530, it was Calvin's catechism, *Formulaire d'instruire les enfants en la Chrétienté,* published in 1541, that had the most influence in France.[16] The first French catechism in dialogue form, it contained fifty-five lessons in four parts: Faith (mysteries of the religion), Law (the Decalogue), Prayer, and the Sacraments. Calvin undoubtedly wrote this catechism for children; he eliminated most of the complicated theology often found in Calvinist literature and added simpler explanations of doctrines like the Trinity and the sacraments. He also tied the catechism to first communion by making memorization of the text a prerequisite for children approaching the communion table in Geneva. Protestant congregations in France followed this practice as well, and even the Catholic clergy found the idea appealing. Henceforth in both Protestant and Catholic churches, catechism and first communion would go hand in hand.[17]

Protestant catechisms met with so much success that Catholic theologians and bishops began to adopt this method during the sixteenth century. New editions of Gerson's *Oeuvre tripartite* appeared, and Charles de Lorraine, archbishop of Reims, issued the first Catholic catechism written in dialogue form in 1550.[18] In Paris, Bishop Eustache du Bellay published the *Institutio catholica quam Vulgus Manuale vocat* in 1562, but he addressed the text to curés and vicaires rather than the laity. Cardinal de Bourbon had a catechism published in Sens in 1554, and a Latin catechism of sorts was published in Châlons-sur-Marne in 1557.[19] None of these catechisms was specifically written for children, however, and they found only limited audiences.

Rome published its own catechism, as part of the Council of Trent, in 1566.[20] Primarily written by the Italian theologian and archbishop Charles Borromeo, the Tridentine catechism had the same format as Calvin's, although the lessons were arranged in a different order: the sacraments came earlier in the text, after an introductory section on the Apostles' Creed and before teachings on the commandments and prayer. Everything about this catechism, however, including the title— *Catechism of the Council of Trent for Parish Priests*—shows that it was written with the clergy in mind. Not only was it too long and detailed for children to understand, it even included pastoral guidelines in the text. The first edition was in Latin, and although translated versions in most European languages appeared later, the text probably reached only a small percentage of the lay population in the sixteenth century.

The most popular sixteenth-century Catholic catechism was instead that of the French Jesuit Edmund Auger, published in 1563. Auger wrote his *Catéchisme et sommaire de la doctrine chrétienne* in French, and it attacked Calvin's catechism point by point. Like Calvin, Auger followed the faith/law/prayer/sacraments structure, and the text was written in question-and-answer format; however, it emphasized the importance of the Roman, Catholic, and Apostolic church: whereas Calvin had only nine questions on the church in his catechism, Auger had nineteen. Two-thirds of Auger's catechism dealt with the sacraments— one of the most important points of disagreement between Catholics and Protestants. Auger's catechism found a wide audience; the first edition sold out within a month, and between 1563 and 1582 at least twenty French editions appeared, as well as Spanish, Italian, and Dutch translations.[21]

Despite its initial popularity, the demand for Auger's catechism in France diminished by the beginning of the seventeenth century as the religious wars ended. Jean-Claude Dhotel argues that both Calvin's and Auger's texts worked well in their own time period but did not have lasting appeal. Once the peak of passions between Protestants and Catholics had passed, catechisms containing question after question dealing with specific but often minor Protestant or Catholic doctrines seemed less relevant than they had in the mid-sixteenth century. Calvin's and Auger's catechisms remained influential, however, because later authors often retained their format and methodology despite significant changes in content.

The German Jesuit Peter Canisius's *Summa doctrinae christianae* (1555) focused more on everyday Catholic living, and it became the most popular catechism after the Wars of Religion had abated. In the seventeenth century Canisius's catechism found a larger audience than Calvin's or

Auger's texts because it did not concentrate solely on heresy and the
ways to combat it, and it included more details on how one could live
a Christian life. Canisius organized his text around the three theological virtues—Faith (the Apostles' Creed), Hope (prayer), and Charity
(commandments of God and the church)—with a final section on the
sacraments. Canisius also included a section on "Christian Justice," or
the necessity to avoid sin and practice virtue. Running two hundred
pages in length and containing 222 questions, the *Summa* was still too
long and too theological for everyday use, so Canisius later published a
short version, the *minimus,* in 1556. It had only 59 questions and most
editions were accompanied by an *abécedaire,* or a text meant to teach
children the alphabet and the basics of reading. Canisius published a
third version of his catechism in 1557; the *minor* had 122 questions and
was intended for use in secondary schools. This final version became
the most popular of the three.[22]

Thus, Canisius accomplished what no other theologian before him
had been able to do: he produced not just one but three catechisms,
containing the same doctrines but with graduated amounts of detail,
meant to teach the basic doctrines of Christianity to people of all ages
and intellectual capacities. All three of his catechisms enjoyed a great
deal of success throughout the early modern period; by the time Canisius died in 1597, there were ten editions of the *Summa* in France (eight
in Latin and two in French) and thirteen of the *minor* (ten in Latin and
three in French). In the seventeenth century it replaced Auger's catechism in all Jesuit schools, and at least twenty additional editions appeared before 1700. Canisius's catechism continued to be published in
the eighteenth century, and there were even editions published after the
Revolution.[23]

Seventeenth-century French bishops and theologians also borrowed catechetical material from the Italians. Robert Bellarmine's *Dot-
trina christiana breve,* first published in Italian in 1597, has the distinction
of being the first catechism designed specifically to be memorized in
its entirety by children. It followed the same format as Canisius's texts:
the theological virtues plus the sacraments and Christian justice. Bellarmine, however, was the first to give an explanation of the sign of the
cross at the beginning of the catechism—this practice became nearly
universal from then on—and he proposed a new, abbreviated method

for teaching the Apostles' Creed using one question-and-answer set for each of the twelve articles that also became popular.

Bellarmine believed that catechism should be practical: he eliminated much of the theology usually found in medieval catechisms, concentrating on the essentials of what a child must know and do, and emphasized the external aspects of Catholicism since visible practices could be more easily grasped by children. Even though this meant he had to omit explanations for many Catholic doctrines and practices and retain only simple descriptions of those practices, Bellarmine held that this method was more appropriate for young children, who had little stamina for complicated theories and expositions. Bellarmine's catechism spread quickly throughout France, aided by the fact that Pope Clement VIII required its use by the Prêtres séculiers de la doctrine chrétienne, or Doctrinaires—the religious teaching order founded by César de Bus in 1592—in their schools and instructions. The Ursulines, France's major female teaching order, used Bellarmine's catechism as well.[24]

Thus, by the mid-seventeenth century the basic catechetical framework and method had become fairly standardized. Although each individual bishop might still put his own unique stamp on the catechism he issued for his diocese, the essential elements would not change until the twentieth century.[25] The Apostles' Creed, the commandments of God and the church, sin and virtue, prayer, and the sacraments were the primary topics, and the question-and-answer format had proved to be the most successful method of teaching religious truths. Clergymen and theologians had also demonstrated that using a written text intended to be read, memorized, and recited was a profitable way to teach both children and young adults.

In the second half of the seventeenth century, however, the popularity of the Jesuit catechisms waned in France with the advent of the diocesan catechisms. At this point bishops began to publish their own catechisms modeled after Calvin, Canisius, Auger, or Bellarmine but adapted for the needs of the people of their own dioceses. Between 1650 and 1700 bishops published at least 57 different catechisms in 48 dioceses in France, as they began to take a personal interest in the instruction of their parishioners in the science of salvation, and by 1800 the numbers had risen to 181 catechisms published in 102 dioceses.

Over the next century the major changes in French catechetical education would not be in the type of texts that were taught, or even in their general format, but simply in the fact that each bishop insisted on the use of a specific catechism in his diocese, and then distributed that text to a greater percentage of the lay population.[26] They wanted to make sure that each parish priest, schoolteacher, and parent had not just any catechism to teach from but *the* catechism: that is, the version of the catechism that the bishop himself had approved and distributed. Furthermore, the content, organization, and overall message of the catechism—the science of salvation—indicates not only the bishops' commitment to reform but also their willingness to adapt to the needs of the laity in order to make the catechism as accessible as possible.

Catechisms: Content

When seventeenth- and eighteenth-century bishops issued catechisms for their dioceses, they borrowed heavily from their predecessors' texts. Catechisms from Luther to Canisius had all begun with a section on faith, and the diocesan catechisms were no different. "Faith," in catechetical terms, meant primarily a discussion of the Apostles' Creed: a twelve-article statement of the basic beliefs of Christianity. Because the Creed begins with the statement "I believe in God, the Father Almighty, Creator of heaven and earth," catechisms usually began with a lesson or two on the attributes of God. Lessons on the birth, life, death, and resurrection of Christ followed, in which catechism authors presented a bit of history as well as discussions of the mysteries of the Incarnation and the Redemption. Article eight of the Creed, "I believe in the Holy Spirit," was usually presented in relation to the mystery of the Trinity, and lessons on the necessity of the church and the communion of saints corresponded to article nine. The final three articles dealt with the "four ends" of man (death, judgment, paradise, and hell) and examined the relationship between Christ, the church, and man.

The material found in the articles of the Creed was included in the diocesan catechisms in a variety of ways. Some of the longer texts devoted at least one lesson to each article, while shorter versions followed

Bellarmine and included only one question-and-answer set per article. Some sections on faith only included material on God, the mysteries, and Christ, while lessons on the church and the four ends were taught in later sections. No diocesan catechism that I have examined omits a discussion of the Creed altogether; in fact, usually between one-fourth and one-third of the material is devoted to the "faith" section.

Just as essential as the Creed were the commandments of God and the church. Shorter catechisms might simply require children to memorize the Decalogue like they would a prayer, but larger catechisms usually devoted at least one lesson to each commandment. In addition, children had to learn the commandments of the church, which regulated parish life and contained details about Mass attendance, feast days, and tithes. The commandments of the church also reminded children that when they reached adulthood they would be required to confess and take communion at least once a year, at Easter. Commandments to fast, pay tithes, avoid dealings with excommunicates, and postpone marriages until after Advent and Lent completed the list of duties children would be expected to fulfill as adults.

Often included in the sections on the commandments were lessons on avoiding sin and practicing virtue. Lessons on sin covered the difference between mortal and venial sins, listed and explained the seven capital sins (pride, avarice, gluttony, lust, sloth, envy, and anger) and sins against the Holy Spirit, and often contained a discussion of original sin as well. Material on the virtues covered faith, hope, and charity at the very least; longer catechisms included lessons on the four cardinal virtues (prudence, justice, fortitude, and temperance) as well as the eight Beatitudes, taken from Christ's Sermon on the Mount.

The longest and most important part of the diocesan catechisms was undoubtedly the material on the sacraments. All seven sacraments — baptism, confirmation, the Eucharist, penance, extreme unction, holy orders, and marriage — were covered in varying detail, along with teachings about the grace bestowed upon the worthy participants in those rituals. The sacraments most relevant to children were divided into a number of lessons, while material on orders and extreme unction was often combined into just one lesson. Catechism authors apparently did not intend their texts to be used by those preparing for marriage, judging by the fact that lessons on that topic were usually short and superficial. For example, a ninety-six-page catechism published in Lyon in 1730 contains two-and-a-half pages on baptism, two on confirmation, ten on penitence, and nine on the Eucharist, but only one page on marriage. The catechism ends with one final question on holy orders—it seems catechisms were not designed for future priests either.[27] Instead, catechisms emphasized the sacraments that the majority of the laity would participate in repeatedly throughout their lives: confession and communion. An average of 20 percent of the material in the catechisms examined here is devoted solely to these two sacraments.

Finally, a ritualized communication with God was also an important aspect of seventeenth- and eighteenth-century bishops' science of salvation, and catechisms included considerable instruction on prayer. Lessons on prayer usually had a number of questions and answers on the two most important Catholic prayers, the *Oraison dominicale* and the *Salutation angélique*. Texts also explained, or at the very least listed, the prayers and recitations used in the Mass. Most catechisms devoted a significant number of pages to the prayers used by Catholics on a daily basis.

Bishops borrowed from their predecessors not only the content of the texts but also their method and organization. Following the example of Canisius, some bishops issued not just one, but two or three catechisms, each adapted for people at different stages in their religious education. They published shorter versions of their catechisms so that even the youngest children had a chance to learn basic religious truths, while more extended versions were made available for members of the clergy or anyone else who wished to have more details and explanations. Of the seventy-eight publications examined for this study, forty-six contain either two or three separate but related catechisms: either a small (*petit*) and an ordinary (*second*) catechism, or a small, an ordinary, and a large (*grand*) catechism.

One of the most well-known sets of three catechisms of the late seventeenth century was the Catechism of the Three Henris, so named because it was issued in 1676 by three bishops of neighboring dioceses—Angers, La Rochelle, and Luçon—who all shared the same first name. In their introductory ordinance to the catechism, the three Henris argued that the effectiveness of religious instructions depended primarily on the manner in which people were taught.[28] For this reason, they wanted to make sure not only that everyone in their three dioceses learned the same catechism but that "children and the weak will find there the milk that they need, and those who are stronger and more robust will find nourishment that is more suitable for them."[29] Therefore, they published a 24-page small edition for "the small children, who have only memory in their tender youth, and are not capable of any greater instruction"; an 85-page ordinary catechism designed to be memorized in its entirety by children preparing for first communion; and a large edition of 383 pages to be used primarily by priests in their preparations for teaching catechism. The organization and lessons of the three catechisms are the same, but there are more questions in the larger versions and the answers are often longer and more detailed. The three-catechism format found a wide audience in the seventeenth and eighteenth centuries; the archbishops of Reims approved the Catechism of the Three Henris for use in their diocese until the mid-eighteenth century, and four other dioceses published three related versions of their own catechisms as well.[30]

Bishops who did not issue three texts usually found just one or two catechisms—a small and an ordinary—adequate.[31] In fact, the large catechisms—those running to more than three hundred pages in length and containing theological details and arguments too advanced for children and even most adults—began to disappear in the eighteenth century. Of fifteen large catechisms published in the seventeenth and eighteenth centuries, only five appeared between 1700 and 1756, when a new version of the Catechism of the Three Henris was issued for Luçon.[32] The existing evidence suggests that no other bishop published a large catechism in the remaining decades of the eighteenth century. The demand for such long and dense texts had diminished, and bishops knew that the laity would not get much use out of catechisms totaling 300, 400, or even 500 pages. The large catechism thus became simply a reference book, despite its question-and-answer format, and no one expected ordinary people to memorize it. Instead, small and ordinary catechisms became the standard texts used by children in schools and curés' catechism classes, and most of the laity would have encountered the large catechism only if their curé used it in his Sunday sermons.

At the same time, bishops did expect the children in their dioceses to learn a significant amount of material; the ordinary catechisms published in the eighteenth century actually contained more pages than those published in the seventeenth.[33] While the seventeen ordinary catechisms published between 1650 and 1700 averaged 127 pages in length, the fifty published after 1700 averaged nearly 149 pages. As the large catechisms disappeared, the ordinary catechisms became longer. The length of the *petit* catechisms, designed for children just learning the alphabet, remained fairly standard throughout the whole period: the fifty-one small catechisms published between 1650 and 1800 averaged 29 pages in length, the smallest being only 7 pages and the largest containing 75 pages of text (not including collections of prayers).[34] These small catechisms served as important introductory texts, but bishops believed that those children who were preparing for first communion should learn more material.

This change in the length and organization of catechetical material indicates several important trends in religious education in the early modern period. First, it demonstrates that Catholic Reformation bishops understood the educational capacities of the laity and responded appropriately to their needs. The fact that bishops stopped issuing long and impractical catechisms in favor of shorter, child-appropriate versions shows that they understood the time constraints and intellectual limitations of their parishioners. Bishops still needed to improve the religious education of the laity, however, and the proliferation of ordinary catechisms demonstrates that their efforts to increase religious education did not abate. Instead of issuing a long catechism and hoping that the laity might learn some of it, bishops published midsized catechisms but expected that children would learn the entire text and learn it well. If the ordinary catechism served as the primary source of religious education for children, then bishops wanted to ensure that it not only suited that age group but also provided adequate coverage of the necessary doctrines and practices; thus, the catechisms became slightly longer and more comprehensive. Finally, while seventeenth-century bishops felt that catechism was an exercise in which all members of the laity, no matter what age, should participate, eighteenth-century bishops recognized that the practices of learning the catechism and taking first communion had become increasingly tied together, meaning that catechism had become a childhood exercise and not a lifelong practice. Thus, as time went on ordinary catechisms more and more became geared toward a specific group of the laity—namely, children and young adults.

Catechisms published in Sens in the seventeenth and eighteenth centuries show the increasing importance of the relationship between catechism and first communion. In the introduction to a 1669 catechism, Archbishop Louis Henri de Pardaillon de Gondrin explicitly argued that the catechetical exercise should not be limited to children. In fact, he urged curés to teach children and parents the catechism together:

> But although the Catechism contains the instructions that are given to those who are only beginning to believe in Jesus Christ, it should not be only for the children . . . it is also necessary to keep the interests of the fathers and mothers in mind, and other people who are advanced in age, who have no less need for instruction than the children, and to try different ways to attract them to your instructions.[35]

He further emphasized that curés had a sacred duty to teach all of their parishioners so that the usual vices would not continue to reign throughout the countryside. Archbishop Gondrin issued just one catechism of 131 pages and told his curés to adapt it to the ages and capacities of all uninstructed people in their parishes. Because catechetical education had not yet become a routine aspect of parish life, in the second half of the seventeenth century bishops like Gondrin had to assume that no one knew their catechism, and therefore they aimed their educational efforts at all members of the parish, both children and adults.

After a generation or two, however, bishops could be confident that the majority of the adults under their care had already been through catechism classes in their youth, so they could focus their attention on the children. One of Gondrin's successors, Jean-Joseph Languet de Gergy, specified in the introduction to his catechism that he had designed it exclusively for children:

> Thus in giving you a new Catechism, we are not giving you a new doctrine, for this would not be pleasing to God. It is the same doctrine, taught in all places and in all times, that we present to you, compiled into a more useful form, and expressed in terms

more proportionate to the weakness of age of those who must be instructed, and more convenient for those who are charged to instruct them.

In fact, the entire introduction is about methods that could be used to make learning the catechism easier for children. Languet noted that each lesson included morals and Christian practices that could be used to show children how to apply what they learned in catechism to their daily lives. He also indicated that scripture stories could be used to illustrate doctrines taught in the catechism: "Nothing is more appropriate to attract the attention of children, and to help them acquire a taste for Catechisms, than to tell them of marvelous events drawn from the holy Scriptures, which pique their curiosity, and which paint in a manner so vivid and admirable, the justice, goodness, and the providence of God, and all of his other attributes." Furthermore, instead of specifying that both adults and children should learn the catechism, as Archbishop Gondrin had, Languet assumed that adults had already memorized it and insisted instead that the parents' responsibility was now to teach. He stipulated that parents should be their children's first catechists and asked them to teach their children the ten-page small catechism at home, even before they were old enough to attend the curé's catechism classes. A reprint edition of this catechism, published in 1747, even includes a fifty-seven-page special catechism specifically on first communion, again demonstrating how closely catechism and communion were tied together in the eighteenth century.[36]

This Sens catechism was not the only one that included a separate catechism on communion: specialized catechisms on topics like communion, confession, and confirmation became increasingly popular in the eighteenth century. Curés did not necessarily teach these catechisms year-round, as they did the small and ordinary catechisms, but they encouraged children to use them like study guides before an exam. Curés usually required children who wanted to take their first communion to attend extra catechism lessons in the months before Easter. Children attending these special sessions would have reviewed the ordinary diocesan catechism, but they also may have learned lessons from a confession and communion catechism so that they would know more details about these important sacraments and be able to participate in

them with decency and dignity. Similarly, the curé might have distributed confirmation catechisms to children who had not yet received
this sacrament once the announcement of a bishop's visit was made.[37]

Even more popular than the catechisms designed for specific sacraments were feast catechisms. Twenty-nine of the catechisms published in the seventeenth and eighteenth centuries included special catechisms with lessons that corresponded to holy days in the liturgical year
rather than the usual Creed/commandments/prayer/sacraments format. Usually between fifty and one hundred pages long, these catechisms were not necessarily read and memorized but instead used by
priests during their sermons on Sundays and feast days. For example,
curés presented lessons on the conception and nativity of Christ at
Christmastime and material on the Holy Spirit on Pentecost Sunday.
Catechisms used on feast days provided an opportunity to reinforce the
doctrine found in regular catechisms and helped to ensure that adults
continued to receive some formal religious instruction.[38]

The development of the feast catechism is further evidence of the
specialization of catechetical material in the eighteenth century; the
ordinary catechism became the standard text used in childhood, especially in preparation for first communion, while short catechisms dealing with more specific topics were used at different times of the year
according to specific needs. These parallel developments in early modern religious education demonstrate that Catholic Reformation bishops could accommodate the needs of the laity by using different forms
of catechisms so that the doctrines and practices they taught could be
learned and understood by both children and adults.

Catechisms: Organization

Every catechism published between 1650 and 1800 included the basic
doctrines of the catechism, but bishops organized the material in a variety of different ways. Many diocesan catechisms followed either Calvin's faith/law/prayer/sacraments structure or Trent's slightly different
faith/sacraments/law/prayer outline, although the material was often
divided into a number of different parts. For example, the 116-page catechism of Cahors follows the Trent outline, but the doctrines are di-

vided into ten chapters: three chapters on the Creed, one long chapter (27 pages) on the sacraments, two chapters on the commandments of God and the church, one short chapter (9 pages) on prayer, and three final chapters on sin, virtue, and the four ends of man.[39] Seventeenth- and eighteenth-century catechism authors often included chapters on sin and virtue borrowed from Canisius's "Christian Justice" section. In fact, several borrowed Canisius's faith/hope/charity/sacraments outline in its entirety. One of France's most famous seventeenth-century bishops, Jacques Bénigne Bossuet of Meaux, organized his 1687 catechism in this manner.[40]

In contrast to the catechisms that used outlines borrowed from sixteenth- and early seventeenth-century texts, about one-third of the diocesan catechisms examined here contain nothing more than a long list of lessons, with no particular organization at all. Most begin with lessons on either the Apostles' Creed or the mysteries of the faith, but the organization of the remaining material is not ordered in any logical or predictable way. For example, an oddly arranged catechism appeared in 1695 in the diocese of Le Mans. The first part of the text contains twenty-six lessons and 54 pages of text on the usual catechism topics in a somewhat irregular order, while part 2 gives 80 pages of more detailed explanations of these topics organized around the Creed, the commandments, and the sacraments. The bishop who issued this catechism, Louis de La Vergne-Montenard de Tressan, explained in his preface that he meant for children aged ten and older to study the first half of his catechism, while children preparing for their first communion would use the second, more detailed, half.[41] But children likely found this type of organization confusing, since the topics were separated from their explanations. Most small/ordinary catechism pairs were complete catechisms in themselves, but each part of the Le Mans catechism was incomplete without the other half and probably not very effective as a result. Perhaps Bishop La Vergne realized this; when he became the archbishop of Rouen he issued a different, more traditionally organized catechism used not only in his new diocese but also by bishops in Bayeux, Dijon, and Sens.[42]

In fact, despite the existence of these haphazardly arranged catechisms, many of the bishops who issued catechisms in the seventeenth and eighteenth centuries felt a sacred duty to find new ways to organize their texts that would facilitate learning in the children for whom they were written. The organization of the material in the ordinary catechisms also shows that bishops and their theologians attempted to make learning the catechism a more meaningful experience and more in tune with what parents wanted for their children's religious education. Each bishop wanted the text of his catechism to be a true science of salvation, not just a list of doctrines to be memorized. For example, Bishop François-Renaud de Villeneuve of Viviers mentioned in the introduction to his 1740 catechism that the people in his diocese had complained about the limitations of their catechism and that their curés had a difficult time with their instructions as a result. His revised version, Villeneuve claimed, included questions and answers that were "plainer, clearer, shorter, and more precise."[43]

Bishop Paul de Ribeyre of Saint-Flour responded to his parishioners' requests for a more appropriate catechism by issuing a new text that included more extended, but also more lucid, explanations of Christian truths. Furthermore, he presented the material in his catechism in a unique way, dividing both the small and ordinary catechisms into three parts: "The Natural Law," "The Ancient Law," and "The New Law." In part 1 Bishop Ribeyre stated that man has three obligations: duties toward God, toward his neighbor, and toward himself. These duties make up a "natural law," Ribeyre explained, because reason alone is sufficient to understand them. It is not enough to obey only this natural law, however, for parts 2 and 3 of the catechism indicate that God had revealed additional laws to his people. The first was the ancient law, or the law of the Jews, included in part 2 of the catechism. Part 3 lists the responsibilities of the "new law," including faith, prayer, grace, the sacraments, the commandments of God and the church, and practicing virtue.[44] By equating Catholic doctrines with laws, Bishop Ribeyre sought to persuade the laity that the catechism was not just a body of knowledge that had to be memorized but a set of guidelines to follow in everyday life.

Similarly, two other bishops organized their catechisms around the concept of duty. Bishop Louis-Sextius de Jarente de la Bruyère of Orléans wrote in 1762 that he wanted to issue a new edition of the diocesan catechism that "was more correct than the last, to clarify and explain more amply some articles which seemed to be a little obscure or too short, and to change certain expressions which are no longer in usage."[45] He indicated that the changes he had made would not fundamentally alter the substance of the doctrine, but the presentation of the material was somewhat different. The catechism is divided into four parts. The first part, on the Creed, is entitled "The First Duty of a Christian." The second part deals with the second duty of a Christian—the commandments—and the third and fourth parts correspond to duties three and four: prayer and the sacraments. The catechism published by Bishop Étienne de Champflour of La Rochelle in 1717 is organized in a similar manner. Bishop Champflour noted that he and his advisors had been working for several years to write a new catechism, "which through the brevity and clarity of its responses, and its methodical organization, could greatly facilitate the children's instruction."[46] The catechism is divided into three parts. The first follows the outline of the Creed, but the second, entitled "The Duties of the Christian Religion," teaches that Christians have six primary duties: to keep the commandments of God as well as those of the church, to fulfill the particular obligations of one's estate, to avoid sin, to practice Christian virtues, and to carry out all one's actions with holiness. The final section, "The Ways to Fulfill the Duties of the Christian Religion," teaches children that through the grace of God and the sacraments, these duties can be fulfilled. By organizing the material in this manner, Jarente and Champflour created a clear science of salvation for the children in their dioceses. Rather than just a collection of prayers and doctrines to be memorized and later forgotten, these catechisms presented a comprehensive set of duties that constituted a method for living a Christian life.

Although the Saint-Flour, Orléans, and La Rochelle catechisms are fairly unusual in the way they present Catholic doctrines, a few other contemporary catechisms were organized in a similar manner, demonstrating that the bishops and theologians who wrote them wanted to present the church's teachings as a comprehensive guide to living a Christian life. For example, an Avignon catechism contains all of the traditional components of the catechism organized around five verbs describing Christian obligations: *croire* (believe in the articles of the Creed), *espérer* (demonstrate hope through prayer), *faire* (keep the commandments of God and the church), *fuir* (avoid sin), and *recevoir* (receive the sacraments). Eleven other catechisms, divided into either four or five parts, were organized in the same way.[47] Children who read, memorized, and recited these catechisms could easily see that their duties as Catholics could be divided into simple steps to be followed one after the other.

By breaking down Catholic doctrine into easy-to-digest sets of morals and practices, catechism authors of the seventeenth and eighteenth centuries emphasized standardization of behavior and religious rituals rather than complex doctrines. Historians of the catechetical method have pointed out that many early seventeenth-century catechisms conscientiously stress external behaviors over internal understanding, and the diocesan catechisms continued and even standardized this practice.[48] Children learning their catechism could not simply believe in Jesus Christ and his church; they also had to profess that belief by memorizing and reciting the Apostles' Creed and then believe, hope, do, practice, and receive. Thus, the entire science of salvation, in its organization and in its overall message, was geared toward producing standardized behavior in Catholic children rather than any profound understanding of Catholic doctrine. At the same time, children would have found this method easier to learn and more applicable to their lives. Accordingly, the catechism satisfied the needs of both the clergy and the laity.

Orthodoxy and Orthopraxy: The Message of the Catechism

The first lesson of many seventeenth- and eighteenth-century catechisms often provided an introduction to the catechism itself, explaining exactly what purpose bishops had in mind for the catechisms that they issued. The catechism first published in 1669 for the diocese of Sens by Archbishop Gondrin began with the following question-and-answer series:

> **Question:** How should one serve God and live in a Christian manner?
> **Answer:** Before anything else, one must be instructed in the principal mysteries of our Religion in order to revere them, and the principal rules of piety in order to practice them.

Q: Where can one receive such important instruction?

A: At catechism, where all of these great truths are explained familiarly, and in few words.

Q: Is it not enough to read a good book, or to listen to sermons?

A: No, because ordinarily we will understand nothing if we have not been instructed in the catechism first.

Q: Is it thus necessary to attend catechism?

A: There is no doubt about it, because one cannot be saved without being instructed in these truths, and it is at Catechism where they are taught.[49]

The purpose of the catechism, at least according to Gondrin, was to teach God's eternal truths and to encourage people to live their lives in harmony with those truths.

Catechisms were supposed to teach both doctrines and the Catholic practices associated with those doctrines; in reality, however, the texts emphasized behavior rather than doctrine. Although the diocesan catechisms contained teachings about the mysteries of the religion and the rules of piety, the texts concentrated on standardizing behavior rather than teaching anything more than basic doctrines. The diocesan catechisms taught children what to believe and do but provided only the most basic and superficial reasons as to why God and the church required these rituals and behaviors. Although a thorough understanding of Catholic doctrines was not completely discouraged, bishops did not design their texts to provide that kind of understanding; instead, catechisms taught that Christians believed, practiced, asked, and received simply because God required it. The emphasis on behavior was ultimately acceptable to both the clergy and the laity: bishops and curés believed that too much doctrinal knowledge was inappropriate—and perhaps even dangerous—for the average peasant, while parents just wanted their children to know enough to participate in the rituals that defined them as Catholics. Both clergy and laity were also interested in teaching the parish children the moral and ethical codes that governed society—codes that make up a significant portion of catechetical material.

Perhaps the most obvious example of the emphasis on behavior rather than doctrine is found in the catechism lessons on the mystery

of the Trinity. The doctrine of the Trinity was one of the most important doctrines of the Catholic Church in the medieval and early modern periods—so fundamental that those who denied the doctrine of
the Trinity were not even considered Christian. From the first day they
attended catechism class, children learned how to make the sign of the
cross, and they were taught to think of the mystery of the Trinity each
time they crossed themselves and said "in the name of the Father, the
Son, and the Holy Spirit." Since children were supposed to make the
sign of the cross many times during the day—upon rising in the morning and before going to bed, before prayer, before and after meals, before working, and any time they felt tempted to sin or were in danger—
it is clear the Trinity was supposed to be a subject on children's minds
continually.[50] In addition, every catechism had at least one lesson devoted to the subject; it would be logical to assume, therefore, that bishops and theologians wanted children to understand this doctrine more
thoroughly than any other. Yet catechisms only scratched the surface
of the theology behind the Trinity, so that children only learned that
God the Father, Jesus Christ, and the Holy Spirit were three distinct
beings yet only one God:

> **Question:** There are thus three Gods?
> **Answer:** No: although they are three distinct Persons, they are
> nevertheless only one God.
> **Q:** How are these three distinct persons only one God?
> **A:** These three persons are only one God, because they have the
> same nature and the same Divinity.[51]

Catechetical explanations of the Trinity actually explained very
little. No child could truly understand that three separate people made
up only one God just because they shared abstract characteristics such
as "the same nature" and "the same divinity." Yet the bishops and theologians who wrote the catechisms ended their explanations at this point
and even justified this choice. In his 1734 catechism, Bishop Charles
de Caylus of Auxerre told his curés to omit theological discussions of
the mysteries in order to prevent confusion. Instead, children were to
be taught to simply trust God:

There is only danger in showing them certain difficulties which will spark their imaginations without them being able to understand such enlightenment; it is infinitely better to accustom them early to submit their weak reason to the yoke of the Faith, and to reject all discussion of difficulties, saying to them: it is enough for me to know that God has revealed a truth to his Church to believe it without hesitating, and without getting hung up on difficulties that are only founded in ignorance or the presumptions of men who have been corrupted by sin.[52]

Similarly, a Valence catechism begins the explanation of the Creed by asking, "What does this mean, *I believe?*"

> **Answer:** It means, although the Mysteries of my Religion are above my understanding, I hold them to be more certain than if I were to see them with my own eyes.
> **Q:** Why such a great certainty?
> **A:** Because our eyes can be mistaken, but not God, who revealed these Mysteries.[53]

The full title of this catechism is, ironically, *Catechism of the Diocese of Valence, Which explains all the Mysteries of the Religion, and its Dogmas.* All that is really explained, however, is that the mysteries must be believed solely because God had revealed them. Many diocesan catechisms contain similar lessons designed to teach children to believe and obey despite incomplete understanding.

Bishops also found it unnecessary to include many details about the theological questions commonly disputed by Protestants and Catholics in the early modern period. For example, because of the intensity of the debate over the real presence of Christ in the Eucharist during the early years of the Reformation, we might expect to find detailed lessons on transubstantiation in catechisms so that children could identify the correct Catholic doctrine and denounce the Protestant view if necessary. Yet not a single catechism examined here provides any instruction on the difference between Protestant and Catholic theology on this subject. In fact, one noteworthy characteristic of the diocesan catechisms is that they rarely mention Protestants at all. One catechism published in 1712 in Grenoble—a diocese that shared a border with Protestant Swiss territories—includes some material denouncing Protestantism in general,[54] but the lessons on the Eucharist are no different from those in catechisms used in areas without large Protestant populations. Most catechisms did not engage in any doctrinal debates, no doubt because these subjects were seen as inappropriate for children. Teaching opposing doctrines would only create confusion and could even result in more heresy. Perhaps bishops hoped that by ignoring Protestantism and emphasizing Catholic theology and practice, the offending Protestant doctrines would eventually disappear. For whatever reason, theologians emphasized Catholic doctrines and definitions in their catechisms and did not dignify Protestantism by debating it.

The Catholic definitions of the Eucharist that bishops included in their catechisms were thus generally basic and cursory. An average of 20 percent of most catechisms was devoted to the sacraments of penance and the Eucharist, but most of this material dealt with confession and communion—the ceremonies surrounding the two sacraments rather than the doctrinal reasons behind them. Out of the eighteen pages in Auxerre's 1751 ordinary catechism that provide instructions about communion, only four pages are about the Eucharist itself, in which the doctrine of transubstantiation is explained very simply:

> **Question:** What do you call the nature, or appearance of the bread and the wine?
> **Answer:** It is what appears to our senses as the color, shape, and the taste.
> **Q:** Are the bread and the wine also in the Eucharist, in its nature or appearance?
> **A:** No: the bread and the wine are changed into the body and blood of our Lord Jesus Christ.
> **Q:** What does the Church call this transformation?
> **A:** It calls it Transubstantiation, meaning the transformation of one substance into another.
> **Q:** How is this transformation done?
> **A:** It is done by the almighty virtue of Jesus Christ that the Priest pronounces with the name of the divine Savior.[55]

The bulk of the lesson gives the history of the institution of this sacrament by Christ and the apostles. The text provides just the basics of an extremely complicated doctrine and then concentrates on how believers were supposed to take part in the outward ritual of communion. The conclusion is obvious: all children had to do was believe that the real presence of Christ was in the bread and wine, and they did not have to understand why.

Even catechisms devoted solely to confession and communion tended to give the doctrine of the Eucharist short shrift. For example, at the end of an ordinary catechism published in Grenoble in 1786, the bishop included a thirty-four-page special catechism, "Method for a good confession and communion." Although a definition of the Eucharist appeared in the regular catechism, no further doctrinal explanation was included in the special catechism; instead, communicants found detailed instructions on the proper way to participate in this sacrament. Along with the dispositions necessary for a good communion (modesty of the body, purity of the heart, and fervor and devotion of the soul), men were told to approach the altar with their hair and beard trimmed and with a clean face and hands, while women were warned not to wear any rouge or makeup and to keep their breasts, arms, and shoulders covered.[56] An entire page of this catechism is devoted to mistakes that people often made when taking communion, including pushing and shoving when approaching the altar, whispering to each other instead of paying attention, letting their eyes wander around the congregation instead of bowing their heads, and chewing the host rather than just swallowing it. The following page of this lesson gives a list of things that one should do during communion instead:

1. Keep your eyes modestly open. 2. Do not look around. 3. Take the cloth and bring it to your chest without using it to clean yourself. 4. Look at the holy Host when the Priest arrives to give you communion. 5. Gently raise your head and hold it still. 6. Open your mouth slightly. 7. Bring your tongue to the edge of your lower lip. 8. Draw your tongue carefully back into your mouth and close it after the Priest has deposited the Host. 9. Let the holy Host be moistened on your tongue for a little while, and then swallow it. 10. If it sticks to the roof of your mouth, be patient, and try to

detach it gently with your tongue. 11. Do not withdraw from the
rail until your row of communicants is finished.[57]

If people had to be given eleven separate instructions on how to approach the altar and swallow the host, the bishops and theologians
who wrote catechisms evidently did not feel that the majority of their
parishioners needed to know anything more than the basics behind the
practices.

When bishops said that they wanted to teach the truths of the religion to the people of their dioceses, they meant truths about the way
that the religion was supposed to be practiced, not complicated doctrines. Multiple examples of doctrines treated only superficially in the
diocesan catechisms could be included here: the doctrines of the Incarnation and the Redemption are dealt with in the same way as the mystery of the Trinity—children were taught that believing in these mysteries, even if they did not understand them, was necessary as a sign of
their faith in an almighty God; the sacramental nature of marriage is almost completely ignored; the complicated doctrine of grace is usually
relegated to a few questions and answers introducing the sacraments,[58]
and some of the shorter catechisms omit it altogether.[59]

Of the religious rituals that the diocesan catechisms do emphasize,
the sacraments are undoubtedly the most important. The entire purpose of the sacraments was to give an outward sign of belief—belief
in the efficacy of God's grace, the divinity of Jesus Christ, the legitimacy
of the church, and the communion of the saints. One of the most important functions of the church was to ensure that people participated
in the sacraments throughout each stage of their lives: from baptism at
birth, to entering adulthood with first communion and later marriage,
to extreme unction at death. Participation in the sacraments was also
important to lay parents, who wanted to make sure that their children
had enough instruction to approach the altar for the Eucharist. Lessons
on the sacraments make up a total of 32 percent of all catechetical material in the catechisms examined here, not including the specialized
catechisms on confirmation, confession, or communion. Usually, instructions on the sacraments made up the final lessons of the catechism
since the church saw participation in these rituals as the culmination of
all Catholic theology. In this sense, the purpose of every mystery, doc-

trine, or truth learned in the catechism was to better prepare the laity
to participate in the sacraments.

Like catechism lessons on the sacraments, lessons on the commandments concentrated on the regulation of religious behavior. This
is especially true of the material devoted to the commandments of the
church, which taught children when to attend Mass, when to take communion, when to feast, and when to fast. But lessons on the Decalogue
also provided regulations for religious behavior. For example, bishops
usually divided lessons on the first commandment into two parts. The
first part examined love for and worship of God, and the second explained that devotion to saints, relics, the cross, and other images was
just another way of worshiping God. The following questions and answers from a Paris catechism are fairly typical for a first commandment
lesson:

> **Question:** What does it mean to worship God?
> **Answer:** It means that we give him the homage that we owe him,
> as the first Being, and our sovereign Savior.
> **Q:** Do we worship the Saints?
> **A:** No: we do not give them the homage that is owed only to God,
> but we honor them as his servants and friends.
> **Q:** Can we pray to the Saints?
> **A:** Yes: it is good and useful to have recourse to their prayers, in
> order to obtain from God the grace that we have need of.
> **Q:** How do we pray to them?
> **A:** We do not pray to ask them to give us grace, but for them to
> ask God for us and with us, for the merits of Jesus Christ.
> **Q:** Can we honor their Relics?
> **A:** Yes, because they are the precious remains of a body which
> was the temple of the Holy Spirit, and which will be gloriously
> resurrected.[60]

In the process of learning the first commandment, then, children were
given more information about external religious practices and appropriate religious behaviors.

Furthermore, lessons on the Decalogue provided an opportunity
for the church to teach not only the way that religious rituals should

be carried out but also the ways in which mundane, secular activities could be done in a manner that was pleasing to God, the church, and the community. Lessons on the commandments can be interpreted as a practical moral code (rather than simply a list of doctrines) that taught children their proper relationship within both the church and the community. For example, lessons on the second commandment, which forbids using God's name in vain, concentrated on the broader topics of swearing and oaths. Children were taught that there are three ways to violate this commandment: swearing against the truth, against justice, and without judgment. Lessons then gave examples of what each of these three things meant. In a Nantes catechism children learned that it was wrong to swear an oath for something that they could not actually accomplish, and that even a small lie, when accompanied by an oath, would greatly offend God. Priests were supposed to explain further that "people of commerce or artisans, who swear so easily over the value of their work or merchandise, must be especially careful of this."[61] The author of this catechism did not stop at giving religious instruction and included business advice as well.

Material on the third commandment, which admonishes believers to keep the Sabbath day holy, also shows how catechisms taught children to live their daily lives in accordance with Christian principles. One of the biggest struggles that bishops and parish priests had with the laity seems to have been the regulation of their activities on Sundays. Curés usually had little difficulty getting their parishioners to attend Mass on Sundays and even feast days. At the conclusion of services, however, lay men and women often spent the rest of the day doing the same things that they would have done on any other day of the week. It should come as no surprise, then, that catechism lessons on the third commandment included lists of appropriate Sunday activities. Besides attending Mass, listening to the curé's sermon, and attending catechism and vespers, children who read and memorized a Châlons catechism learned that Sundays should be spent reading good books (the text recommends *Le Bon Laboureur* and the *Guide des Pécheurs* by Grenada, among others), visiting the poor and the sick, and working to reconcile those of the community involved in quarrels and lawsuits.[62]

Catechism lessons on the fifth commandment—thou shalt not kill—regulated behavior not just on Sundays but on every day of the week. It seems logical to assume that material on such a simple commandment would be brief and to the point, but catechism authors expanded this commandment into a lesson on community relationships rather than simply an admonition against murder. As a result, lessons on the fifth commandment were often the longest and most specific of any of the commandment lessons. In an Auxerre catechism, children learned that if they harmed their neighbor in any way, they had broken the fifth commandment. The text outlines three sins against one's neighbor: harm against body, soul, or reputation. Harming in body meant killing, wounding, or striking another; children learned that if they sinned in this way they had to apologize to the offended party and compensate them for any harm caused. Harming a neighbor's soul is described as causing scandal and leading others to commit sin as a result:

> **Question:** How do we do wrong to our Neighbor's soul?
> **Answer:** By encouraging him to offend God, through words or bad examples; this is what is called the sin of scandal.
> **Q:** What are those who are the cause of a scandal obliged to do?
> **A:** Repair the scandal as much as possible, especially by being a good example.

There were two ways that one could harm another in reputation: slander (*calomnie*) and gossip (*médisance*). Those who committed these sins were told that they had to publicly recant in order to be forgiven. Finally, the Auxerre catechism ends with a list of additional sins forbidden by the fifth commandment, including hatred, injuries, mockery, and curses.[63]

Lessons on the seventh commandment (in combination with those on the fifth) covered nearly every possible relationship that one might have with other members of the community. While the fifth commandment deals with physical and emotional harm, the seventh—thou shalt not steal—forbids children to steal or harm their neighbors' goods and belongings. And, like most of the other commandments, the lessons on the seventh commandment covered more than just the obvious sins. For example, an Arras catechism published in 1745 listed three general categories of theft: taking knowingly and unjustly the goods of others; dishonestly retaining other people's things; and causing damage to the goods of another. The lesson then included numerous examples of the most commonly committed "thefts" by people of all social categories. The word "steal" thus took on new meanings: the rich stole from the poor through unjust lawsuits, through usury, or by overcharging them for "trifles"; merchants stole from their customers when they sold bad merchandise, when they sold goods at a higher price than necessary, or when they consciously bought goods from others for less than their true value; workers stole from their employers when they did not use their workday wisely and honestly. Even magistrates who made poor judgments or submitted to bribery had broken the seventh commandment.[64] Other catechisms provided similar lists of common thefts, including fraud, unjust lawsuits, usury, nonpayment of wages to workers and servants, destruction of crops or vines, and unfair distribution of the *taille*.[65] Thus, a seemingly simple commandment became a lesson in community ethics.

The Decalogue lessons also included instruction on family relationships tied to material on the fourth commandment. This is another aspect of catechetical education that the clergy and the laity could easily agree on, so fourth commandment lessons were often quite extensive. It was advantageous to families, to the parish, and to society as a whole for children to learn to properly respect their parents and other authorities.[66] In a Grenoble catechism, for example, children learned that to honor their parents they had to respect, love, obey, and assist them. The text then listed dozens of instructions surrounding these four duties, including having esteem for parents, helping them acquire good things in their lives (especially things related to their souls and their salvation), obeying them immediately and happily in all things, and praying for them in sickness and affliction. The lesson included an equal number of inappropriate behaviors toward parents, from simple disobedience to abandoning parents in their old age.[67]

But many fourth commandment lessons did not stop at this point. Some catechism authors extended duties toward parents to include all superiors: masters, husbands (in regard to their wives), clergy, lords and magistrates, godparents, tutors, and the elderly. Following this list of the parish community's principal authorities, the 1665 Agen catechism provided details on each of these relationships; thus, children learned not only their own place in society but also the roles that they would one day play as adults in the community.[68]

The remaining commandments of the Decalogue were dealt with in much less detail in the diocesan catechisms. The subject of the ninth and tenth commandments, against coveting your neighbor's wife or goods, was usually covered sufficiently in the material on the fifth and seventh commandments. The eighth commandment, against bearing false witness, was presented in relation to the second commandment, reminding children again of the importance of honesty in legal depositions and providing further injunctions against lying, slander, and gossip. The sixth commandment, forbidding fornication, had to be taught very carefully. Bishops and theologians had to be able to make sure that children knew of their responsibility to remain pure in body and soul, but they did not want to give them details that might put inappropriate ideas into their heads.[69] Lessons on the sixth commandment were thus intentionally short and vague. A Besançon catechism included only seven questions and answers in a lesson on the sixth commandment, admonishing children to avoid "dances, conversations with the opposite sex that are too free, vanity, immodest clothing, going out with the breast uncovered, excess in drinking and eating, reading novels and comedies, and, especially, idleness." The word "chastity" is used in only one question-and-answer set, and the wording of most of the text is so ambiguous that if the commandment itself had not been printed at the beginning of the lesson, it would be hard to know exactly what it was about.[70]

Yet the sins of adultery and fornication, and even covetousness, are primarily private sins, while the other commandments, and the diocesan catechisms in general, emphasized the repercussions of public sins. Catechetical education in the seventeenth and eighteenth centuries focused on how to regulate public, outward behavior in both the religious and the secular spheres. Lessons on the sacraments and the commandments of the church taught children about the outward rituals that they would participate in throughout their lives, while the lessons on the Decalogue provided the religious, ethical, and moral code by which the church hoped society would be governed. Catechisms therefore taught children their proper place in society—subordinate to the

God who created them and to the church and its priests who performed the sacraments and were as such the conduit of God's grace. But children were also part of a larger community, and specific rules governed that relationship, from respecting the lives and property of others to refraining from gossiping and backbiting. Because children did not need to have a knowledge of sophisticated doctrines in order to understand and follow these rules and prescriptions, catechisms left out much of the theology and concentrated on behavior. This did not mean that true belief was considered unimportant, or that bishops wanted children to obey the commandments and take communion without really knowing what they were doing. In fact, Bishop Bossuet of Meaux explicitly taught that outward behavior was actually a sign of belief:

> **Question:** How do we obtain Faith in so many inconceivable things?
> **Answer:** The desire to see them one day.
> **Q:** Where will we see them?
> **A:** In Heaven, when God will reveal himself clearly to us.
> **Q:** Why then do we believe all of these things?
> **A:** Because God revealed them.
> **Q:** And why has God obliged us to believe these inconceivable things?
> **A:** Because it is pleasing to him to exercise our Faith.
> **Q:** Is a wrong done to us because we are obliged to believe things which are above us?
> **A:** On the contrary, it honors us.
> **Q:** Why?
> **A:** Because it elevates us above ourselves.[71]

The seventeenth- and eighteenth-century bishops' science of salvation was thus a science in only a particular sense. Diocesan catechisms were not the ultimate repository of religious knowledge, nor were they meant to be. The early catechisms of Calvin, Auger, and the Council of Trent engaged in theological debates, and anyone who studied those texts carefully certainly would have come away with a thorough understanding of Christian theology. But as the catechetical method evolved over the years, catechisms emphasized a knowledge, or "science," of practical religious behavior. Bishops wrote their catechisms exclusively for children, so the texts became shorter and more specific. They limited the material included in the text to only those doctrines deemed appropriate for a child about to take communion for the first time. The organization of catechetical material emphasized behavior over doctrine as well, with four- or five-part catechisms telling children specifically what they had to believe, do, and receive in order to be saved. Each part of the catechism was further divided into chapters, lessons, and questions and answers, with lists of sins and virtues, multiple "dos and don'ts," and practical moral lessons to be applied in everyday life. In this way the science of salvation became a set of step-by-step instructions on both religious and secular behavior: a how-to manual for those seeking salvation.

The Catholic Reformation at the parish level was not meant to make every believer a theologian or a monk. Reform for both the laity and the clergy meant a more faithful and respectful adherence to Catholic rituals and practices and the acceptance of an ethical code infused with Catholic truths; therefore, this is what seventeenth- and eighteenth-century catechisms were designed to teach. The compromises and accommodations that bishops and their theologians accepted in order to make their catechisms more acceptable to, and useful for, the people of their dioceses demonstrate that reform did not mean indoctrination or a rigid enforcement of uniformity. In fact, bishops and parents wanted much the same thing: obedient and respectful children who would grow up to participate in the sacraments of the church and fulfill their obligations to the community. They both used the catechism to help them accomplish these goals. By the end of the eighteenth century, the catechetical method was an established part of both childhood and parish life, as both the clergy and the laity worked together to ensure that the Catholic "science" would indeed lead to salvation.

CHAPTER TWO

The Catechetical Method
Theory and Practice

By the end of the seventeenth century, efforts to reform the Catholic Church were well under way in most French dioceses. Bishops were more committed to residing in their dioceses and overseeing both administrative and spiritual affairs. Accordingly, many bishops dedicated themselves to creating smoothly running administrative systems in their dioceses, and through their pastoral visits they made sure that their churches, chapels, and monasteries were in working order. They also preached, instructed, and admonished as they tried to bring about a higher level of spirituality in the souls under their care. The French bishops made a concerted effort to establish educated and dedicated priests in their parishes, and, with the institution of seminaries and regular synods, managed to ensure that curés conformed to fairly rigorous ecclesiastical standards. They also tried to make certain that their curés were willing and able to provide instruction and guidance for the uneducated members of their flock—primarily the children and young adults. Because the diocesan catechism was the most effective tool that bishops had for ensuring this instruction took place, the reforming clergy maintained a strong commitment to their catechetical science of salvation and continued to publish and endorse catechisms for their dioceses throughout the seventeenth and eighteenth centuries.

Bishops did not limit themselves to publishing and distributing these catechisms to curés and the laity, however; they also prescribed a specific pedagogical method for teaching the catechism. Bishops believed that the curés, schoolteachers, and parents who taught catechism needed a sound and exact method for their instruction that was appropriate to the needs of their pupils. Even instruction in perfectly orthodox doctrines, if presented in a confusing manner, could lead to misunderstandings or heresy—a bishop's greatest fear. Consequently, bishops were extremely careful to provide curés and other catechists with a particular method for instruction, which was just as significant as the catechisms themselves.

The bishops' catechetical method essentially had three components. First, bishops and educational theorists believed that education for both boys and girls had to begin when they were young, with minds and spirits free from corrupting influences. At the same time, because of the tender age of the students, the material to be learned had to be broken down into small parts that could easily be engraved onto children's impressionable minds. The second part of the bishops' method was their insistence that children learn through memorization, which required no critical thinking and inspired little independent thought. Although the recitation of page after page of questions and answers might seem tedious and even useless to those of us in the twenty-first century who have been taught that education should develop powers of reason and imagination rather than rote memory, early modern bishops believed the training and exercise of the memory was the fundamental principle of all education. Once the laity had this solid, orthodox foundation, they would be able to build upon it throughout their lives as they listened to sermons, participated in the sacraments, and read pious books on their own.

The third part of the bishops' catechetical method involved the regulation of children's behavior. Catechism classes were meant to teach much more than just the actual questions and answers of the catechism itself. Learning proper religious and moral behavior while receiving instruction was just as important as memorizing the doctrines. Children learned how to sit still in church, listen to religious authorities, and bow their heads during prayer, among other things. Over and over again, bishops told their curés in pastoral letters and elsewhere to reward children who behaved with modesty and restraint, even if they had failed to memorize their catechism lesson for the day. Similarly, students who may have learned the text of their lesson perfectly but who were caught carousing with their classmates were to be admonished and made to kneel at the front of the class in penance. Thus, just as the content and organization of catechisms emphasized behavior over doctrine, the method of instruction advocated by bishops also highlighted the catechist's priority as teaching proper behavior, often at the expense of children reaching a true understanding of the doctrines of the catechism.

If placed in the context of early modern educational theory, the bishops' method corresponds to what most educational theorists of the time prescribed for their students, whether clerical or lay, child or adult, male or female. It has often been assumed that the dryness of the catechetical method would be a detriment to any program of religious education, but in reality the catechism was taught with the same principles that guided anyone attempting to master a particular body of knowledge in the early modern period. A belief in early education and the use of repetition and memorization were in no way new or unique teaching methods; as we shall see, bishops built upon a long tradition of theories about proper methods of both secular and religious education dating back to Roman times. Bishops were heavily indebted to both humanist and Jesuit pedagogical theories as well, and the Jesuit system remained the dominant method of education throughout the early modern period.

The only serious challenge to the pedagogical method that bishops had adopted came toward the end of the eighteenth century with the

Enlightenment. The new educational theories, typified by philosophers such as Locke and Rousseau, emphasized reason and empirical learning rather than memorization. Bishops in general were reluctant to embrace Enlightenment ideas about education, but since most of the pedagogical and curricular changes applied only to the children of the upper classes, historians would be mistaken to label the bishops as backward or reactionary. Bishops knew that the primary audience for their catechisms was the boys and girls of the lower classes—children for whom learning by rote was still the ideal method of instruction. Most Enlightenment thinkers, no matter how radical their ideas about secondary and university education, still believed in the necessity of religious education for the masses and did not question the utility of the catechetical method. Thus, bishops should not be accused of ignoring contemporary pedagogical theories; in fact, they relied on a proven method of instruction that was most applicable to the majority of their parishioners.

The catechetical method, emphasizing early education, memorization, and conformity to standards of behavior acceptable to both church and society, was one of the primary tools of both religious education and social discipline in the early modern period. Bishop Bégon of Toul told his curés that if they would teach the catechism in the way that he outlined, they would banish ignorance in their parishes and form a holy nation. He also told the parents in his diocese what the foundation of this holy nation would be:

> Exhort Fathers and Mothers to have the catechism in their homes, and to read it frequently as a family . . . Help them to understand that a child well brought up and well instructed brings joy and honor to his Father and Mother; that parents will be the first to taste the fruit of their children's education; and that the way to make sure their Children are submissive to their will, is to teach them to know and respect the will of God.[1]

Bishops presented catechetical education to parents as a way to make their children more obedient, but by extension it was also a way to ensure that society would run smoothly. Children who respected God and their parents would also respect other authorities, whether clerical or lay. Furthermore, respectful children would grow up to be responsible members of the community as well as practicing Catholics, providing order and stability for the village as a whole.

Educational Theory in the Early Modern Period

One of the most well-known historians of childhood is Philippe Ariès, whose work *Centuries of Childhood: A Social History of Family Life* has been the subject of great controversy since its first appearance in 1960. Ariès is famous for arguing that the concepts of childhood and adolescence, as stages of life separate from infancy and adulthood, did not exist until the seventeenth century. Using evidence drawn from art and literature as well as demographics, Ariès insists that because young children died so frequently in the medieval period, parents did not allow themselves to become too attached to their children and had little interest in developing their character until they were older and their survival more certain.[2] The reaction to Ariès has been passionate; many medieval historians have vehemently objected to his conclusions and have produced evidence that parents did in fact care deeply about their children in the Middle Ages, insisting that seventeenth- and eighteenth-century changes in ideas about childhood and adolescence were not nearly as significant as Ariès describes.[3]

Yet much of what Ariès says about the relationship between ideas about childhood and early modern educational theories has been subject to less controversy. In a fascinating chapter entitled "From Immodesty to Innocence," Ariès uses the meticulous record kept by Louis XIII's childhood physician to analyze contemporary ideas about young children's moral education. The physician's diary shows that there was very little concern over Louis's moral development because his caregivers believed that he was too young to commit or even understand moral infractions. Things of an overtly sexual nature were not hidden from the future king until he was about seven years old. Ariès believes that this practice was not limited to the royal family. In the first half of the seventeenth century, he argues, no one worried about children's innocence and few precautions were taken to protect it.[4]

Ariès then draws upon the writings of theologians and moralists who demonstrate a significant shift in thinking about early childhood education in the mid-seventeenth century. By the time of Louis XIV's reign, these writers began to insist that children were by nature innocent but also weak and pliable; the impressions that they received in their earliest years would have the most influence on them throughout their adult lives. If parents and other members of society did not make efforts to both guard children's innocence and strengthen them against the evils of the world, they would grow up corrupt and debauched. Both clerical and lay educational theorists believed that a lack of attention to children's education would lead to not only undisciplined children but also a dangerously libertine society. Ariès insists that this change in attitudes toward children and childhood contributed to the increased number of *collèges, petites écoles,* and other educational institutions in the late seventeenth and eighteenth centuries.[5]

The idea that children needed to be molded in their youth was not entirely new; in fact, the most influential ideas about education in the early modern period can be dated to the Roman era and the first-century writings of Quintilian. Overall, Quintilian's method of education emphasizes discipline, morality, memory, and repetition; each of these characteristics became indispensable to later educators and moralists who looked to Rome for examples of effective educational practices. In his *Institutio oratoria* (The Orator's Education) Quintilian sets out to educate a child as an orator. His plan of instruction begins when the child in question is just learning to speak, and he criticizes those who would argue that children should not be taught their letters before age seven. He says that children had to do something to occupy their time, and what better to busy them with than learning both morality and reading and writing? Quintilian also notes that children learn things much more easily than adults; as an example, he describes foreign slaves who never mastered Latin despite living in Rome for nearly all of their adult lives. Quintilian further emphasizes that what was learned in childhood would be retained throughout adulthood as well: "I should like to suggest that the lines set for copying should not be meaningless sentences, but should convey some moral lesson. The memory of such things stays with us till we are old, and the impression thus made on the unformed mind will be good for the character also."[6]

Quintilian continued to be influential in the Middle Ages and was much admired by two groups of scholars that would have a tremendous

effect on education in the early modern period: Renaissance humanists and the Jesuits.[7] Of the humanists, perhaps none was more influential than Erasmus, and the importance of early moral and character-
defining education for children was a crucial component of his thought.
Like Quintilian, Erasmus argues that children's minds should be occupied with morality and letters at a very young age. He claims that the
mind of a child is flexible and tenacious but must be taught correct
principles before becoming warped by superstition or incorrect phi-
losophies. Erasmus provides a metaphor for children's education based
on a fascinating, albeit erroneous, view of the way that animals raised
their young:

> It is said a bear's cub is at birth but an ill-formed lump which by a
> long process of licking is brought into shape. Nature, in giving you
> a son, presents you, let me say, a rude, unformed creature, which it
> is your part to fashion so that it may become indeed a man. If this
> fashioning be neglected you have but an animal still: if it be con-
> trived earnestly and wisely, you have, I had almost said, what may
> prove a being not far from a God.[8]

Human children too, in Erasmus's view, had to be licked into shape in
their earliest years while their minds and natures were still soft and
malleable.

Erasmus's works do not provide a complete plan of education, nor
does he recommend any one method for teaching young children; he
and many of his humanist colleagues were more interested in criticizing
the existing educational system than in building a new one. The task of
creating and implementing an early modern program of education was
instead taken up by the Jesuits, who, in the sixteenth century, began to
create the largest and most unified network of secondary schools that
Europe had ever seen. The Jesuits were the first to apply, on a broad,
comprehensive basis, the ideals of humanist educational theorists in a
practical and systematic way. Their schools were (theoretically) open to
both clerical and lay students, from any economic or social background.
From the University of Paris they borrowed and adapted a system of
classes that each boy would follow in his educational career, bringing
much-needed uniformity and compatibility to the secondary educa-

tional system. By the time the order was suppressed in 1773, the Jesuits had opened more than eight hundred educational institutions in Europe and Latin America. In France in the seventeenth century they opened new *collèges* and took over existing institutions, and they continued to administer these schools until the order's expulsion in 1762. Most of the bishops and theologians who wrote or issued catechisms would have attended Jesuit schools, and since the Jesuit system was adopted by nearly all other religious orders who were involved in education, no bishop could have escaped the Jesuit method entirely.[9]

The Jesuit *Ratio Studiorum* (the rules for their educational institutions adopted by the order in 1599) outlines an entire program of study infused with the desire to inculcate morality and good character in their students. This program had a great influence on early modern French bishops. Schools that the Jesuits administered had three basic purposes: to teach "letters," meaning humanities and the arts; to intertwine a religious education with secular studies; and to form the religious and moral character of their students. The *Ratio* is divided into sets of rules issued for each teacher or prefect, and the first rule given in each list always reminds the teacher to have for his ultimate goal the development of good character in his students: "The teacher shall so train the youths entrusted to the Society's care that they may acquire not only learning but also habits of conduct worthy of a Christian. He should endeavor both in the classroom and outside to train the impressionable minds of his pupils in the loving service of God and in all the virtues required for this service."[10] The rules also show that students had to be carefully monitored in order to keep them from coming into contact with anything of a questionable nature. Teachers scrutinized the books that their students read, and any plays that students memorized and performed had to be approved by the faculty. The daily schedule was kept so busy that students had few opportunities to get into mischief— if they were not in class or at recitation, students were supposed to be at confession or Mass, or studying under the supervision of one of the teachers. The Jesuits' basic philosophy for instilling morals and virtues in their students was quite clear: keeping children away from sinful or dangerous behavior and ideas, and exposing them only to pious books and role models would ensure that their own morals and activities reflected solely the latter.

Although Jesuits taught only boys, their methods became so dominant that they influenced educational systems for girls as well. The female teaching congregations that spread rapidly throughout France in the second half of the seventeenth century depended heavily on Jesuit methods.[11] The women of the teaching congregations were perhaps even more dedicated to the idea of a solid Catholic education in catechism and morality than their Jesuit contemporaries because their role as purveyors of moral education for girls from all walks of life was at times the sole justification for their existence.[12] The Jesuits saw themselves as providing a classical education in a religious context, but women like the Ursulines and the Soeurs du Saint-Enfant-Jésus had no such mission. Their job was simply to catechize young girls and then help them prepare for their futures as wives and mothers, and instruction in Catholic doctrines and morals was at the center of that education. As far as religious and moral education was concerned, the same educational theories that applied to boys applied to girls as well. Girls who attended schools run by the religious orders, either as boarders or as day students, learned the same catechism and read from the same religious and devotional books as their male counterparts in the Jesuit *collège*.

In addition to an emphasis on religion and morality, the Jesuits and other teaching orders insisted that their students spend the bulk of their time memorizing and reciting both classical and religious texts. To the modern mind, an education centered solely around memorization seems unbelievably tedious and ineffective, and in fact several historians and educational theorists have criticized not only the Jesuits but any religious or secular group that taught primarily through memorization. Gerald Strauss argues in his work on Protestant religious education in sixteenth-century Germany that the catechetical method was one of the main reasons that Protestant reformers failed to instill a thorough knowledge of Christian doctrines in their followers. Memorizing a catechism, he insists, was a wholly useless form of instruction since the doctrines were broken down into such small bits that children failed to grasp the bigger picture. In addition, the process of memorizing these long texts was so dull that children quickly became bored and lost interest in obtaining anything but a superficial knowledge of Protestant doctrine. He claims that Protestant leaders who visited congregations to question people on their catechism found that children only parroted the doctrines and had no real understanding of what they were saying. Strauss concludes that the disadvantages of the catechetical method were responsible for the larger failure of Protestant leaders to establish a truly reformed version of Christianity at the parish level.[13]

Yet perhaps Strauss is too hard on those Protestants who chose to use the catechism to teach religious doctrine—after all, the catechists were only following the educational theories of the time period. Anyone involved in education, from Quintilian to Locke, strongly believed that a trained memory was the basis for all learning. As Quintilian wrote in his chapter on memory in the *Institutio oratoria,* "all the effort I have described up to now is futile unless the other parts are held together, as it were, by this animating principle. All learning depends on memory, and teaching is in vain if everything we hear slips away."[14] Furthermore, during the Middle Ages a person with a prodigious memory was regarded as the highest sort of genius. Thomas Aquinas, for example, was known for having an excellent memory. When he wrote his famous *Summa theologica* in the thirteenth century, Aquinas did not scribble away at a desk cluttered with books, notes, and previous drafts; rather, he composed his text in his head and later dictated it to a scribe from memory. Having a good memory was also equated with a good moral character; authors of saints' lives often praised their subject's capacity for memorization.[15]

The primary purpose of medieval education was to develop one's memory and then fill it with knowledge that could be drawn upon in any situation. The powers of reason were not innate, as Enlightenment thinkers would later emphasize; for medieval scholars, reason was impossible without memory since one had to have a base of knowledge stored in one's memory to allow the exercise of reason. The process of learning in the Middle Ages, therefore, involved inscribing onto the mind mental copies of texts. When medieval scholars and their students read, they did not take notes—they memorized. Texts were read over and over again, analyzed, and digested in the memorization process. Writing was often thought of as an aid to memory but not as a replacement for it. This was as true for the humanists as it was for medieval scholars, as Erasmus notes: "Personally I disapprove of the practice of taking down a lecture just as it is delivered. For this prevents reliance upon memory which should, as time goes on, need less and

less of that external aid which note-taking supplies."[16] Scholars before
the age of printing even felt that having a text memorized was more
important than owning a physical copy of the text itself. They believed
that while manuscript copies might have errors, a carefully trained
memory was entirely trustworthy.[17]

With the arrival of the printing press, having a trained memory
may have become less important in the early modern academic world,
but memorization was still a significant part of children's education.
Although the Jesuits' *Ratio studiorum* does not provide an example of a
typical school day, it is clear that students spent their time in three main
activities: listening to lectures, memorizing the material presented in the
lectures, and then reciting it. Students took oral examinations; written
compositions were assigned as well, but these compositions were more
like in-class exams. Students were expected to write from memory without the aid of notes. No matter what stage a student in a Jesuit school
was in, it was expected that he would spend a significant part of the
day working to memorize a variety of material, from grammar rules,
to passages from Greek and Latin texts, to professors' lectures.[18]

The memorization of texts, along with religious and moral instruction begun at an early age, are the most significant aspects of
early modern educational theory. Ariès may have overemphasized the
novelty of this philosophy in his work, but he is certainly correct to suggest that by the end of the seventeenth century this idea was not an
isolated or obscure hypothesis but a pervasive, comprehensive theory
that influenced any group, religious or otherwise, engaged in the education of youth.[19] Any child who enrolled in a *collège* or other secondary
school would have encountered a curriculum based on memorization
of texts—religious or secular—infused with a heavy dose of ethics and
morality. As pedantic and backward as these methods may seem to the
modern mind, seventeenth- and eighteenth-century educational theorists saw them as classic techniques that had stood the test of time and
would continue to produce results.

The bishops who issued catechisms for their dioceses in this same
period subscribed wholeheartedly to these methods, and they asked
their curés to apply them when they taught the catechism to the children in their parishes. Even though Erasmus and later the Jesuits had
written primarily for members of the elite classes—few peasants

would have had the opportunity to attend a Jesuit *collège*—bishops had to provide a religious education for children from all levels of society. The fact that the bishops adopted a program of education based on teaching young children both doctrines and morals through the memorization of prayers and the catechism demonstrates that Jesuit theories of education had penetrated all levels of society and applied to more than just the children of the elites. Jesuit teaching methods were also deemed appropriate for girls as well as boys; just as the Ursulines and other female teaching orders adopted them, bishops applied those same methods to both the boys and the girls in their dioceses. The bishops' catechetical method, far from being backward or ineffective, was very much in tune with the educational theories of the day, and they believed it would be successful. For Catholic Reformation bishops, an education in Catholic doctrines and morals, engraved onto the hearts and minds of children from their earliest years, was the only way to ensure that the laity would conform to Catholic norms and practices in their adult years and, consequently, contribute to the success of the reform movement.

Catholic Reformation Bishops and the Catechetical Method

When a bishop published a catechism for his diocese, he often included several pages of introductory material outlining his ideas about religious education and instructing his curés in catechetical pedagogy. Bishops usually opened these *mandements* with a plea to their curés, reminding them that their most important duty as representatives of the church was the instruction of their parishioners. Without this instruction, the laity would be unable to participate in the sacraments that were so necessary to their salvation. Bishops had to be sure, however, that when providing this education curés were teaching appropriate subjects without creating misunderstandings that might lead to heresy. Although religious education was necessary, imparting information to the masses could also be very dangerous. Several bishops emphasized the words of Paul in his epistle to the Corinthians and warned against giving people bread and meat before they even knew how to chew: "Because the flock of Jesus Christ is composed of sheep and lambs, it is not enough to give to the former whole bread that they are not capable of digesting, as is found in ordinary Sermons and Speeches, if one does not take care to break it, and give it to them in bits, or rather change it to milk for the latter, who otherwise could not be fed."[20] The catechism was a type of education that mitigated much of the perceived danger of teaching complicated material to innocent and uninitiated children. Clerically sanctioned church doctrines were presented in the catechisms as simply and clearly as possible, using terms that the laity were familiar with and that would prevent confusion. The catechism was literally the church's attempt to break up the bread of instruction into pieces that the laity could easily digest.

In order for this instruction to be most effective, the bishops insisted, it had to come at an early age. One author of an Angers catechism wrote that it was more difficult to teach adults the truths of their religion than it would be to engrave them onto a piece of marble. Archbishop Michel Phélypeaux de la Vrillière of Bourges compared an ignorant adult to an old, crooked tree and said that it would be easier to straighten the tree than it would be to get a man whose habits had been base and worldly for all of his life to look toward heaven and his salvation instead. Like the educational theorists of their time, the bishops believed that the first impressions a child received would last throughout their lives. They felt children were much like Erasmus's bear cub, needing to be molded into shape, or, as an archbishop of Lyon wrote in 1665, like a lump of soft wax "which is not yet corrupted by the ugliness of vices, neither soiled by bad habits; they can easily be molded, with care and affection, and made into clean and pure Images of the living God."[21]

More often than not, bishops compared the children of their dioceses to young plants that needed to be fed and watered with Christian doctrine and carefully tended as seedlings so that they would grow to be healthy adults, whose spirits, turned toward the things of God, would be the church's greatest harvest. The plant metaphor was apparently borrowed from John Chrysostom, as noted by Bishop Jacques de Grasse in his 1762 catechism: "Look, said St. John Chrysostom, at the young plants growing in your fields . . . These plants symbolize the youth: be attentive and vigilant to give them a Christian education, and to bring them to virtue. The first impressions are decisive, and they are the most solid, since the building depends on its foundation."[22] Other bishops made similar analogies to the plant world in their introductions; they wrote of sowing seeds in prepared soil, rooting out bad habits like separating the tares from the wheat, and guiding vines so that they would grow straight and upright. The doctrines found in the catechism were supposed to be the guiding force for curés' young charges, the water and nourishment that young plants needed to grow up healthy and strong.

Nearly every bishop who wrote an introduction to his catechism emphasized the necessity of a standardized text in order to ensure that everyone memorized the same doctrine in the same terms. Thus, the catechism is an interesting mix of medieval and modern: it is a printed text, widely available at an inexpensive price, but it was supposed to be memorized in its entirety. It must have been fairly simple to find a catechism to consult, yet no one was supposed to have to resort to that— its doctrines were to be stashed away in the memory for easy access in times of need. In his work on concepts of childhood within English Puritanism, C. John Sommerville notes that educational theorists argued that orthodoxy would become second nature for children who had memorized their catechism. He compares catechism to the memorization of multiplication tables—both were necessary first steps in a long process of education.[23]

Yet young children could not be expected to memorize page after page of text without some sort of help. During the Middle Ages, individuals working to commit a large amount of material to memory often used some sort of memory technique to help them achieve their goals. Most of these techniques involved breaking down the material into small, coherent sections and associating them with some sort of visual image.[24] By the end of the seventeenth century, the most erudite of these techniques were no longer widespread, but the basic principles of the development of a strong memory remained. In fact, the catechism itself can be seen as a memory technique. The most basic component of all of the memory arts was the careful division and presentation of the subject matter to be memorized, and this is exactly what the catechism did for religious doctrines. The question-and-answer method is also a useful aid to memory—children used the catechist's question as a prompt that told them which passage to recite. Learning the catechism was probably the easiest form of memorization that a child would encounter. Answering just a few questions in a catechism lesson would have been much less daunting than trying to memorize a page of uninterrupted text.

Despite the fact that the question-and-answer method found in nearly every seventeenth- or eighteenth-century catechism had been proven effective, not every catechism was easy to memorize. Bishops had to make sure that they organized the material in their catechisms clearly and concisely and in a way that would facilitate memorization. They often noted in their introductions that they had decided to issue a new catechism simply because their curés had complained that the previous catechism was too difficult for children to memorize. For example, Bishop François-Renaud de Villeneuve of Viviers noted that the organization of the catechism his curés had been using was not methodical enough, and he had discovered that curés often threw out the text altogether and followed whatever method they thought was best. In Villeneuve's view, this kept the children from making any progress in their religious education, so he issued a new catechism, "in which the truths that are taught through Questions and Answers are more plain, more clear, shorter, and more precise."[25]

Once a clear and well-organized catechism was issued, along with a solid method for instruction, bishops had no doubts that dedicated curés would be able to teach the children of their parishes to memorize it. Bishops and educational theorists believed that the capacity to memorize was a quality inherent in all children, even those without a great deal of education. In fact, the ability to memorize was supposed to be even stronger in children than in adults. Erasmus wrote that "the beginnings of learning are the work of memory, which in young children is most tenacious," and he was echoing Quintilian, who insisted that one of the reasons an orator's education should begin early was that the memory was most retentive in childhood.[26] Bishops also felt that children had a large capacity to memorize both their prayers and the questions and answers of the catechism. In fact, they emphasized that memory was often the only tool that the youngest children had to draw upon since they had not yet sufficiently developed their powers of reason and judgment: "For the youngest children, recognize that because they do not yet have enough reason to learn by judgment, it is necessary to limit yourself to teaching them nothing except by memory."[27]

At the same time, bishops knew that they had to be careful not to force children to memorize too much material, or they would be in danger of causing confusion. They urged curés to teach only a few questions and answers at a time to prevent their students from becoming frustrated. Bishops recognized that the process of memorizing the catechism could not be accomplished in a hurry—children were allowed literally years of weekly catechism classes to complete it. Curés began teaching children their first communion catechism at age seven or eight, at least three or four years before they would be required to give their official recitation, allowing them to teach only small amounts of material at a time. Although the standard catechism lesson was meant to be learned in one sitting, bishops encouraged curés to be sensitive to the needs of their students and divide lessons into shorter segments if necessary. Even single responses that were too long could be broken up into shorter pieces; according to most bishops, it was much better to adapt the material to the individual capabilities of the students than to try to teach them something that was too difficult for them to understand.

There is thus an interesting contradiction in the theory behind the bishops' catechetical method: catechisms had to be memorized, but at the same time children were supposed to understand the words that they were reciting. Could the two processes happen at the same time? Or, as Strauss argues happened in Protestant Germany, did focusing on memorization automatically preclude any real understanding? Some bishops did in fact insist on memorization only and were not overly concerned with imparting a thorough knowledge of Christian doctrine. The heavy emphasis on uniformity in catechetical education certainly demonstrates that many bishops and curés cared more about teaching everyone the same words and phrases than they did about making sure that the doctrines were thoroughly understood. Several bishops justified their decision to designate a single catechism for use in the entire diocese by noting that the existence of a variety of catechisms was causing frustration among both the curés and the laity. If people moved from one parish to another, where a different catechism was taught, they often became completely confused by the text since it used different words and terms. Newly appointed curés who wanted to introduce an alternate text found that their parishioners rebelled against them if the new catechism contained even the slightest differences in phrasing.

If curés had been stressing understanding when they taught catechism, would people have become so discomposed by the fact that different texts used slightly different words and phrases? Instead, curés were emphasizing memorization alone, and when their parishioners had worked so hard to memorize one catechism, they resented being told that what they had learned was no longer acceptable. Bishop François de Bonal of Clermont wrote in 1789 that he had delayed issuing a new catechism for a number of years primarily because he knew that it would cause an uproar among the people when they found out they would have to learn a different text. Bishop Gabriel Cortois de Quincey of Belley was careful to reassure his curés and parishioners that he had not changed the order of the material in his new catechism in the slightest. Not wanting to make people feel as if they were being asked to rememorize doctrines in different terms, he wrote that he had only added a few short explanations at certain points in the text that curés could use at their discretion.[28]

Furthermore, the pedagogical advice that many bishops gave in their introductions shows that the process of memorization was still the most important part of catechism class. Archbishop Vrillière of Bourges told his curés to use the exact same terms each time they asked a student a question and to make sure that the student always used the same words when he or she responded. Curés were told to ask the questions in the precise order that they were presented in the catechism as well. He admitted that some critics might argue that this practice would turn children into parrots, who could only repeat what they heard without understanding it, but he disagreed with this notion:

> Experience demonstrates that this is an error, and makes us see that by these variations and frequent upheavals, you will obliterate in one day what had been previously imprinted in the minds of the Children; you will build but then destroy, you will confound their memories, their thoughts will be troubled, they will no longer know what to hold on to, what to believe or say; in a word, they will retain nothing, their knowledge will be only confusion and uncertainty, they will worry about not appearing smart, and about not understanding what is being asked of them.[29]

Archbishop Vrillière's primary pedagogical strategy was to repeat the questions and answers of the catechism over and over again, until even the slowest and stupidest child could respond appropriately. He told his curés not to be afraid of repeating things too much; constant repetition would only cement the doctrines into the children's minds. Vrillière believed so strongly in the utility of the catechism that no doubt about the catechetical method ever entered his mind. He noted that he had received complaints from curés that people were lax about attending catechism; his advice to those curés was, simply, try harder: study more, prepare better, live a more virtuous life, make sure that children attend catechism from a young age, and visit homes and hamlets to encourage attendance. The method was not the problem, only the level of commitment on the part of both the curés and the laity.

Many other bishops show a similar trust in memorization in their introductions; like Vrillière, they believed that teaching the same doctrines with the same terms in the same order was the only way to educate, prevent confusion or doubt, and preserve orthodoxy at the same time. Yet there were some bishops who demonstrated a certain level of concern that children who simply memorized the catechism might not have a deep enough understanding of Catholic doctrine. Bishop Ennemond Alleman de Montmartin of Grenoble dedicated a significant portion of the preface to his 1712 catechism to this problem:

> Faith, without which it is impossible to please God, does not consist, said St. Augustine, in the sound of syllables, nor in the pronunciation of certain words that one learns by heart: it consists in the understanding of the things signified by the words. However, those who take pains to interrogate the *petit Peuple* in the confessional or elsewhere, find that the majority only know the words, and are in a state of profound ignorance of the truths that these words signify.[30]

He continued that he had found that when the catechist changed the order of the questions, people who were supposedly well instructed became confused and could not respond correctly; Montmartin took this to be a sign of a lack of real understanding. His solution? More explanations. He added more material on the mysteries, the Mass, penitence, and the Eucharist to the new catechism, as well as explanations that curés could use to provide further information to their students but that would not have to be memorized. He also urged curés to use scripture stories to make catechism more interesting for children. At no point in his advice, however, does Montmartin ever suggest that his pedagogical method should be changed: he clearly did not think that memorization and comprehension were mutually exclusive activities. Despite recognizing that memorizing the catechism did not always provide true understanding, bishops still believed that constant repetition, with a few stories and explanations mixed in, was the best way to instruct children. Even if children did not always understand what they memorized, there was still hope that they would learn more as they got older. Bishop Bossuet said as much in his introduction: "If you sometimes find things which seem to surpass the capacity of children, you must not tire of teaching them, because experience has shown that provided that these things are explained to them in short and precise terms, although the terms are not always understood at first, little by little they meditate on them and acquire an understanding."[31]

Bishops also blamed the curés' lack of dedication for some children's memorization difficulties. Bishop Montmartin noted that his curés tried to excuse themselves by saying that most of their parishioners were too stupid to learn the catechism properly. Although he admitted that the people of the countryside had little intellectual capacity, Montmartin countered that Protestants somehow taught their converts very complex religious ideas; thus, there was no reason that faithful Catholic curés should be unable to teach true doctrines to even the most simpleminded believers. Other bishops made this comparison as well and recommended that questions and answers be rephrased so that those with unrefined intellects (*esprits grossiers*) just had to answer "yes" or "no" if necessary:

> Instruct these sorts of people by way of acquiescence, and not by questions and responses: for example, say to them:
> *My Child don't you believe that there is only one God?*
> *Yes, Sir.*
> *Don't you believe that there are three Persons in a single God?*
> *Yes, Sir . . .*[32]

Unlike Erasmus, who recommended that unintelligent students be removed from the classroom and sent to the fields, Catholic Reformation bishops had to insist that every soul could be taught the basics of religious truths—even farmers and manual laborers had to know their catechism.[33] They believed that it was just a matter of dedication and effort on the part of the curés, who had to do whatever it took to drill the material into the heads of the parish children and simply hope that something would eventually get through. And, if children never fully understood the meanings behind the catechism, at the very least they would be able to respond to the curés' questions and thus demonstrate their faith. Even bishops who did worry that catechism classes focused too much on words and not enough on meaning ultimately trusted in the catechism because both their lay and religious colleagues held this method in such high regard. It was only a matter of hard work and dedication—the method itself was not in question, just the application of it. This confidence in the catechism continued in the eighteenth century, despite the arrival of tremendous challenges to all established thought during the Enlightenment period.

Catechisms and the Enlightenment

Most of the previous examples of the conflict between understanding and memorization in the catechetical method are drawn from bishops' introductions written either in the late seventeenth or early eighteenth century, but by the end of the eighteenth century very little had changed in the bishops' beliefs about how catechism should be taught. The best example of this is found in a rather unique Angers catechism, published in three volumes from 1801 to 1803. The first volume is entitled *Explication et développement de la première partie du catéchisme du diocèse d'Angers,* and the text is not in question-and-answer format; this publication was supposed to explain and expand upon the existing Angers catechism. In an introduction the author of this text wrote that making children memorize a catechism without ensuring that they understood it was like giving a torch to a blind person—useless.[34] Much like Bishop Montmartin, he urged catechists to use stories, pictures, and songs to make catechism classes more interesting. He felt that applying the material in the catechism to the students' daily lives was also an effective strategy, but the basic method of helping students to understand the concepts had not changed at all during the eighteenth century: "But how to make children understand what is easy to teach to them? First of all, it is necessary to make them retain well each article of the catechism word for word, without however overtaxing their memory, but go step by step, and don't move on to a second subject until the first is known perfectly . . . it is necessary to make the students recite a lot, and repeat the same thing often."[35] Only after the catechism had been completely memorized were catechists supposed to provide extra explanations to the children. It should also be noted that volumes two and three of this catechism reverted back to the question-and-answer format because people had complained that the change in method in the first volume presented too many difficulties.[36] This catechism, and other late eighteenth- and early nineteenth-century texts like it, shows virtually no changes in the basic catechetical method. Catechisms still had to be memorized and recited—supplemental activities and explanations were just window dressing.

At the same time, the eighteenth century was a time of innovation in educational and pedagogical theories.[37] The most important educational theorist for the first half of the eighteenth century was undoubtedly John Locke, whose ideas about man's capacity for learning and understanding would have a profound influence on educational theories and systems for years to come. Locke is perhaps most famous for his *tabula rasa* theory—the idea that a child's mind is a blank slate, empty of any inherited ideas or influences. This implies, of course, that the first impressions a child receives are the most important, as they are engraved most deeply on the pristine surface of the mind; Locke says as much in the first paragraph of *Some Thoughts Concerning Education*: "Of all the Men we meet with, Nine Parts of Ten are what they are, Good or Evil, useful or not, by their Education. 'Tis that which makes the great Difference in Mankind: The little, and almost insensible Impressions on our tender Infancies, have very important and lasting Consequences."[38] This idea was, as we have seen, not particularly new; Locke was merely codifying an idea that had been gaining popularity for decades.

Instead, Locke's main innovation was his emphasis on reason and observation in education. Catholic Reformation bishops and other clergymen, including Jesuit educators, distrusted children's powers of reason and made little attempt to help their charges develop those powers, but Locke argued that children could learn to use reason as early as they learned language. He felt that even the youngest children should be treated as rational creatures; while children could not reason deductively from abstract principles, they were capable, Locke believed, of reasoning out correct principles for themselves through observation and experience.[39] This had an important effect on pedagogical techniques in that Locke argued children should spend much less time memorizing and more time developing their powers of rational thought through observation and critical thinking. He thought early education should be as much like play as possible—learning to read, for example, was explained not as an odious task but something as natural as a sport or a game. Locke also suggested tailoring methods and material to the individual, arguing that children of limited capacity should not be forced to learn more than they could handle, and nor should children who would have no need to use Latin or Greek in their adult lives be made to slave away at grammar during their time at school. Furthermore, Locke criticized the traditional secondary school curriculum's heavy emphasis on Latin for any student regardless of his social status. He felt that a knowledge of Latin was still essential for men of the upper classes, but the language should be learned naturally, the same way that children learned their first language. Grammar was only to be studied once the student could speak easily and in order to improve and polish expression.[40]

These innovations in educational theory are not the only important aspects of Locke's thought, however. In many ways, Locke and the Catholic Reformation bishops agreed about the overall purpose of education. First of all, Locke believed that the most important aspect of a child's education was the development of a moral character. More than half of the sections in *Some Thoughts Concerning Education* deal with the appropriate ways to teach a child how to live a virtuous life.[41] This was the same goal that Catholic bishops had when they issued their catechisms. They might have had a slightly different idea of what virtue was and how it should be expressed, but the method was the same: provide examples of virtuous behavior, shield children from immoral or indecent examples, and instill in them a desire to live an upright life. Secondly, Locke believed in a Christian education, and his ideas on imparting religious knowledge are remarkably similar to those found in both seventeenth- and eighteenth-century catechisms. He felt that the idea of God should be imprinted very early on children's minds and that they should be taught to love and esteem God. At the same time, Locke warned against trying to explain some of the more incomprehensible doctrines that might cause confusion: "I am apt to think, that keeping Children constantly Morning and Evening to acts of Devotion to God, as to their Maker, Preserver and Benefactor, in some plain and short Form of Prayer, suitable to their Age and Capacity, will be of much more use to them in Religion, Knowledge and Vertue, than to distract their Thoughts with curious Enquiries into his inscrutable Essence and Being."[42] This reasoning is nearly identical to that of bishops and theologians who consistently glossed over mysteries like the doctrine of the Trinity in their catechisms.

Locke also reserved a place for memorization in his educational theories. Although he deplored the common practice of having schoolboys learn whole pages from books by heart, he thought that children should be required to memorize "wise and useful sentences," which they could remember and apply throughout their lives. He had little faith in the medieval memory arts, yet he still believed in the utility of memorizing religious doctrines using a catechism. He felt that children should learn by heart the Lord's Prayer, the Creed, and the Decalogue before they even learned to read, recommending that they learn one question from their catechism each day, until they "ha[d] this Catechism perfectly by heart, so as readily and roundly to answer to any Question in the whole Book."[43] This advice coincides exactly with what Catholic Reformation bishops recommended and with their overall program of providing a basic religious education to the children of their dioceses.

Perhaps the bishops' ideas about children's education were not completely out of sync with the times, but a significant challenge to their method emerged in the second half of the eighteenth century, with the expulsion of the Jesuits from France and the publication of

Jean-Jacques Rousseau's *Émile,* both in 1762. The main trend in French educational thought during this period was the belief that the church should not be allowed to dominate education, either at the secondary or the university level. The church fought against this, of course, and their efforts were somewhat successful in the short term; the removal of clergymen from France's public educational system was not complete until the nineteenth century, when there were enough qualified lay teachers to run the schools. But the loss of the Jesuits as the main providers of secondary education caused quite an uproar in the French educational system, at least until the events of the Revolution eclipsed most debates over pedagogy.[44]

Rousseau proved to be a much greater challenge to the church than Locke since nearly every aspect of his educational program appeared contrary to the church's teachings. Rousseau agreed with Locke's emphasis on observation and experience and the utility of inductive rather than deductive reasoning. But in *Émile* Rousseau advocated a rather extreme and controversial method for the proper education of a child: he proposed to completely separate a child from society and allow his education to be entirely self-directed. Rousseau felt that man was naturally inclined to moral, virtuous, and reasonable behavior from birth but was quickly corrupted by society. Only by removing all influence of that society could a child receive a truly effective education. As far as the teaching of religion was concerned, Rousseau's tone was decidedly acerbic; although he seemed to believe in God and in spirituality, he had no real trust in organized religion. Catechism was certainly not a pedagogical method that Rousseau advocated: "If I had to depict sorry stupidity, I would depict a pedant teaching the catechism to children. If I wanted to make a child go mad, I would oblige him to explain what he says in saying his catechism."[45]

Thus, it is not surprising that we see little of Rousseau's influence in bishops' thoughts about children's education; however, we should be careful not to label church authorities as backward and completely behind the times. In fact, clergymen were not the only ones to disagree with *Émile;* in the first few years after its publication, it was nearly universally derided. The Parlement of Paris condemned the work immediately, citing its dangers to both the church and the state. Even many of the most well-known *philosophes* of the time disagreed with Rousseau's method. Man in Enlightenment terms was inherently social, and many simply could not agree with the idea that a child raised in complete isolation could ever be useful to society. Since the primary purpose of education for most eighteenth-century educational theorists was to produce enlightened French citizens, they could not advocate a method that involved withdrawal from civil society. At the very least, Rousseau's method was criticized for being impractical—not even the wealthiest and most elite members of society could have supported an *Émile*-style education without a complete restructuring of ideas about family life and childhood.[46]

Recent historians insist that much of the negative reaction against Rousseau was due to an almost complete misunderstanding of the overall message of *Émile*. Rousseau was most likely pointing out the pitfalls in a traditional education in order to draw attention to the need to reform society as a whole. In other writings Rousseau indicated that in a society that had been reformed according to the principles laid out in his other works—primarily the *Social Contract*—public education would be entirely appropriate. But until that reformed society was in place, Émile would have to be removed from society in order to avoid its corrupting influence. Even Rousseau himself, then, may have agreed that *Émile* was not supposed to provide a model for France's educational system.[47]

Despite the fact that not all of Rousseau's thoughts on education found acceptance in society at large, he encouraged people to think about education in general, and especially about national education. At the center of the debate over national education was the question of the extent to which the state should support or provide education for the children of the lower classes. Most of the participants in the debate believed that if any education was provided to the masses, it must have as its ultimate goal the strengthening of the moral and ethical values of society and the nation itself. In his study of the writings of some eighty eighteenth-century authors, both clerical and lay, Harvey Chisick argues that Enlightenment thinkers feared advocating a universal education in reading, writing, and arithmetic.[48] They recommended against allowing more poor children to enter the *collège* system, worrying that too much education would make the poor dissatisfied with their God-given position in society. If everyone went to a *collège*, who would be left to plow the fields? Despite their overall belief in "enlightenment," the authors Chisick examines certainly did not believe that everyone in society could or should be "enlightened." While they wanted to stamp out superstition, they did not support replacing it with an education in the arts and humanities; rather, they advocated occupational training and a strong sense of loyalty and duty toward both the state and society. The overall purpose of any type of education for these authors and for Enlightenment thinkers in general was to teach children what they would need to know in order to become responsible members of society.

Perhaps the most influential contributor to this debate was Louis-René de Caradeuc de La Chalotais, a lawyer and member of the Parlement of Brittany. La Chalotais spoke out vehemently against the Jesuits and most other religious teaching orders and called for a state-controlled educational system that employed lay teachers who would teach children how to become useful subjects of the state. In his "Essay on National Education," published just one year after *Émile,* La Chalotais argued that the memorization of long texts only bored children and did not lead to real understanding. He urged teachers to introduce their students to history, geography, and the physical and mathematical sciences at the same time as they taught reading and writing.[49] But the most important point La Chalotais makes is that children should only be taught subjects that would be useful to them later in life. He meant for the program of study that he outlines in his "Essay" to apply to just a small percentage of the population and insisted that most children needed only occupational training. He went so far as to argue that not everyone should learn to read and heavily criticized groups like the Christian Brothers for teaching reading and writing to peasants, who he believed should only receive the instruction necessary to handle the plane and the file.[50]

The fact that someone like La Chalotais, who campaigned vigorously for the expulsion of the Jesuits and detested any educational system run by religious orders, still believed in the utility of religious education and even the catechetical method demonstrates that the reason Catholic Reformation bishops were uninvolved in most of the debates over education and pedagogy in the eighteenth century was not because they were out of touch with current theories; rather, religious education was never part of the debate in the first place. Despite his disagreements with the religious orders, La Chalotais was not in any way against basic religious education. He thought that lay teachers should teach catechism in schools and *collèges* (he especially recommended Fleury's historical catechism) and that priests should teach it to children of both sexes and of all social classes in their parishes, along with instruction in religious observances and rituals.[51] Bishops did not need to respond to Enlightenment innovations in education because no one (aside from Rousseau, who remained on the fringes of eighteenth-century pedagogical debates) thought those innovations applied to the catechetical method. Thousands of schoolboys might have been able to throw away their Latin grammars as a result of new educational theories, but they could not do the same with the catechism, which remained the standard method of religious education throughout the eighteenth and even the nineteenth centuries.

Furthermore, most of what Enlightenment thinkers said about educational methods applied only to the children of the upper classes. No one questioned the fact that the children of the poor—both boys and girls—were supposed to memorize their catechism as part of a basic religious education provided by bishops and curés at the parish level. Enlightenment thinkers may have questioned the validity of many of the practices of organized religion, but they did not question Christianity's role in inducing loyalty to the state and conformity to society's norms, and they had no desire to force the masses to give up their religious belief. Simply put, everyone, even *philosophes* and those who subscribed wholeheartedly to the Enlightenment movement, believed that religious education was necessary and appropriate for all boys and girls.

The Catholic Reformation bishops themselves generally agreed with the main point that Enlightenment educational theorists were trying to make—that education, religious or otherwise, should serve the larger needs of society and the state. In fact, many bishops actively encouraged such a belief. Bishops did not believe any more than lay thinkers that the children of the lower classes should be given more education than was appropriate to their estate. Religious education, however, was appropriate for children from all levels of society and would in fact serve to strengthen the state. Bishop Louis-Marie de Nicolay of Cahors told his curés in the introduction to his 1781 catechism that teaching the catechism had broader effects than simply providing children with a bit of religious knowledge: "It is through these wise Instructions that you will form good Fathers of Families, virtuous Citizens, and Faithful Christians."[52] Another common statement was that children were the hope of both religion and society, as Bishop Gabriel-François Moreau of Mâcon wrote: "It is the children (whom Jesus Christ said should be allowed to come unto him), these young and precious Plants, who are the hope of Religion and Society . . . the more dangerous their first steps are, the more the wrinkles and habits acquired in childhood harden and strengthen with age, the greater our duty is to work to prevent bad habits and form good habits by wholesome instructions."[53]

The catechetical method was not just about memorizing doctrines; it was also designed to teach children the correct way to behave, in religious and social settings. Because children were the future of both church and state, they had to be taught how to conduct themselves appropriately. Catechism classes, in the minds of early modern bishops, were the perfect place to teach children how to become French Catholic citizens. Behaviors learned in catechism class were just as important to bishops as the catechism itself, and they provided just as many instructions about the proper way to produce appropriate behavior as they did about memorization and recitation. The routine of the catechism class, and the activities that took place during the hours that children were under the direct supervision of the curé, shows that bishops believed catechism would standardize not only doctrinal beliefs but also behavior, and it was thus one more step in the long process of Catholic reform.

Catechism Class and the Standardization of Behavior: Social Discipline in the Parish

The idea that the early modern period was a time when both religious and state authorities were trying to institute social discipline into European society has been tremendously influential in the academic world for the past several decades. Max Weber, Norbert Elias, and Michel Foucault are considered three of the most important pioneers in the movement, and each focus on different aspects of the discipline process.

Elias examines the notion of manners and the relationship between civility and the state, while Weber focuses on the internalization of the values of capitalism. Foucault has a particular interest in the influence of state power on morals, and in several works he describes a variety of disciplinary institutions built by the state during the early modern period—especially the army, the prison, the workhouse, and the school. All three, however, are essentially investigating the same issue: the relationship between religion, discipline, and state power and the internalization of codes of ethics and civility.[54]

Reformation and Catholic Reformation historians following the more recent trend of confessionalization studies have also applied these same theories to religious history and argued that the Reformation is the true origin of ideas about social discipline. Whereas Foucault, Elias, and Weber are more apt to see the state as the prime instigator of the civilizing process, confessionalization historians like Wolfgang Reinhard and Heinz Schilling demonstrate that church and state worked together to ensure discipline and social order, and that it was the different religious confessions' need to define the boundaries between the two institutions that created the drive for standardization and strict personal discipline in the first place.[55] Thus, the confessionalization model is more than an application of ideas of social discipline to the Reformation period; it is a complete reimagining of the theory, placing the Reformation and the Reformation state at the center.[56]

Although the confessionalization and social discipline models have found more success among German rather than French historians, the process of social discipline was taking place in villages and towns all over France.[57] Whether they were acting on their authority as representatives of the church or the state (they still possessed both in the seventeenth and eighteenth centuries), the Catholic Reformation bishops essentially were attempting to institute social discipline in their dioceses. When bishops published their catechisms, they often included short handbooks that listed rules for curés and others involved in teaching catechism.[58] Along with the bishops' introductions, these handbooks explain exactly how the hour set aside for catechism was supposed to be spent. Although the handbooks do provide some insight into how actual doctrines were to be taught, they provide more information about the bishops' ideas about social discipline.[59] Every hour that children spent on a church bench under the watchful eyes of their curés or vicaires was supposed to teach them something about how to behave as proper French Catholics. These lessons would last longer than the text of the catechism itself, as adult parishioners put into practice the behaviors they had learned as children.

Curés were supposed to hold a catechism class for approximately one hour every Sunday and feast day. Bishops indicated that catechism should take place at whatever time was most convenient for the people of the parish, although it was supposed to be held at the same time throughout the year (except during the harvest in the countryside, when classes were often canceled). Usually, catechism was taught either before or after vespers, although in places where children were sent out to pasture with the family's animals in the afternoons, curés often held catechism class directly following Mass.[60] In larger parishes curés were supposed to teach (or arrange for) two catechism classes, one for the younger children and another for those preparing for their first communion and learning the ordinary catechism. Curés also scheduled extra catechism classes during Lent and Advent, primarily for those preparing for first communion, either twice or three times a week in addition to the usual Sunday classes.

Bishops advised their curés to conduct their classes in the same way every week. Catechism class began, predictably, with prayer. As soon as the curé or catechist entered the room, students were supposed to kneel, make the sign of the cross, and repeat a designated prayer. Bishops recommended that curés then spend a few minutes reviewing the previous lesson to make sure that their students still remembered what they had memorized. The bulk of the hour centered around the new lesson. Bishops advised curés to prepare their material for catechism class well in advance. They had to decide exactly how many questions and responses the children could learn in one class period and then divide the lessons up if they seemed too long. Curés also had to make sure that they knew the questions and responses perfectly so that they could conduct class without looking at the book.

The central activity of all catechism classes was the repetition of the assigned questions and responses. The curé began the new lesson by repeating the first question and answer himself several times. Then he asked one of his students to repeat the answer, followed by another, until as many students as possible had a chance to respond. When the curé called on a student, he or she stood up, made the sign of the cross, and responded to the curé's question in a loud, clear voice. Some bishops recommended that curés simply go down the roll, asking students one after another, always in the same order, to repeat each response, while other bishops thought the questioning should be done randomly to keep the students on their toes. Bishop Claude Joly of Agen wrote that a curé should first interrogate a child that he knew would be able to answer correctly, thereby creating an example for the other children, giving them a chance to hear the response again, and engraving the text deeper into their memories.

For the students who usually had a hard time learning their lessons, Bishop Joly recommended that the curé should "question two or three of those who are sitting nearest to them, so that by listening to them with greater attention, they will learn the response that they must give, and their ignorance will not cause confusion."[61] It was important that curés try to keep mistakes to a minimum, not only to avoid confusing others but so that each child would feel confident and successful as he or she learned the catechism; bishops felt that students who came away from catechism class feeling slow and ignorant would be less likely to come again, although they needed the most instruction in the first place. Curés were never supposed to make fun of or strike students who gave wrong answers: "without this precaution, you will surely disgust the Children, and give them an aversion for the Catechism."[62] Students were not allowed to ridicule their peers either; Bishop Vialart of Châlons urged curés to tell their students that such mockery was inspired by the devil.[63]

To prevent students from disliking catechism, the curé should refrain from giving long lectures. If the children obviously did not understand something, the curé could explain further, using as few words as possible. On the whole, bishops reminded the catechists to speak very little and interrogate a lot. Every student, no matter how large the class, was supposed to have the opportunity to recite at least once, and curés had to mark on the roll the number of times that students responded during each lesson so that those who participated very little one week could be called upon frequently the next. Bishops also encouraged curés to allow some time for students to question each other on the day's lesson; the archbishop of Auch noted that a bit of competition was beneficial and might even encourage students to repeat their lessons outside of class.[64]

After the day's questions and responses were finished, curés were supposed to end class with some kind of moral lesson or scripture story: "It is nevertheless necessary to conduct class so that not all of Catechism is spent in interrogation, since this makes class cold and boring; but add into the interrogations explanations, short and animated morals, and sometimes some short stories."[65] Bishops believed that moral reflections and stories would inspire in children a love of God, a fear of sin, a distaste for things of the world, and a desire for eternal life; they also provided children with a practical application for the doctrines they learned. Finally, catechism class ended as it had begun, with the recitation of at least one but usually several prayers. Children went home with the admonition to apply what they had learned in their daily lives and to repeat the day's lesson to friends and family members.

The procedure for teaching catechism was fairly simple—students came to class, said a few prayers, and memorized and recited the responses that the curé taught them—but the rules issued by bishops reveal that there was much more going on during the classes than just memorizing and moralizing. The majority of the rules in the bishops' handbooks and introductions deal with policing the students' behavior rather than with how best to teach them the necessary doctrines. The real lessons of catechism class began even before the curé stood to lead the children in prayer, when he rang the bell announcing to the village that the time for catechism had arrived. Bells were very significant in early modern religious life; people living where they could hear the sound of a church bell were tied to that church and obligated to obey its call.[66] It was as though the bell was announcing the separation between time that belonged to the secular world and time that belonged to the church. When the bell rang on Sunday afternoons, children knew that it was time to go to catechism and to put on their proper church behavior, just as they might put on proper church clothes.

The fact that catechism class was a public event, held at the church and open to all members of the community, is highly significant. By requiring curés to hold catechism classes on a weekly basis, the church had effectively taken the primary responsibility for religious education out of the hands of parents and given it to the curés. Curés and bishops expected parents to have a copy of the diocesan catechism in their homes so that they could read from it often and be their children's first catechists. Yet when bishops warned parents of their duty to educate their children, what they meant was that it was the parents' responsibility to send their children to the curé for instruction. Parents were told that their children would be returned to them not only better educated but better behaved, as the archbishop of Auch noted: "Parents will be the first to taste of the fruit of the pains that they have taken for their children, because they will be more submissive to their parents, just as they will be better instructed in the will of God and in his Laws."[67] By teaching all the children of the parish together, with the same method, the curés could not only make sure that the doctrines children were taught were strictly orthodox, but they also could teach them the right way to behave. It gave the bishops one more opportunity to exercise control over the laity and make sure that their activities conformed to the regulations of the church. It seems that parents simply could not be trusted to provide a proper religious education for their children, so bishops asked that they be sent directly to the church for that education.[68]

Once they entered the church, children's behavior was supposed to be carefully monitored. The description of the entry into the church provided by Paul de Ribeyre, bishop of Saint-Flour, is typical of the bishops' rules on the subject: "At a certain hour the Bell will be rung to call the People, who, having entered [the church] devoutly, will salute the Holy Sacrament or the Crucifix, take a seat modestly, and remain silent until the Catechist arrives."[69] It was crucial for children to understand their responsibility to demonstrate respect for the church and its holy contents each time they crossed its threshold; all loud or boisterous behavior had to stop immediately when they entered. Children were told to use the time waiting for class to begin reading, praying, or even singing hymns led by the curé's assistant—anything, that is, but talking amongst themselves or wandering around the church.

Bishops were also very specific about the seating arrangements in the church during catechism class. A bishop of Montpellier wrote that it was absolutely necessary that there were enough benches to accommodate all of the children: "experience has shown that without this it is impossible to avoid trouble and confusion."[70] Furthermore, students sat in assigned seats, and they were not allowed to leave their places without permission. And, just as the adult villagers sat on church benches according to rank and privilege during Mass, children sat in a certain order as well. Bishops instructed their curés not to play favorites with the children of village notables; rather, modest and well-behaved students of any social status could earn the privilege of sitting in reserved places at the head of each row. In a handbook issued for Avignon, curés were advised to choose different "officers" from among "les plus sça-vans" or "les plus sages" children. Students chosen as the "Premier du Catéchisme," or as assistants, councillors, or intendants, were given special places on the benches as a reward.[71] These arrangements provided incentives for children to behave properly and helped the curé or catechist to keep order during class.

The most appropriate arrangement of the "classroom," according to the bishops, was to place benches on each side of the nave of the church, with a gap between them that allowed the curé to easily walk up and down the aisle and have a good view of the students on each bench. But even more importantly, girls sat on one side of the classroom and boys sat on the other. Bishops strongly urged curés in the larger towns to hold separate classes for boys and girls, but if this proved impossible, curés were absolutely forbidden to let boys and girls sit together or, as the archbishop of Bourges recommended, even sit where they could see each other:

> It would be much better to teach the Catechism to Girls and Boys separately, than to assemble them in the same place at the same time—avoid this as much as you can; it is necessary to separate them at least, seating one on the right and the other on the left or at an angle, so that they cannot see each other well, or otherwise they will fool around together, and become too familiar with each other. It has been noted that Children are much more modest when they cannot see others of the opposite sex during their instruction.[72]

Curés had to be careful about the way that they warned against sins of a sexual nature in their catechism classes, but their actions spoke louder than their words—by keeping boys and girls separate from each other as much as possible, they would have few opportunities to conduct themselves indecently or immodestly.

Bishops recommended that curés use a system of rewards and punishments to further encourage good behavior. Several bishops outlined a point program in their handbooks, in which children earned a good point for good behavior and a bad point for bad behavior. After a student collected a certain number of good points he or she received a prize—a better seat on the bench, a pious book, or a religious picture. Students who earned bad points were punished in a variety of ways. They might be given prayers to say, told to spend a certain amount of time kneeling in front of the class, or demoted from their rank on the bench. Bishops vehemently warned against corporal punishment; the worst penalty that bishops allowed curés to issue was suspension from class and, if necessary, from first communion.[73]

It is important to note that very few of the behaviors for which students received rewards or punishments had anything to do with the catechism itself; instead, the rewards and punishments were based on how students conducted themselves in class. The Avignon handbook recommended handing out bad points to students who were caught talking during class, who swore or blasphemed, or who were observed associating too freely with children of the opposite sex; however, children who did not know their lesson should never be punished.[74] If a student was unable to give a correct response, the curé was told to simply move on to the next student until someone else answered correctly. Similarly, prizes were not given to children who memorized more quickly than the others, or to those who could recite more lessons correctly. Instead, students who sat quietly and obeyed the curé received prizes. In a section on prizes and rewards in a Poitiers handbook, curés were told to reward children for four things: diligence, modesty, knowledge, and good morals at home.[75] Clearly, good behavior was valued much more than knowledge of Catholic truths and doctrines.

Because children's behavior was supposed to be monitored constantly during class, bishops recommended that curés find an assistant to help them with this task. Then the curé could give his full attention to individual students, while the assistant made sure that the other children sat still and listened. The assistant might be another clergyman, if the parish was large enough to have a vicaire or chaplain, or the school-

The Catechetical Method   93

master might step into this role. Assistants did not actually teach the catechism, however; their function was strictly limited to supervising every aspect of the children's behavior. The Avignon catechism contained a long list of the assistant's duties, from arranging the benches before class began to keeping the roll and warning the curé about students who were often absent or habitually late. But most importantly, the assistant was supposed to keep an eye on the children constantly, "to keep them modest, warning them of their misbehavior by a sign or by a quiet whisper, without listening to their excuses."[76] The author of the Nantes handbook insisted that the children should fear the assistant so much that he would be able to reprimand them with just a look: "He must try to gain so much authority over the children that a glance or a sign can bring back into line those who misbehave." He could use a baton to regain the attention of students whose minds or eyes were wandering, although he should never use it to hit anyone.[77] The assistant could give good and bad points as well, and students knew that they had at least two sets of eyes on them for the duration of catechism class. Under this constant surveillance, children learned to sit still, respect their elders, and act appropriately when in the church and in the presence of the clergy; they would perhaps find these skills more useful throughout their lives than any doctrines their curés taught.

Catechism and First Communion

There was a point, however, when knowledge of both the doctrines of the church and proper religious behavior came together, in a public ceremony meant to provide religious inspiration for the entire community and reinforce the church's teachings for both children and adults: first communion. The designation of the first communion ceremony as a major rite of passage in a child's life was, like the catechism itself, a development related to the Catholic Reformation. In the early church Christians focused primarily on baptism as the most significant community ritual; any person who had been baptized could participate in the Eucharist, including children. In the centuries before Lateran IV (1215), however, the Eucharist became more than just a symbolic event as the doctrine of transubstantiation took hold, and increasingly the clergy excluded children from the ritual. After Lateran IV children usually took their first communion at some point after the age of ten; the Council of Trent confirmed this practice. In the post-Tridentine period, as reformers paid more attention to the sacrament of the Eucharist and the education of the laity, the two came together in the first communion ceremony. The ceremony began to mark a rite of passage for children into adulthood—or at least adolescence—as well as a way for adults to be reminded of their own religious responsibilities.[78]

The ceremony of first communion can be seen as the culmination of the entire religious education process. The sacraments of confession and communion were the two most important rituals that Catholic believers participated in throughout their lives. Being able to approach the altar during Easter demonstrated that the communicant knew two crucial things, both of which were taught through catechism: the basics of the doctrines behind the sacraments (since no curé was supposed to allow an ignorant person to take communion) and the proper religious and ritual behaviors that allowed participation in the communion of saints.

Each year, in the weeks leading up to Easter, curés made lists of the children in their parish who were between the ages of ten and fourteen and ready to approach the altar for the first time. In preparation for first communion, the curé held special catechism classes several times a week, beginning about six weeks before Easter. Extra lessons on confession and communion were taught, and after about three weeks the hopeful communicants made the first of several general confessions. The curé met with the parents of his students to find out if their children were obedient at home and behaving in a manner that proved that they were ready to participate in the sacraments. About a week before the day set aside for first communion, children faced their first big test—a public examination on the catechism. At least once a year curés were supposed to hold something like a catechism recital, where children's parents could gather at the church to see what progress their children had made in memorizing their catechism lessons. Children received congratulations, prizes, and encouragement to continue their religious education. But the examination for those hoping to take first communion was much more serious; children who failed had to wait another year before they could take communion.

Once the day for the first communion ceremony had been set (usually a weekday in the first week after Easter, so the importance of the first communion ritual would not be overlooked while all the adults in the parish fulfilled their Easter duty), the entire parish was notified so that everyone could attend and pray for those participating in the ceremony. First communion was an important public ritual, and it was meant to involve the entire community in addition to the children and their parents. The church bells were rung the evening before, as well as the morning of, the ceremony, and the altar was decorated as if it were a feast day. The communicants made a final confession in order to make sure that they would be worthy to take the Eucharist in the morning. The next day, after the Mass, prayers, and a special sermon on communion, it was time for the children to approach the altar. Describing this moment of the ceremony, Bishop Jean-Claude de La Poype de Vertrieu of Poitiers wrote: "The beauty of the first Communion ceremony consists in the order and modesty with which the children approach the baluster for communion, and in returning to their place after having taken communion, thus the Catechist must take care to ensure this." The bishop then included a three-page description of how the ceremony should be carried out as the communicants approached the altar, first row by row and then one by one.[79] This was the ultimate profession of faith: by taking communion, children demonstrated that they had been educated in the mysteries of their religion and were willing to apply that knowledge through public participation in the sacraments. They had learned to approach the altar with "order and modesty," showing their priest and the entire village that they were ready to be seen as a part of the Catholic community. The adults of the parish witnessed the event, celebrated it, and welcomed the new communicants into full membership in parish life.

⌒ When seventeenth- and eighteenth-century French bishops published catechisms for their dioceses, they had two closely related goals in mind. First, they wanted children to memorize some basic Catholic doctrines. In order to guarantee uniformity and orthodoxy, both boys and girls had to be able to recite their catechism in the precise language that bishops prescribed. Second, children who attended catechism classes regularly and memorized the doctrines demonstrated their faith and proved that they had a foundation of Christian doctrine on which they could build throughout their lives. In many ways the second goal of the bishops' catechetical method was even more important than the first. Bishops knew that a profession of faith without its extension into daily activities was worthless:

> But do not limit yourselves, My dear Brothers, to teaching and having those who are dependent upon you memorize the lessons contained in the catechism. The holy truths of the religion are the object of our faith and the immutable laws for our morals. It is necessary to thus believe them with our hearts, and to apply them to our conduct. It is not enough to commit them to memory and to decorate our minds, neither to believe them with a faith that is dead and sterile: their true effect must be to purify our hearts, and to permeate our hearts with respect, piety, and thankfulness toward God.[80]

The catechism was a critical part of the confessionalization process—it was perhaps the ultimate instrument of social discipline. Bishops knew that the parish children might not always understand every question and response that they memorized, but the rituals of memorizing, reciting, and attending class would leave an impression that would last longer than any doctrinal explanation or theological argument. Having children of all segments of society learn their catechism at a young age was seen as the most effective way to create Catholics who had thoroughly internalized religious and civic values and who could police their own behavior as adults. Creating honest, moral, and practicing Catholic believers and citizens was the true goal of the Catholic Reformation, and the catechism, with its emphasis on behavior rather than doctrine, was an essential tool in the reform process. Thus, by the end of the seventeenth century Catholic Reformation bishops had a clear plan for reform through education, with catechism at the center. They published catechisms and distributed them, they issued ordinances to curés and schoolmasters requiring them to teach catechism in churches and schools, and they insisted during their periodic visits that children publicly recite what they had learned.

But how successful were their efforts? The bishops' plans depended entirely on the compliance of curés, village authorities, schoolmasters, and parents. Just how willing were these individuals to follow the prescriptions of church authorities? We cannot assume that the laity simply accepted the bishops' plans for catechism with no questions asked, yet neither can we assume that they automatically tried to oppose any ordinance or regulation that bishops imposed. As the following chapters will demonstrate, the laity usually had a number of options at the parish level regarding how much religious education their children needed. They accepted the fact that the catechetical exercise was necessary, but they let their curés and bishops know if a particular catechism was unacceptable. Many parents surely believed that their children would be more obedient as a result of their religious education, just as their bishops promised them. Catechism was an important childhood exercise, but parents refused to make catechism an adult activity, despite admonitions from church authorities. The process of compromise between clergy and parents on the subject of catechism and religious education demonstrates that lay men and women were not powerless in the face of Tridentine reforms.

This is one of the central themes of Catholic Reformation and confessionalization studies: if we are to understand the history of reform, we must examine how those reforms were applied in individual dioceses and parishes. Thus, the remaining chapters investigate the reform process at the parish level. The chapters in part 2 examine local records to determine how, and how well, catechism was taught in the dioceses of Auxerre, Châlons-sur-Marne, and Reims. They focus on the relationship between curés and their parishioners and the position of schoolmasters, as providers of primary education, in local communities. An analysis of visitation records and other sources shows that the bishops' plans for reform were indeed implemented in these three dioceses, but it was largely as a result of lay efforts that curés' catechism classes and village schools found any sort of success. A close examination of primary education shows that the laity had a great amount of influence in how the reform movement played out in their own communities and demonstrates to the historian the necessity of a local perspective in Catholic Reformation and confessionalization studies.

Primary Education in Auxerre, Châlons-sur-Marne, and Reims

CHAPTER THREE

The Curé and the Catechism
The Birth of a Childhood Ritual

When Bishop Félix Vialart de Herse of Châlons-sur-Marne issued a catechism for his diocese in 1660, he outlined his views of the Catholic Reformation in his introductory ordinance. He described the Catholic Church as a "bonne Mère" and the spouse of Christ, whose goal was the eternal salvation of her children. In order for them to be saved, the church, in its maternal incarnation, had to provide instructions to her children—instructions as important to believers' souls as a mother's milk is to her infant. Sadly, Vialart lamented, the ministers of the church had not always done their duty, and many had allowed their flocks to languish in profound ignorance, subject to dangerous vices.

The church had then been forced to take steps to correct this deplorable situation and attempted, through the reforms of the Council of Trent, to

> return to all of our Dioceses their former discipline, in its greatest strength, by commanding on the one hand the Curés to take great pains to fulfill their duties toward their flocks with faithfulness, and on the other hand asking Bishops to hold them to their duties, if they were to rebel against them, by the just fear of the most serious Censures.[1]

Bishop Vialart then detailed his own attempts at reform during his tenure in Châlons, citing his many ordinances and *mandements* dealing with proper ecclesiastical behavior, the synods and other meetings that he held, and the efforts that both he and his rural deans made to visit curés and set them on the right path. He concluded with joy that his parishes now contained capable and zealous pastors who were ready to teach their parishioners the doctrines and practices necessary for their salvation. He warned his curés that if they failed to correct and instruct the souls that Christ and his church had bound them to care for, they would one day be held accountable for the loss of those souls.

In the eyes of early modern French bishops, the Catholic Reformation was a two-step process. The first step involved the reform of the Catholic clergy itself. In the seventeenth and eighteenth centuries, reforming bishops all over France used a variety of tools to ensure that they had educated, capable, and dedicated priests to care for the souls in their dioceses. Bishop Vialart was just one of many bishops who issued ordinances, held synods, and made regular parish visits in order to enforce church standards and ecclesiastical discipline. Bishops had to make sure that their curés were willing and able to work for the salvation of the souls in their parishes.[2] Only then could the second step in the reform process—the religious education of the laity—begin. Seminary-trained curés who performed the ceremony of the Mass and administered the sacraments on a regular basis were now asked to fulfill another duty: teaching catechism. Bishops insisted that their curés teach catechism for at least an hour every Sunday and feast day, and when they visited the parishes in their dioceses they expected to find both children and adults who could recite catechism lessons when asked.

Furthermore, bishops indicated that parents should bear part of the responsibility for the religious education of their children by sending them to catechism class. Vialart included a text on the Christian education of children at the end of his catechism and told both parents and clergymen to apply its principles to their instructional efforts. Similarly, in the *mandement* to his catechism, Bishop Charles de Caylus of Auxerre reminded parents of their duty to make sure that their children were instructed: "We exhort Fathers, Mothers, Masters, Mistresses, and all Heads of Families to send their Children and Domestics to Catechism faithfully, and to attend class themselves, and to regard this religious exercise as one of the most useful for their salvation."[3] These *mandements* and ordinances were common in all types of catechisms; by the end of the seventeenth century bishops expected that their educated and zealous curés would hold catechism classes on a regular basis and that parents would send their children to those classes.

Yet the most essential question we must ask about the Catholic Church's program of religious education during this period does not center around the reform work undertaken by bishops but rather the parish clergy and the laity: How well did curés and parents actually follow their bishops' prescriptions? Did their ordinances, synods, and visits produce the desired reforms? Bishops' pronouncements can only tell one side of the story. What did the bishops find when they visited curés and observed their efforts at instruction? This chapter and those that follow provide some answers to these questions using visitation records and other sources from the diocese of Auxerre in Burgundy and two dioceses in Champagne, Châlons-sur-Marne and Reims.

As noted in the introduction to this volume, visitation records are particularly abundant in these three dioceses, as are supplemental sources like the *enquête* of 1774 in Reims.[4] But these three dioceses were chosen for study not just because of the quantity of visitation records but also for the quality of those records—a result of the increasing focus on the necessity of consistent episcopal administration at the diocesan level. One of the most important changes in the highest levels of the French church brought about by the Catholic Reformation was the bureaucratization of the episcopate. The bishops themselves still came from noble families,[5] but, as Joseph Bergin points out, noble sons and brothers who chose the church as their profession had to show more concern for the everyday administration of their dioceses than their pre-Trent predecessors. By the mid-seventeenth century a candidate for a bishopric had to be educated in theology and able to preach, conduct visits, and keep the parish clergy under control.[6] Yet because they often had public, political roles to play as important representatives of the church, many bishops had to depend on bureaucratic institutions that could keep the diocese running even if they could not be there to do it in person. Many of these administrative systems were put into place in the seventeenth century and then extended and improved in the eighteenth.[7]

The bureaucratization of the episcopate is reflected in the visitation records themselves. Beginning in the second half of the seventeenth century, bishops and their administrators used printed forms and surveys to record their observations during visits.[8] Specific spaces on the forms were designated for secretaries to record information about various aspects of parish life, from the background and education of parish priests to the religious habits of the laity. Usually, these forms included questions about the instruction of the parish children — such as the frequency and regularity of the curé's catechism classes and whether the community employed any schoolteachers. Bishops also questioned some of the children on their catechism and made notes on their responses. Except for the 1626 visit, all the Châlons records use printed forms, and Auxerre's bishops stopped using free-form notes by 1705 at the latest. Bishops in Reims did not use printed forms until the very end of the century, but visitors did respond to a series of specific, numbered questions designated in the diocesan *rituel,* or handbook. The standardization of visitation records enables us to get a more complete picture of the reform process in the parishes of these three dioceses and allows for general comparisons of religious education from parish to parish and from diocese to diocese.

Thus, visitation records are a crucial resource for the study of Catholic reform at the parish level. Records from Auxerre, Reims, and Châlons-sur-Marne demonstrate that by the end of the eighteenth century, catechism — as a preparation for first communion — had become as important as the sacrament itself, and the majority of Catholic parents made sure their children attended the curé's classes and memorized the doctrines that he taught. At the same time, neither clergy nor the laity followed the bishops' rules to the letter—by the end of the eighteenth century curés and parents had reached a compromise over religious education. Parents made sure their children knew enough of their catechism to be able to take first communion, and curés looked the other way when the parents themselves could no longer recite the text word for word. Early modern Catholicism, as it was practiced in parishes all over France, was not simply the result of bishops imposing the will of the church on the laity; curés and parents together implemented their own program of catechetical education.

The Background and Education of Curés in Auxerre, Châlons-sur-Marne, and Reims

Parish curés before the Protestant and Catholic reformations are usually described as, at best, mediocre servants of the church. Certainly not all curés were as corrupt and debauched as some of the Protestant reformers intimated, but there is a large amount of truth behind the sixteenth-century anticlerical propaganda. In his analysis of late medieval parish religion in France, Paul Adam portrays curés as lacking in discipline and uneducated—sometimes the only instruction they had received was from their own parish curé. They often did not know how to perform the sacraments properly, and they took very little care to keep their vows of chastity. Their illegitimate children lived openly in their parishes, and bishops did nothing to stop this practice. Some curés did not even live in their parishes, and, again, bishops either could not or would not enforce residence rules. Adam does note that there were many calls for reform in the fourteenth and fifteenth centuries, usually centered around the need for a standardized moral and theological education for future priests.[9] After the Council of Trent the church began to take steps toward the reform of the parish clergy, but it took nearly a century for the reforms to take effect. Robert Sauzet indicates that between 1620 and 1656, curés in the diocese of Chartres still were not following rules regarding trouble with drunkenness, nonresidence, and sexual immorality, in addition to exhibiting a general lack of pastoral zeal; visitors were so preoccupied with the morals of the clergy that they had no time to concern themselves with the behavior of the laity.[10] Not until the end of the seventeenth century, or even well into the eighteenth, did real progress in clerical reform become evident.[11]

Eighteenth-century images of parish priests are generally much more favorable than those from earlier periods. Pamphleteers and *philosophes* berated indolent cathedral canons, outrageously wealthy and worldly bishops, and idle monks living off the produce of their large landholding monasteries, but the curés were praised for their dedication to the improvement (religious or otherwise) of the peasantry. Gone was the parish priest who mumbled his way through Sunday services because he was as unskilled in Latin as his parishioners. Curés living like peasants, with a female "servant" as a common-law wife, or with two or three illegitimate children in the parish, had largely disappeared by the eighteenth century. Instead, curés served as the spiritual and social leaders of the parish, responsible for maintaining order and for looking after both the spiritual and temporal welfare of their parishioners. Any complaints about curés concerned eccentricities and minor foibles rather than serious lapses in morality or behavior. As long as curés took care to help the poor and perform the sacraments with regularity and decency—and they generally did—the laity did not express any dissatisfaction.[12]

This improvement in the image and status of curés resulted in large part from education: eighteenth-century curés, as products of the *collège* and seminary system, received a more substantial and comprehensive education than any of their predecessors had in the past. The most basic aspects of a future cleric's education were learning to read and write in Latin; no young man could hope to enter a diocesan seminary without these skills. Some curés taught Latin to promising young boys in their parishes in hopes of securing a scholarship to a seminary for them, but for the most part parents who wanted one of their sons to enter the priesthood had to finance his education themselves and either hire a tutor or send him to a *collège*. At the *collège* boys spent between three and six years studying Latin grammar, literature, philosophy, and rhetoric. A few may have learned some Greek as well. Since members of the religious orders ran most of the *collèges,* future clerics learned how to

Table 3.1. Social Origins of the Parish Clergy in Reims, 1774

Profession of the Cleric's Father	*Number of Clerics*	*Percentage of Clerics*
Nobles	9	2.4
Bourgeois	9	2.4
Officiers	73	20.0
Textile Merchants	34	9.3
Other Merchants	86	23.6
Schoolmasters and Surgeons	81	4.9
Artisans	59	16.0
Laboureurs	70	19.0
Unknown	9	2.4
Total	367	100

Source: Julia, "Le clergé paroissial," 207.

reconcile this classical education with the teachings of the church, and their daily schedule included attendance at Mass, regular prayers and scripture readings, catechism, and other devotional exercises.[13]

In the early modern period, however, secondary education was fairly expensive and beyond the reach of much of French society. A father who had the means to send his son to a *collège* in preparation for a career in the clergy came from the upper levels of society; very few curés came from peasant stock. Dominique Julia has shown that out of 367 secular curés serving in the diocese of Reims in 1774, more than half of the clerics' fathers (55 percent) claimed to be royal officers, merchants, or simply "bourgeois" (see table 3.1). Nearly one-fifth were from the *laboureur* class—the wealthiest part of the peasantry. Julia notes that most of the fathers listed as artisans had achieved the status of master in their trades and had relatively high social positions. Clearly, the parish clergy of Reims came from the more prosperous members of non-noble French society—those of the lower classes simply could not afford to give their sons the education they needed to enter the priesthood.[14]

In order to ensure that future clerics had access to additional education beyond the *collège,* at the Council of Trent the church decreed that bishops should open seminaries in their dioceses as soon as they could procure adequate resources. Consequently, many dioceses established their first seminaries in the early modern period, including Reims, Châlons-sur-Marne, and Auxerre.[15] In 1574 Reims became the first French diocese to open a seminary when Archbishop Charles de Guise, the Cardinal of Lorraine, founded a building to house young men studying for the priesthood. However, the Wars of Religion soon put a halt to any sort of standardized clerical education (at one point the seminary building had to be used to quarter League troops), and the seminary ceased to function after 1600. Archbishop Charles-Maurice Le Tellier permanently reestablished the institution several decades later (1676) and entrusted it to the administration of the Génovéfains, an Augustinian order. Châlons also had a seminary in the sixteenth century, but it was soon absorbed by a Jesuit *collège*. Bishop Vialart obtained official *lettres patentes* for a new seminary in 1650 and spent nearly his entire episcopate working to create an institution that would improve and standardize clerical education. Vialart and his cathedral canons administered the seminary themselves until 1660, when it was turned over to various religious orders. The Lazarists finally took over its permanent administration in 1681 and continued as its directors until the Revolution. The Lazarists also ran the seminary in Auxerre, which was founded by Bishop Nicolas de Colbert in 1671.[16]

Young men usually entered the seminary in their late teens or early twenties and at that time made the necessary spiritual and financial commitment to the priesthood. Most would be tonsured upon entry, and in the course of their studies they took two orders: the subdiaconate, only given after age twenty-one, and the diaconate, which conferred the right to baptize and preach. The subdiaconate was a critical stage in a cleric's career. Before he could be given this the first of the major orders, he had to have proof that his family would support him financially during the time it took him to complete a clerical education. This income was usually in the form of a patrimonial title backed by a family member, and it consisted of at least one hundred livres per year, to be paid until the young man entered the priesthood and could claim a benefice. The future priest gave up his right to any family inheritance by accepting the patrimonial title, thus making the subdiaconate the point of no return for most young men. The one-hundred-livre minimum for the patrimonial title also further ensured that curés only came from the upper classes of society—no *manouvrier* or *journalier* could afford to give his son at least one hundred livres a year for a clerical education.[17]

The amount of time a cleric spent studying at a seminary varied depending on the type of seminary he attended. Degert lists four common types of seventeenth-century seminaries. The first was little more than a spiritual retreat—a place for priests and curés to gather and spend some time away from the world. Although most seminaries in the eighteenth century continued to offer similar retreats, very few made this their sole purpose after midcentury. The second type offered preparation for each of the minor orders over a one-year period. The "seminary year" did not have to be completed all at once—seminarians often took time off to study elsewhere. The third type of seminary offered a similar program but also housed clerics studying at a nearby university. As a result, seminary and university classes could be taken concurrently. The final type of seminary offered upper-level courses in philosophy and theology at the seminary itself, as well as the usual clerical preparation courses.[18] At the very least, a young man preparing for the priesthood could expect to spend a year in the seminary learning the practicalities of the clerical profession.

The core of seminary education did not center around the study of complex doctrines and theology; instead, seminary training was designed to be practical and spiritual rather than intellectual. Theology and philosophy could be learned elsewhere, but only at the seminary could future priests learn both the practical skills they would need to administer a parish and the ways that they could spiritually prepare themselves for a lifetime of service to the church. The daily schedule for seminarians illustrates this.[19] The clergymen who administered the seminaries expected their students to live as much like monks as possible and to withdraw completely from the world. Students rose as early as four thirty in the morning and spent the next three hours before breakfast praying and studying. Seminarians were given topics upon which to meditate for much of this time, and they read from both scripture and approved pious books. After Mass at about eight, students spent at most two hours in classes on theology or philosophy and then retired to their rooms for personal study. After lunch and a short recreation period, the entire seminary gathered in the chapel for

New Testament readings and vespers. In the afternoon students spent only one and a half to two hours in classes, devoting the remaining hours to personal study or individual preparations for taking holy orders. At the end of the day there were more common prayers and meditations before students retired at nine. Seminarians thus spent only a small fraction of their day in class; their time at the seminary prepared clerics spiritually, rather than intellectually, for their careers.

Students also dedicated a large amount of their time to preparing to administer the sacraments and attend to other parochial duties. They learned the doctrine behind each ceremony, as well as the practical aspects of sacraments and services and how to perform the Mass correctly and with dignity. Using wooden dolls, they practiced baptizing infants. They learned how to give confession and the types of penance appropriate for different situations. They certainly studied the diocesan catechism and, perhaps, received instruction on the best ways to teach it to their future parishioners.[20] Overall, the seminary was meant to provide a future curé with the skills he needed to be the spiritual head of a parish, as well as instill in him a monastic-like discipline and a sense of the serious nature of the ecclesiastical life.

In addition to seminary training, some young clerics spent time taking university courses. A university education might be obtained in a number of different ways. In towns with both a university and a seminary, students might live at the seminary, eating and associating with other clerics and following the monastic lifestyle as much as possible, while attending university lectures during the day. Other clerics, after being ordained to the priesthood and leaving the seminary, might elect to spend several more years at a university before accepting a position in a parish. Clerics who held a vicariate or a chaplaincy in a university town could continue their education while serving in their parishes. Because university education was not absolutely necessary for most priests, the amount of time clerics spent at a university usually depended on financial considerations, as well as proximity to a university and personal inclination.

Considering the cost of a university education, few curés took any university courses, except in dioceses that had a university nearby. Timothy Tackett notes that in 1789 in Gap, a diocese without a university, only 13 percent of the parish clergy—curés or vicaires—had

Table 3.2. Curés with a University Education in Reims, 1774

Time at University or Degree Acquired	Number of Curés	Percentage
No university education	302	60.7
Some university education	196	39.3
At least five years of university education	154	30.9
University degree acquired	183	36.7
Maître ès arts	29	5.8
Gradué	117	23.5
Licencié	13	2.6
Doctorat	24	4.8

Source: 1774 enquête, in AD Marne, 2 G 253–87.

Note: The total number of curés was 498. There were 506 parishes in the diocese, but only 498 of them provided details about their education in the 1774 enquête.

obtained university degrees.[21] In Reims, a diocese with a prestigious university, significantly more curés completed a university degree. After two years of philosophy at the university in Reims, students could obtain the degree of maître ès arts; 36.7 percent of the curés working in Reims in 1774 had received this degree (see table 3.2). Many of these men continued their studies and completed three years of theology, earning them the title of gradué en théologie. Priests with gradué status were generally more attractive candidates for a position as a curé, so priests in Reims had both motive and opportunity for a university education. It took several more years of education to obtain the licencié and the doctorat; only thirty-seven curés in Reims had earned either degree. In total, nearly 40 percent of the curés serving in Reims in 1774 had attended a university, and 31 percent had spent at least five years in university-level studies.[22]

Hands-on training comprised the final, and perhaps most essential, stage of clerical education. Curés usually did not go straight from the seminary to running a parish of their own; they first spent some time serving in other ecclesiastical positions. According to the 1774 Reims questionnaire, some new priests had obtained chaplaincies as their first clerical position, and thus were responsible for taking care of a small chapel and saying a few Masses there. Some served as clerks or sacristans in urban churches, helping the parish priest with his duties. Many of these clerics taught catechism on a regular basis as part of their duties. A few priests had worked at a local *collège,* teaching philosophy or theology for a few years before a parish became available. Other priests spent a few months as a substitute priest at various parishes, perhaps covering for a curé who needed to be out of town for a short period of time. Some were even designated as *desservants*—priests who held a parish temporarily until the official curé could be installed.

The most significant post that priests held before obtaining a parish of their own, however, was that of an assistant parish priest, known in France as a *vicaire.* The vicariate provided an excellent opportunity for a priest to perform all or most of the duties of a curé (including teaching catechism classes) under the supervision of a more experienced priest. In 1774 there were 150 vicaires serving in the diocese of Reims. Vicaires did not hold benefices but instead were either paid by the curés they assisted or by their parishioners, or, most commonly, by both. Large parishes often had vicaires because one priest simply could not perform all of the duties required of a curé. In other parishes, old or infirm curés who did not want to give up their positions sometimes enlisted the help of a vicaire and paid him themselves, preferring to take a cut in pay rather than lose the benefice. In parishes with one or more annexes, vicaires often lived in the annex itself and performed all of the duties that a curé would, although the people of the parish still had to go to the official curé for their Easter communion. Some vicaires might stay in a parish for only a few months, while others stayed for several years at a time. Many priests served as vicaires in a number of different parishes, working under several different curés. The time spent by young priests in these temporary positions became a crucial aspect of Tridentine clerical reform; it gave priests more time to learn the skills that they would need as curés, provided an opportunity for them to prove themselves, and gave them the chance to spend time with other priests, thereby creating a clerical identity and ensuring more uniformity in practices and standards.

Most of the curés serving in Reims in 1774 had worked as a vicaire or some other type of clerical assistant, demonstrating how seriously the church felt about providing future parish priests with hands-on experience. Out of 498 curés who provided information about their ecclesiastical careers, 258 (51.8 percent) had been a vicaire for at least six months before becoming a curé. One hundred and forty-four other curés had served in some other ecclesiastical capacity, as *desservants,* chaplains, or clerks. Many had worked in other clerical positions as well and consequently possessed a variety of potentially beneficial skills. For example, curé Jacques François Gridaine worked as a catechist in two different parishes as soon as he had taken orders; he was given permission to preach in those parishes as well. Then he received a position as a vicaire, followed by a stint as a *desservant* in another parish. Finally, at age twenty-nine, he became the curé of Suippes, having had at least five years of unofficial, but vital, training in clerical duties.[23] Only ninety-six curés (19.2 percent) gave no indication that they had worked in other capacities before receiving their first job as curé.[24] Thus, four-fifths of the curés in the diocese had received a rather comprehensive—and unprecedented—education in parish administration from their fellow ecclesiastics.

Because of the time curés spent as assistants, the average age of priests when they obtained their first parish benefice was quite high in the eighteenth century. Parishes were no longer assigned to young men who had not yet become priests or who had not completed their education. Parishes were rarely left vacant while parishioners waited for their curé to grow up, and they did not have to endure the reign of an entirely inexperienced and immature curé. Of the 441 curés working in the diocese of Reims in 1774 who noted their age upon first becoming a curé, only two had not yet reached the age of 25: one was 23, and the other 24. The average age stood at 32, and nearly two-thirds of the curés obtained their first parish between the ages of 27 and 34. By this age, it was hoped, curés had matured enough to be a voice of authority in the parish—someone that parishioners could respect and trust.

The fact that curés obtained their benefices at a mature age further demonstrates the increasing professionalization of the parish clergy in the seventeenth and eighteenth centuries—a professionalization that would help them in their attempts to impart Catholic doctrines to their young parishioners. Curés from respectable, upper-middle-class families entered their parishes with a solid classical education obtained from *collèges,* seminaries, and universities and after having completed several years as a priest in training. They had a working knowledge of Latin and could perform the sacraments properly, say Mass, and put together passable, if not always spectacular, sermons, *prônes,* and catechetical instructions. They knew how a curé, as the primary representative of the Catholic Church at the parish level, was supposed to dress, speak, and act. During their time as seminarians, they learned the diocesan catechism and the methods required to teach it, and they practiced their catechetical skills as clerks, *desservants,* and vicaires. As curés they understood their duty to impart Catholic doctrines to the children of their parishes through weekly catechism classes, and they were remarkably well prepared to carry out that duty.

Duties and Morals

Of course, even the most comprehensive training and preparation could not ensure that every parish priest fulfilled his responsibilities as faithfully as bishops hoped. Using records of the eighteenth-century clerical synods held by bishops in Châlons, as well as records from episcopal visitations to Auxerre and Reims, we can assess whether curés' behavior conformed to their training in the seminary and beyond.[25] Nearly every year from 1705 to 1744 the bishops of Châlons-sur-Marne called a synod of archdeacons and rural deans to discuss the behavior of both the parish clergy and the laity.[26] The ordinances issued at these synods reveal that most of the problems with ignorance and immorality had been resolved. Usually bishops reminded curés that their female servants had to be at least fifty years of age, but this seems to have been encouraged in order to avoid any appearance of immorality rather than because of any actual illicit affairs between curés and servants.[27] It seems that curés were performing the sacraments diligently as well—the bishop only noted ways that they could continue to improve. Many ordinances asked curés to be as consistent as possible in the confessional and to conform to the rules prescribed in the ritual. Bishops did not complain that curés were failing to confess their parishioners; rather, they just wanted to make sure that the penance handed out was consistent throughout the diocese. Similarly, curés said Mass when they were supposed to, but perhaps not with as much sincerity and gravity as they could. No ordinances dealt with nonresident curés, although there were many admonishments for curés who took trips to neighboring parishes to visit with other curés. In 1705 Bishop Gaston-Jean-Baptiste-Louis de Noailles warned his curés to avoid social gatherings and to stay home and study instead: "[Curés] should reside assiduously in their parishes, occupying themselves with the prayer and study that is so necessary for both their own sanctification and that of the souls who are under their direction."[28]

The synodal ordinances demonstrate that bishops in Châlons held their curés to very high standards of conduct and expected them to live in strict accordance with the ecclesiastical regulations for the secular clergy. Any business affairs needed to be conducted as discreetly as possible, and curés were not supposed to be involved in any sort of commerce unless they had to sell wine or grain that came to them as part of their benefices. Bishops admonished curés to avoid lawsuits with the laity or with other ecclesiastics as much as possible. Parish celebrations, either for weddings or for feast days, were off-limits for curés, as well as meals held at their parishioners' homes. With bishops setting such high standards for their curés, it is no wonder that they fell short of the mark and that the same ordinances had to be repeated year after year. At the same time, there is no indication that curés failed to perform their basic clerical functions—even if curés got a little tipsy at parish celebrations or went out hunting from time to time, they must have performed the sacraments and said Mass on a regular basis or the ordinances would have addressed those problems as well.[29]

In addition to synods, bishops found that visiting curés in their parishes on a regular basis was an effective way to ensure that they performed their duties properly and conformed to ecclesiastical standards. Bishops needed to visit their dioceses in order to perform the sacrament of confirmation, but pastoral visits also served as an important tool that bishops used to establish their authority at the parish level. By visiting his parishes personally, a bishop could carefully scrutinize both the curé and the laity and ensure that everyone conformed to the behaviors prescribed by the church. The mere presence of the bishop or archbishop exerted a powerful effect on the behavior of the laity, and because priests knew that their parishes could be visited at any time, they were more likely to follow the diocesan rules. Pastoral visits became much more common in the seventeenth and eighteenth centuries, as bishops worked to ensure the progress of Catholic Reform in their dioceses.

For both the curé and the laity in the seventeenth and eighteenth centuries, the prospect of a major event like a bishop's visit caused a significant amount of trepidation and required considerable preparation. In small rural parishes the entire village turned up for a visit; at the very least bishops expected all village notables, schoolteachers, midwives, and clergy to attend. Everyone knew they had to be on their best behavior for a visit since bishops had the authority to punish recalcitrant individuals much more swiftly and harshly than curés. People who had not taken communion at Easter quickly forgot their disagreements with their neighbors and completed whatever penance their curé prescribed so that they would be worthy to approach the altar. Others paid any outstanding tithes so that they too might persuade the curé to remove them from the list of noncommunicants. Curés and churchwardens cleaned the church and made whatever repairs they could. Curés made lists of those in the parish who had not yet received confirmation and gave them a crash course in catechism in case the bishop decided to quiz them.[30]

The formal part of the visit usually began with a lengthy church service; the Mass was celebrated by either the curé or the bishop and followed by special prayers, a sermon, and confirmation ceremonies. The curé next conducted the bishop on a tour of the church—the building itself (including the cemetery), the ornaments, the baptismal font, the holy water, and the church books and records. Visitors also inspected the curé's home, as well as any chapels or shrines within parish boundaries. These inspections allowed bishops to determine whether curés and churchwardens took proper care of church buildings and their ornaments, which constituted a significant investment for the church. Bishops usually spent a good part of the visit examining the records of the fabric (money and endowments that belonged to the parish) with the curé and the churchwarden, making sure that they administered church funds properly.[31] At some point during the visit, the curé or one of the village notables hosted a meal for the bishop and his entourage, at which further church business could be discussed.

Once the bishop completed the inspections and formalities, he began his interviews, which were designed to ensure that both the clergy and the laity in his parishes had been following all of the necessary ordinances and prescriptions. He asked the village midwife to appear before him and tested her on the formula for emergency baptism. He met the village schoolmaster and schoolmistress to inquire about their backgrounds, morals, and teaching practices. He summoned the children to test them on their catechism. And finally, he questioned the curé. In front of the parishioners, he asked the curé if he performed the Mass with regularity and decency, and if he made himself available to administer the sacraments when needed. The curé reported on his faithfulness in teaching the catechism and other instructions and whether or not his parishioners attended services and took communion at Easter. Often, the bishop told the curé to leave the church for a few minutes so that his parishioners could speak more freely. In this way, the bishop discovered the level of dedication of his curés, how faithfully the laity performed their religious duties, and how well the curé and his parishioners got along with each other.

By questioning both curés and the laity, bishops hoped to discover their true behavior and then change that behavior if necessary. Sometimes curés and parishioners tried to cover for each other—the people might not bring up their curé's hunting trips if the curé did not mention the rowdy festivals on holy days, for example. Some parishes may have succeeded in deceiving their bishops on these minor matters, but bishops seemed to have ways of uncovering hidden weaknesses, for they often noted both curés' and parishioners' shortcomings in their written reports of visits. If a bishop asked either the clergy or the laity a direct question, both parties found it difficult to lie to the man who was ultimately responsible for their spiritual well-being. At the end of the visit, bishops often issued ordinances for the parish, reminding its members of regulations that they had failed to follow or giving them new rules to which they would be accountable in the future.

Bishop André Colbert of Auxerre visited the parishes in his diocese in 1688 and 1689. Despite the fact that only twenty-six of the *procès verbaux* survive, the bishop's detailed comments and ordinances after each visit provide a great deal of information about the parish curés. In sixteen of the parishes the people issued no complaints about their curé, and the bishop made no comments to suggest that the curés had failed in any of their responsibilities. Other curés had a few, relatively minor, bad habits; the list included failure to keep proper parish records, saying Mass at inappropriate times, hunting, and card playing. While the laity did not have a problem with these activities, they likely mentioned them only because the bishop specifically asked about them.

Bishop Colbert dictated that four curés needed more severe reprimands, however. When he asked René Crochain, curé of Escrignelles, why he had not obeyed diocesan ordinances against hunting, the offending priest exclaimed, "I keep the commandments of God and the Church, and my conduct is so irreproachable that no one can rebuke me for any failures." Colbert, probably infuriated more by his curé's blatant disrespect than by his propensity for hunting, ordered him to spend some time at the seminary to think about how he could better serve God and his parishioners.[32] The curé of Saint-Privé was accused of hitting altar boys if they made mistakes (he hit one boy so hard the child had to run out of the church during the Mass to keep from bleeding all over the church linens); parishioners also complained of his ignorance and his inability to govern the parish. They were especially worried about the fact that at least one person had died without receiving the sacraments due to the curé's negligence. The bishop ordered him to spend some time at the seminary as well.[33] Colbert discovered that another wayward curé, Hector Delabarre, did not live in his own parish but rather in a house in a nearby town that shared a courtyard with a *cabaret*. Even more troubling was the eighteen-year-old niece who lived with him. They slept in the same room but in separate beds. Even if the curé was telling the truth, and his "niece" was not actually a common-law wife, Colbert expressed some concern that Delabarre lived too far from his parish to be able to fulfill his parochial duties adequately. He ordered the curé to find other housing arrangements within parish boundaries.[34] Finally, the bishop forced the fourth curé, an elderly octogenarian named Louis Saunier, to give up his parish entirely after he made several large errors while performing Mass during the visit and was unable to provide basic responses when questioned about how to administer the sacraments properly.[35]

Further information about the behavior of parish curés can be found in eighteenth-century visitation records for Auxerre as well. Between 1705 and 1712, Bishop Charles de Caylus conducted a comprehensive visit of Auxerre; the 163 *procès verbaux* that survive include the bishop's regulations at the end of each visit, specific to each parish and curé.[36] In those regulations, the bishop ordered four curés to spend between six weeks and three months at the seminary in Auxerre for failing to perform their duties properly. For example, the curé of Andryes did not take the time to confess anyone under the age of eighteen—he simply told his parishioners that children did not need to go to confession. The curé of Changy had a young female servant, failed to instruct his people properly, and spent too much time hunting. Two other curés (of Oudan and Dompierre-sur-Nièvre) seemed to be beyond the help of the seminary: so many people complained about them that the bishop announced he would begin the proceedings to remove them immediately.

Problems with the remaining 157 curés were of little importance. A few received a reprimand for hunting, and a handful were told to say Mass at the times prescribed by the bishop. Nearly thirty were reminded not to make announcements about secular affairs during the time set aside for *prône*. Three curés were harshly reprimanded for failing to give any sort of instruction to their parishioners, and others were reminded that they were supposed to teach catechism every Sunday and feast day throughout the year. Finally, three curés were told that they needed to pay for a vicaire to help out in the parish. Thus, the vast majority of the curés visited—over 95 percent—performed their basic duties with few difficulties and in general conformed to the clerical lifestyle.

The final comprehensive visit of Auxerre was carried out between 1733 and 1736, and the deficiencies discovered by Bishop Caylus during this visit were again rather unremarkable. Of the 129 curés visited, the bishop removed three from their positions or ordered them to spend time at the seminary for failing to perform their duties properly. He admonished several curés for confessing people in the sacristy and reminded others to say Mass at the proper time, but his *procès verbaux* report no serious moral lapses.[37] Overall, the vast majority of the ordinances dealt with relatively inconsequential problems, demonstrating that even if curés did not behave exactly the way that bishops hoped, they were hitting close to the mark. It is also important to note that these visitation records rarely note any complaints from the laity themselves—and when they did complain, the bishop took them seriously and attempted to bring about reform by sending errant curés to the seminary.

Strict celibacy, diligence, and conformity had become the standard of behavior in Reims, as well, by the beginning of the eighteenth century, according to the nearly one hundred *procès verbaux* from visits carried out in 1716.[38] In his reports the archbishop's secretary made notes about the character, capacity, and morals of the curés in the parishes they visited. For the most part, the archbishop seemed quite satisfied with the work that his curés were doing. He described sixteen of the eighteen curés in the deanery of Saint-Germainmont as good men with satisfactory morals who performed their duties with zeal. For example, in the parish of Avaux-la-Ville, the archbishop noted that "everything is in order and well regulated in the parish, due to the zeal and care of the curé."[39] In only two parishes did the archbishop indicate problems of any significance. In Hannogne the curé had a young female servant living with him. Because the servant was the curé's cousin, the archbishop did not suspect any real cause for concern, but the situation had become the subject of gossip in the parish. Therefore, he thought it prudent to move the curé to another position. In Renneville the archbishop found the curé and his parishioners in the midst of a dispute over tithes. Except for these minor disputes, the parishes in Saint-Germainmont appeared well regulated and were served by capable, dedicated curés.

The state of the deanery of Charleville in 1716 comes across as slightly less regular, however; the archbishop's assessment was more critical for half of the twenty parishes that he visited. He described curés in four of the parishes as good men with good morals, but they possessed only mediocre talent and very little intelligence. Another curé, François Paris of Montcornet, was evidently diligent in performing his duties and scrupulous in his morals but also a little stubborn. Jacques Gerdré of Renwez was an extremely zealous curé—so zealous that he was accused of treating his parishioners too severely. Curés in Launois and Warcq were noted as negligent and inexact in the performance of their duties; the curé of Warcq was also argumentative, often absent from the parish without permission, and involved in some sort of dispute with his parishioners. Several parishioners in Lonny complained that their curé neglected his duties in favor of his personal and financial affairs as well as his "love of wine."[40]

Yet the badly behaved priests in the deanery of Charleville seem to be the exception rather than the rule. On the whole, the curés visited in 1716 were described as faithful servants of the church, despite a few limitations. A significant number of curés with little intelligence or few real capabilities did exist (at least ten out of ninety-four), but they performed their duties as best they could. Another five or six were willfully negligent and more occupied with secular affairs than their religious responsibilities. The archbishop suspected only three curés of any sort of immorality, and in one of those cases he felt sure that the rumors were untrue. The archbishop initiated the process of removing only two curés—the curé of Gespunsart, who was from the Belgian diocese of Liège and in trouble with the secular officials, and the curé of Tarzy, a monk from the abbey of Sept Fontaines who openly traded cattle and had been involved in some sort of pistol contest with another monk.[41]

These types of curés—the badly behaved, negligent, and argumentative—were nearly ubiquitous in the sixteenth and early seventeenth centuries but were rare exceptions by the end of the seventeenth century. At least three-quarters of the curés in these five deaneries were intelligent, educated, and capable men who performed their religious duties and gave their parishioners nothing more to complain about than Masses said at the wrong hour or suppression of processions.[42] When bishops visited the majority of the parishes in Reims, Châlons, and Auxerre, they found seminary- and university-educated curés who respected their authority, conformed to ecclesiastical standards of behavior, and performed the sacraments appropriately. Thus, by the end of the seventeenth century the Trent-inspired reform of the parish clergy had made significant progress. Some curés tended to be a little worldly at times, succumbing to the temptations of wine and a well-laid table, but they kept their vows of chastity much more faithfully than their medieval predecessors, and they generally did not neglect the duties that their bishops—and their parishioners—required of them. As the following section will demonstrate, the religious education of the children of the parish became one of the most important of those duties, as Sunday catechism classes became an integral part of parish life.

Curés and Catechetical Education

The instruction of the people is for all pastors an indispensable necessity; it is a duty of their estate, an obligation imposed upon them by God himself, on which they will be judged.

—Bishop Claude-Antoine de Choiseul-Beaupré

Because religious education was considered so vital, as Choiseul-Beaupré noted, bishops gave clear guidelines for catechetical instruction.[43] Curés were required to hold catechism classes for an hour on Sundays and feast days throughout the entire year, and they had to judge whether children were knowledgeable enough to take their first communion. Bishops also wanted curés to make sure that the adults of the parish were sufficiently instructed in catechism as well. After issuing catechisms and ordinances about them, what did bishops find when they visited the parishes in their dioceses and questioned the children? Had the priests fulfilled the duties that their bishops expected of them? Based on visitations records from parishes in Auxerre, Châlons-sur-Marne, and Reims, the implementation of the reforms dealing with religious instruction may have begun in the seventeenth century, but the real fruits of the church's efforts arrived in the eighteenth century.

When Bishop André Colbert of Auxerre visited the parish of Bonny in June of 1689, he questioned the individuals who attended his visit on the principal mysteries of the faith and noted that the people were badly instructed. The curé complained that the people of the parish neglected to come to catechism, but from the ordinances that Bishop Colbert issued at the end of the visit, it is clear that he felt the curé himself needed to do a much better job of teaching and encouraging people to attend. He told the curé to "teach the catechism exactly, on the days noted in our synodal statutes, and apply himself to give good and solid instructions."[44] He ordered parents to send their children and servants to catechism every Sunday as well as to attend the curé's classes themselves, and he reminded them that eternal damnation awaited those who were ignorant of basic Catholic teachings.

Out of the twenty-six surviving *procès verbaux* from Colbert's 1688–1689 visit, eight classified parishioners as either badly instructed or "very ignorant" of the principal mysteries of the faith, due to the negligence of either the curé or the people themselves. The curé of Saint-Fargeau, who taught catechism three days a week between November and Lent, complained that only the people living in the town itself attended catechism regularly, while the people of the countryside only sent their children for a few months before they took their first communion. In Saint-Martin-des-Champs, the curé complained that the adults in his parish did not come to catechism; as a result, the bishop declared that "the curé is obliged to refuse absolution to all men and women who, by their negligence, are ignorant of the principal mysteries of the faith."[45]

These visits illustrate that catechetical teaching was not as regular and effective as Bishop Colbert hoped; his expectations were perhaps too high, while the curés' and the laity's were rather low. Curés either shirked their instructional duties, or the laity found excuses to remain home when the curés did hold catechism classes. Bishops also expected catechism class to be a weekly event for the entire parish, not just for the children. Yet it seems that adults balked at attending a second church meeting on Sundays, and curés had difficulty persuading parents to come to catechism classes along with their children.[46] Bishop Colbert continued to emphasize that catechism should be taught regularly and repeatedly told curés in his ordinances that they should refuse absolution to anyone who was ignorant of basic Catholic doctrines, although curés usually did not follow through with this prescription.

It seems that Colbert's efforts eventually produced results, despite a rough start. When his successor, Charles de Caylus, visited the diocese in the early eighteenth century, he found that curés provided instructions to their parishioners with a much greater degree of precision. Out of 160 parishes visited, the bishop gave ordinances ordering curés to teach catechism at the prescribed times to only ten curés. Furthermore, many parishioners told Bishop Caylus that their curés instructed the children of the parish "very well," and that they held catechism classes regularly. As bishops put an increasing amount of pressure on curés to fulfill their educational responsibilities, regular classes became more and more common. Teaching catechism was established as a clerical duty, and bishops regulated their curés' performance of parish instruction just as diligently as they regulated the Mass and the sacraments. In the eighteenth century curés taught catechism more often and with greater regularity than they had in the past, and by the end of the century learning the catechism had become an essential rite of passage and a regular Sunday event for children preparing for their first communion.

During his visits, Bishop Caylus made a point of questioning children in each parish before he gave them confirmation in order to assess the thoroughness of their instruction. Unfortunately, the secretaries who filled out the printed *procès verbaux* forms were not always exact in recording information about instruction; only about half of the forms note how well the children knew their catechism. The bishop found the children in two of these eighty-seven parishes so ignorant that he refused to give them confirmation: the children in Andryes, whose curé was found to be negligent and sent to the seminary, and the children in Clamecy, one of the largest parishes in the diocese. The bishop classified children in thirteen other parishes as ignorant or "badly instructed," although he confirmed both adults and children in those parishes. He found the children in the remaining seventy-two parishes (83 percent of the total number) to be sufficiently instructed and even very well instructed: children in thirty-four parishes (40 percent) received a rating of "perfectly instructed," "very well instructed," or "well instructed."

Despite paying a significant amount of attention to the children's religious education during this visit, Bishop Caylus did not question adults on their catechism. Although he and Bishop Colbert had succeeded in making catechism a childhood ritual, they recognized and accepted that parents sent their children to class regularly but did not attend themselves. To make up for this fact, the bishop instructed curés to read through a part of the catechism every other Sunday after the *prône*, reminding everyone in the parish of the questions and answers of the catechism at least every two weeks.[47]

Improvement in catechetical teaching for children continued throughout the eighteenth century in Auxerre. When Bishop Caylus visited his diocese between 1733 and 1736, he again interrogated the children on their catechism. Children in 15 percent of the parishes visited were reported as ignorant or very poorly instructed, and the bishop refused to confirm any children in seven parishes. Yet just as in his previous visit, he classified the majority of the children as at least sufficiently instructed. Furthermore, the ordinances demonstrate that, for the most part, the bishop felt satisfied with the way that his curés taught catechism. Instead of having to remind curés of their duty to instruct, he simply asked them to continue the efforts in teaching that they had already made.[48] Visits carried out by Bishop Champion de Cicé between 1767 and 1786 illustrate a similar situation. The bishop learned that curés taught catechism every Sunday and feast day and that they gave extra lessons in the weeks leading up to Easter. He did not reprimand a single curé for failing to instruct his people, nor did he issue any ordinances reminding curés of their instructional duties— instead, he praised his curés for their diligence in holding catechism classes.[49]

Patterns of catechetical teaching were quite similar in the diocese of Reims. At the end of the seventeenth century many curés taught catechism in their parishes but did so inconsistently, according to the reports of rural deans who visited the parishes in their jurisdictions. In a 1689 visit to the deanery of Le Châtelet, fewer than half of the thirty curés visited followed the archbishop's ordinances regarding catechism: only thirteen taught catechism every Sunday. Others reported that they taught at least every other week, but most reported that they only taught "sometimes," or "from time to time." Worst of all, in six of the parishes visited curés provided no consistent instructions whatsoever.[50] Overall, the deans' visits show that curés held catechism classes regularly in only about half of the parishes in the diocese. Instruction was not entirely lacking in the other parishes, but it seems that many curés did just enough to get by. They made sure that the children in their parishes could answer the most important questions in the weeks before they took their first communion, but they did not think of catechism classes as a regular part of the Sunday schedule.

The questionnaire of 1774 demonstrates that a dramatic change in attitudes toward catechism classes had taken place in the eighteenth century.[51] The questionnaire asked curés to provide the exact hour that they taught catechism on Sundays and feast days, and curés for all but 41 of the 724 parishes and annexes (94 percent) gave specific responses. Curés no longer reported that they taught catechism only from time to time; they instead indicated that they held regular classes every Sunday, usually either before or after vespers (sometime between one and four in the afternoon). Only two curés noted that they taught catechism only during Lent and Advent. A few admitted that they did not hold classes during the time of the harvest, or even during the summer, but the overwhelming majority of curés indicated that catechism had become an established part of the Sunday schedule for most of the year. Many curés even went out of their way to hold extra classes so that all the children could attend. For example, the curé of Alles instituted regular catechism classes on Tuesday and Thursday evenings, largely because many of the children in his parish had to tend livestock on Sunday afternoons and would miss catechism completely otherwise. The curé of Mairy-Meuze taught one catechism class on Sunday afternoons and had the schoolmaster teach another; he also made sure that children continued to attend class for at least a year after they had taken their first communion. He denied communion to any young adults who forgot their catechism until they could prove they were once again sufficiently instructed.[52]

Of course, since the curés filled out these questionnaires themselves, it would have been relatively simple for them to provide false information about how often they taught catechism; it is doubtful, however, that this occurred frequently since curés were subject to regular visitations. While it is certainly true that catechism class could be easily omitted from a hectic Sunday schedule every once in a while, it is probably unlikely that the curés who responded to the 1774 questionnaire completely neglected the catechism. They knew that they could be visited at any time and would have to produce a good number of children who could respond to the archbishop's questions. In fact, the archbishop's *grands vicaires* visited 143 parishes between 1772 and 1776,[53] and in only two parishes did the visitor note that the curé was anything less than exact in teaching catechism: the curés of Cunel and Souain taught catechism rarely, but the rest fulfilled their instructional obligations diligently. By the end of the eighteenth century, as a result of regular catechism classes taught by curés and vicaires on Sunday afternoons, Catholic children knew the basic doctrines of their religion better than they had at perhaps any time in the past—and certainly better than their forebears had at the end of the seventeenth century.

It seems that it also took the clergy in the diocese of Châlons-sur-Marne until the last century of the Catholic Reformation to make catechetical instruction a significant focus of their ministry. Not until a visit made between 1746 and 1752, by Bishop Claude-Antoine de Choiseul-Beaupré, did the printed *procès verbaux* form used for visits in this diocese even include a question specifically about catechism.[54] The bishop visited eight deaneries during this four-year period, comprising 333 parishes and annexes, and expressed concern about curés who were not teaching catechism as well as they could in just 14 of these parishes. The rest fulfilled their duty "exactly" or "exactly enough." As in Reims and Auxerre, by the middle of the eighteenth century curés taught catechism on a regular basis in Châlons-sur-Marne, and they were held accountable for instructions as well as the sacraments and the Mass. It had taken nearly two centuries for the French church to institute the program of religious education outlined at the Council of Trent, but once the behavior and education of the parish clergy were elevated to a higher level, the curés were willing and able to pass on some of what they had learned to the laity. In most seventeenth-century parishes, catechetical education was sporadic and incomplete, but by the end of the eighteenth century it was routine—in all but a handful of parishes, at least one catechism class was held in every parish church on most Sundays throughout the year.

Yet the visitation records from Châlons also demonstrate that persuading curés to teach catechism classes with regularity was only half of the battle—parents had to send their children to class in order for the church's program of reform to work. Catechism classes would be useless if the curé taught to an empty church. Despite the fact that the *procès verbaux* forms used between 1728 and 1732 did not specifically ask for information about instructions, 47 out of 294 curés (16 percent) who filled out an additional questionnaire at the time of the visit complained that their parishioners neglected instructions and catechisms. In 42 of the 333 parishes visited at midcentury (13 percent), either the visitor or the curé himself complained about lackluster attendance at Sunday catechism classes. This information thus begs the question: While it is certainly true that curés taught catechism with greater regularity than they ever had, were the laity as diligent at attending as bishops hoped? Did parents make sure that their children spent an extra hour in church on Sundays, memorizing and reciting the questions and answers of the catechism?

Catechism Attendance: Preparation for First Communion

In 1774 the principal residents of two small villages, Champigneul and Mondigny, wrote a letter to their archbishop, Charles-Antoine de La Roche-Aymon of Reims, providing a detailed list of reasons why they believed the church should pay for a vicaire for their communities. Champigneul contained ninety communicants and Mondigny had seventy; neither had the status of parish and thus no curé or priest lived in the villages. They were annexes of the neighboring parish of Évigny, which, in 1774, was served by the curé Pierre Paté. Paté was responsible for the spiritual needs of the people in all three villages; he alone held the authority to hear their Easter confessions. In addition to the parish Mass he performed on Sundays and feast days in Évigny, he alternated saying Mass in Champigneul and Mondigny. The residents of these annexes complained about the inconvenience of having the curé say Mass at only one of their churches each Sunday; every other Sunday parishioners had to travel to the other village and leave their homes and farms unguarded. In addition, the time of the Mass was not fixed because the curé could not be sure when his Sunday duties in Évigny would be finished.

In their letter the residents of both annexes complained bitterly about the lack of religious services in their villages. They described occasions when the curé had arrived more than an hour after the two villages had assembled, and other times when he had been too early and had nearly finished the service by the time everyone arrived. They complained that when the weather was bad and the roads were impassable, people in both annexes missed Mass altogether. They worried that the curé might not be able to reach injured parishioners or those who suddenly fell ill and needed to receive extreme unction before they died. They feared for the health and safety of the babies who had to be carried to the church in Évigny in all sorts of weather to be baptized, putting them at risk for illness and even death.

The first item on the residents' list, however, was their fear that they and their children were not being sufficiently educated in the doctrines and beliefs of the Catholic Church:

> It is absolutely impossible for the parishioners in the two annexes to be sufficiently instructed in even the basic elements of religion. The only days that the curé can catechize and preach are Sundays and feast days, but even on these days he cannot fulfill this essential part of his ministry, so necessary to the supplicants, for the annexes are so far away from the parish—they are at least a league away, and separated by woods and roads that are impassible during the greater part of the year—so that all the curé can do is to celebrate the two masses. After he returns to his residence in the parish, sometimes around noon but very often much later, it is impossible for him to return to the annexes and the supplicants find themselves in the difficult necessity of being neglected, and remain habitually in ignorance of the things that are the most necessary for their salvation.[55]

The residents of Champigneul and Mondigny felt their children were being shortchanged. They believed that catechism class was an essential part of the Sunday schedule and hoped that having a vicaire in the parish would ensure that the Mass could be said and catechism taught in each village on every Sunday.

The inhabitants of these two villages were not aberrations among a sea of ignorant and negligent parents—requests for additional curés and vicaires in Reims' rural parishes were common throughout the eighteenth century, and village notables repeatedly expressed their fears that their children lacked sufficient religious instruction because of an inadequate number of resident clergymen. Their letters reveal that parishioners viewed a basic religious education as one of their fundamental rights as members of Christendom and, especially, as tithe payers. In their 1769 request for a vicaire, the inhabitants of Menil and Hurlus,

annexes of Perthes, complained to the archbishop that the owners of
the tithe in their villages left them without spiritual aid, causing their
children to languish in ignorance:

> But what will affect your excellence's heart even more is the fact
> that during the seasons that our work allows us to hear the word of
> God . . . it is very rare that we can enjoy this advantage; the rain,
> snow, and frost are constant obstacles, and what is even more lam-
> entable is that our children cannot stay for catechism in the parish,
> since their feet are cold and wet with rain or snow. For you know,
> Monseigneur, that the children are ignorant of the religion, and that
> it is sad to see us thus abandoned to ourselves, deprived of the most
> precious advantages of religion, and to see us treated like a flock of
> no value while the eight or nine tithe-owners harvest the fruit of
> our sweat and labor—at least 1,000 or 1,200 livres—while insen-
> sible to our needs.[56]

Catholic believers did not take education in basic Catholic doctrines
for granted, nor did they feel that education was forced upon them by
reforming bishops. Parents wanted their children to have a religious
education, and they considered the instruction their curés provided as a
necessary component of raising productive adults and members of the
village community. Learning the catechism was an important childhood
ritual, the first step toward confession and communion—the sacraments that Catholics participate in over and over again throughout their
lives. And through their weekly catechism classes, the curés were primarily responsible for the children's religious education.

On the other hand, not all children attended catechism classes with
regularity, and curés pointed out problems with parental negligence
to their bishops. In questionnaires completed before visits to parishes
in Châlons, a few curés lamented the fact that everyone in the parish
seemed to completely disregard catechism. The curé of Montmort,
who taught catechism "very exactly," stated in 1746 that "the majority
of the people take no care to instruct themselves in the duties of the
religion, neither do they have their children and servants instructed;
they don't send them to confession or to catechism." In Thonnance in
1728, the curé told the bishop that the people in his parish spent their

Sunday afternoons arguing in the cemetery, making so much noise
that he found it nearly impossible to teach catechism adequately. He further noted that his parishioners had "no care whatsoever to send their
children to catechism class or to school; they let them live as they please."
Several curés complained that card games, gambling, and *cabarets* interrupted catechism classes as well.[57]

Other cures, however, revealed that problems with attendance were
usually limited to certain groups of people—especially the children
from poor families. For example, the curé of Triaucourt complained in
1748 that he had difficulty getting the poor children to attend catechism,
despite frequent exhortations: "A large number of the poor people is in
complete ignorance of religion . . . they are the first to miss instructions,
prônes, catechisms." The curé details how this negligence for education
led to all kinds of vices in his parish—from swearing and gambling
to theft, vengeance, and slander. Children and servants who had to
spend their Sunday afternoons guarding livestock also seemed to miss
catechism often. The curé of Les Grandes Côtes lamented in 1730 that
some of the parents in his parish "keep most of their children home
during the service to watch their animals, so that the children older than
age ten attend neither the Mass nor catechism class, despite the warn-
ings that have been given to them both in general and individually."[58]

Yet even the negligence by poor families was not the biggest problem that curés faced in instructing their parishioners—the real problem
concerned parents who sent their children to class just long enough
for them to learn what they needed to take first communion. Curés
were unlikely to let too many completely ignorant children approach
the communion altar, and since very few individuals in the eighteenth
century failed to take communion at least once in their lifetime, everyone had to know at least the rudiments of the catechism. The rite was
important enough that even the most recalcitrant parents made sure
that their children could take communion. The difficulty came in the
months and years *after* first communion. Curés who, by the end of the
eighteenth century, placed as much importance on religious education
as did their bishops had trouble prevailing upon young adults over the
age of twelve or thirteen to retain the knowledge that they had learned
and to keep the questions and answers of the catechism engraved upon
their minds.

Visitation records and questionnaires from Châlons contain many examples of parents who neglected the religious education of their older children and adolescents. When listing the individuals in his parish who hoped to receive the sacrament of confirmation during the bishop's 1727 visit, the curé of Épense noted that the youngest among them were the best instructed, but the teenagers and adults had forgotten what they had learned and refused to attend any instructions. The curé of Pringy told the bishop in 1747 that the adults in his parish resisted going to catechism classes because they "believe falsely that it is enough to attend catechism class just until they have taken their first communion, and then it happens that they forget what they took so much trouble to learn." The curé of Saint-Etienne-au-Temple made the same observation: too often people simply forgot their catechism after they took first communion. One woman in his parish had not taken communion in five years because she did not know her catechism; the woman repeatedly told the curé that catechism was for children and she did not need to know it. Every year when she came to confess he told her otherwise, but she refused to re-memorize the necessary lessons and failed to do her Easter duty as a result. The curé felt that the solution to this problem would be to require catechetical tests for young people who wanted to get married, but he did not say how this would help mature adults remember their religious education.[59]

According to the visitation records, the practice of parents sending children to catechism class only at the time of their first communion was common in the dioceses of Reims and Auxerre as well as in Châlons. For example, several curés in Auxerre complained that parents sometimes neglected to send their children to catechism; as a result, the bishop issued ordinances requiring parents to take more care for their children's religious education. The curé of Entrains noted in 1785 that the parents in his parish only sent their children to catechism when they were of an age to take first communion. The bishop's response was the following ordinance: "We exhort all fathers and mothers, masters and mistresses, to send their children and servants to catechism as soon as they have the use of reason, and not to wait to send them until they have reached the age at which they normally take their first communion."[60]

In Reims, out of the 143 parishes visited between 1772 and 1776, sixteen curés and/or visitors noted that parents neglected to send their children to catechism classes *exactement*—meaning that they did not insist on attendance after first communion. The curé of Liry indicated that many of his poor parishioners could not send their children to school and that the children did not come to catechism early enough. He added that no one refused to send their children altogether; he had not been forced to deny anyone the opportunity to take their first communion due to ignorance. In Moronvilliers the curé had given up on trying to make catechism a regular part of the Sunday schedule for all of the children in his parish; he stated in a 1773 questionnaire that he only taught catechism classes when he had a large enough group of children preparing for first communion.[61]

Curés complained about poor attendance at catechism in the 1774 *enquête* as well. The curé of Pouru-Saint-Remy lamented the fact that most of the young people in his parish had to tend livestock on Sunday afternoons, "which is the reason why the majority of the children do not come to catechism class or instructions, and in consequence remain in the greatest ignorance of the things necessary for salvation." The curé of Trois-Puits grew so frustrated with his parishioners' neglect of catechism that he decided to use the time set aside for *prône* to test the children and thus publicly unmask their ignorance. Unfortunately for the curé, this only made the parents angry at him.[62] These parents would certainly have had no problem with their children being tested in the weeks before they took their first communion, but they did not like "pop quizzes" at other times. The laity accepted that children had to learn their catechism in order to take communion, but they also believed that catechism was a childhood ritual that did not need to be extended into other spheres of parish life.

❧ In the dioceses of Auxerre, Châlons-sur-Marne, and Reims, the bishops' task of keeping their curés in line remained an ongoing battle, but the ferocity of that battle diminished by the end of the eighteenth century. As toleration for curés who did not maintain strict celibacy or who could not perform the sacraments properly decreased, fewer and fewer parishes had to live with negligent priests. During their visits bishops found a few curés who showed only lackluster dedication to their ecclesiastical office, but for the most part curés were educated, experienced, and willing to fulfill their duties. Most importantly for my purposes here, they increasingly performed one of their most important duties—catechetical instruction—with more dedication than they had in the past. In the last few decades of the seventeenth century, curés began to make weekly catechism classes a regular element of the Sunday schedule, and the process of regularizing catechetical instruction continued in the eighteenth century. When the church bells began to ring an hour before vespers, children between the ages of five and thirteen knew to file into the church, where they would sit quietly, pray, and repeat their catechism to their parish priest.

But the responsibility for parish instruction did not rest solely on the shoulders of the curé; the bishops' program of religious education depended on the cooperation of the laity as well, and that cooperation often was not easily obtained. As noted in the previous chapter, bishops adapted their catechisms to the demands of the laity, so it should come as no surprise that curés also had to modify the bishops' prescriptions at the parish level. Bishops initially had conceived of the catechism as a tool that could be used to instruct entire families instead of just children, and during their visits they insisted that adults who wanted to get married or be godparents had to demonstrate their knowledge of the catechism. Many even advocated withholding absolution as an incentive for ignorant adults to attend instruction.

This part of the bishops' vision never materialized, however. Instead, curés and the laity reached a compromise: they sent their children to catechism classes before their first communion but did not attend themselves. Parents accepted the need for catechetical education for their children and even insisted that curés provide that education— no Catholic parents, no matter how poor or provincial, wanted their children to be denied the sacrament of communion. Just as diligently as they made sure that their infants were baptized, they encouraged their children to memorize the questions and responses of the catechism so that when they reached their early teens, they would be able to approach the communion altar with the rest of the adults in the parish community. But after their children had been through the first communion ritual, they no longer required them to attend catechism classes. The instructional phase of their religious lives was finished.

Consequently, the compromise between bishops, curés, and the laity meant that catechetical education did not reach every Catholic soul equally. The children of the poor and the marginal remained noticeably absent from catechism classes, and they most likely remained ignorant of the truths of their religion throughout their entire lives. Teenagers and adults from the more well-off peasant families may have forgotten many of the questions and answers they had once worked so hard to memorize. The vast majority of curés—despite their bishops' injunctions to hold the adults in their parishes to higher standards— ignored what they heard at seminaries and synods and gave absolution to individuals who could no longer recite their catechism. Knowing that if they asked every person who passed through the confessional to re-memorize the catechism the list of noncommunicants would include nearly the entire parish, they concentrated their attention on the children and tacitly excused ignorant or semi-ignorant adults. Even the new, educated Catholic Reformation curé knew that he had to compromise with his parishioners on this issue, or the parish system would collapse altogether.

Even if the evidence demonstrates that just some children attended catechism for a portion of their lives, the catechism and the catechetical exercise still exerted a larger influence on the parish and society as a whole. We should not forget that catechism was designed for a larger purpose than simply teaching doctrine and theology. In their formative years, the children who attended catechism learned the practices of the Catholic faith that they would use throughout their lives. Perhaps even more importantly, through the lessons of the catechism and the methods curés used to teach it, they learned the moral and ethical code that governed their society. The bishops' program of religious education succeeded in firmly wedding the ritual of first communion to religious instruction—a practice still maintained in modern times—and made standard the idea that men and women of the Catholic faith should not be simply believers, but instructed believers. Thus, the catechism represents the very essence of the Catholic Reformation.

CHAPTER FOUR

The Village Schoolmaster
Another Agent of the Catholic Reformation

At the end of the seventeenth century in the diocese of Reims, two clergymen shared jurisdiction over the teachers of the *petites écoles:* the archbishop and the *écolâtre* (one of the cathedral canons). By virtue of his benefice, the *écolâtre* had the right to both approve and dismiss village schoolmasters and schoolmistresses, and any schoolteacher in the diocese was required to have his written permission in order to open a school.[1] Although teachers did not have to receive approval from the archbishop (except during a vacancy in the position of *écolâtre*), they could be fired by him or his representatives during pastoral visits. Thus, the duties of the archbishop and the *écolâtre* with regard to the *petites écoles* overlapped, creating the potential for disputes between the two officeholders.

In the early eighteenth century two archbishops of Reims brought two separate cases to court, arguing that control over the *petites écoles* belonged exclusively to the office of the archbishop. The two cases, one in 1718 and the other in 1736–1737, ended the same way—with the *écolâtre* maintaining his rights as long as he agreed to grant the archbishop the power to dismiss schoolteachers during pastoral visits.[2] The documents for the cases provide no specific information as to why the archbishops wanted to divest the *écolâtres* of their authority over the *petites écoles*. The income for the benefice of *écolâtre* was not large (Louis Joseph de Sugny, who held the office of *écolâtre* in 1729, listed his income as 634 livres for that year), and schoolteachers usually earned such small salaries that *écolâtres* certainly could not have expected much in the way of bribes.

The cases do show, however, that both archbishops equated control over schoolteachers with control over religious reform at the parish level. Essentially, they hoped to place the *petites écoles* under a clear authority in the church hierarchy. The *écolâtres,* despite the fact that they were also cathedral canons and clergymen by definition, represented more individual interests, and the archbishops feared they did not share the same dedication to Catholic reform. Bishops and archbishops, on the other hand, had a vested interest in securing control over village schools since the content of the education provided therein represented a significant component of the church's reform program.

Philip Hoffman has made a convincing argument that French parish priests served as "agents" of the Catholic Reformation, yet they did not act alone: schoolteachers could exert an equally significant influence over the religious and moral life of the parish. Hoffman describes his clerical "agents" as well-trained representatives of the church who spread Tridentine Catholicism to even the most remote parishes throughout France.[3] The village schoolmasters (and in some cases schoolmistresses[4]) of Auxerre, Châlons-sur-Marne, and Reims fulfilled many of the same duties that curés did, thus acting as agents of the Catholic Reformation as well. Not only did the schoolmaster function as a disseminator of moral, religious, and secular education; he was also a semiclerical representative of the church and a community leader. During school hours he taught catechism to his students as well as appropriate moral behavior, and he supervised their participation in the sacraments of confession and communion. All told, schoolteachers had more regular contact with, and influence over, the children of the parish than curés or any other member of the clergy.

As a result, bishops knew the successful reform of their parishes depended on their ability to persuade schoolteachers to operate their schools in accordance with the principles of Tridentine Catholicism. In fact, most of the literature on primary education in the sixteenth, seventeenth, and eighteenth centuries assumes that the Catholic Reformation movement and the increasing amount of control bishops exerted at the diocesan and parish levels allowed the church to dominate all primary education in the early modern period.[5] This is perhaps most clearly demonstrated by the fact that the term *petites écoles* is often mistranslated as "parish schools" by English-speaking historians, implying that the church itself had established and administered the schools. The curriculum of the *petites écoles* certainly centered on religion; besides learning the catechism, children learned to read from religious literature and copied out Christian scriptures and moral proverbs as writing exercises. But just because children studied religion does not mean that the church maintained complete control over the schools—the laity believed in the idea of religious and moral education as well, and parents and village notables had a significant influence on the administration of the schools in their communities.

The *petites écoles* and their schoolteachers were in fact subject to several layers of competing authorities; the *écolâtre* and the archbishop represented just two of a large cast of characters with interests in controlling primary education. The state maintained a rather distant and indirect authority—Louis XIV issued an edict in 1698 requiring each parish to have a schoolmaster and a schoolmistress, but neither he nor his successors created any institutions to support or finance those schools.[6] Bishops and other clergymen had grand visions of creating semiclerical schoolmasters and schoolmistresses who would teach religion and support the curés, but they, too, could only admonish and issue ordinances and exhortations since they provided no funds for the schools. Thus, with neither the church nor the state opening or maintaining primary schools, the confessionalization model in its classic form falls apart when the *petites écoles* are factored into the equation.

Consequently, the most important impetus for schools came from parents and local village authorities, who shared the responsibility for the administration of the *petites écoles*. At the village level, curés interacted with schoolteachers on a daily basis and certainly had some say in how the schools were run; however, the village notables and parents who provided housing and salaries for their children's teachers exerted the most direct influence over primary education. While the laity took advice from bishops and curés, they made the most significant decisions about primary schooling themselves, essentially setting the curriculum. Schoolmasters and schoolmistresses taught catechism along with reading and writing, but the laity accepted and even encouraged this: if they had not wanted schools that taught religion and morals, they would not have paid for them. It was at the instigation of the laity that agents of the Catholic Reformation were brought into their communities, and thus the laity's role in the reform process cannot be ignored. Schoolmasters and schoolmistresses can indeed be described as agents of the Catholic Reformation, but not necessarily as agents of either the church or the state. Instead, schoolteachers answered to several authorities and served several purposes in the communities in which they taught.

Because the village schoolteacher was at the nexus of these competing authorities, and because all levels of society had a stake in what and how schoolteachers taught, an examination of the role of the *petites écoles* in French villages can clarify and refine our understanding of the implementation of Catholic reform in the seventeenth and eighteenth centuries. The implementation was not a one-dimensional movement but rather the result of a complex interaction between a variety of people. Bishops, curés, and village notables all had their own ideas about how the schools should be run, and each influenced primary education and the religious reform movement in their own significant way. Together, they created a system of schools in Auxerre, Reims, and Châlons-sur-Marne to teach Catholic children to read, write, and recite their catechism.

The Village Schoolmaster: The Bishops' View

At an assembly of clergy held in November of 1662, Bishop Vialart of Châlons-sur-Marne issued a regulation encouraging the leaders of each parish in the diocese to find money to support a schoolmaster. To his curés Vialart wrote: "Neglect nothing which depends on your zeal, to bring about the establishment of a good schoolmaster in your parishes; this being the safest and most appropriate way to ensure that the youth are always well instructed in their duties and raised in the fear of God, on which depends the complete reformation of your parishes."[7] He recommended that curés and village notables review the accounts of the parish fabric to determine if any parish funds could be used to contribute to a schoolmaster's income. He asked the curés themselves to donate to the cause rather than give money to less worthy charities. Vialart even prompted his curés to canvass the parish for donations and to exhort parishioners to set aside money for education in their wills. Speaking to the parents in his diocese, Bishop Vialart urged those with school-age children to take advantage of the schools that did exist and to spend their money on securing an education in *bonne conduite* for their children rather than on more frivolous affairs.

Because the village school was one of the first places where children received formal Catholic instruction, the upper clergy knew that a significant part of their reforming mission depended on securing schoolteachers for their parishes and on maintaining the honesty, dedication, and doctrinal orthodoxy of those teachers.[8] Vialart certainly understood this, as his regulation reflects. Indeed, bishops serving in dioceses all over France agreed that schoolteachers should teach the young children in their care basic Catholic doctrines and imprint proper Catholic behaviors on their souls while they remained tender and malleable. Educated children would then grow up to be faithful Catholic parents, communicants, and tithe-payers.

Bishops indicated that formal Catholic instruction should take up a significant portion of the school day. Both class sessions, morning and afternoon, began and ended with prayer. Students all knelt together, in front of some devotional painting or image, to repeat prayers and make the sign of the cross. Schoolteachers had to teach catechism at least twice a week, on Wednesdays and Saturdays, with lessons lasting anywhere from one to three hours.[9] Bishops also recommended that teachers take their charges to Mass at some point during the school day. Instruction on how to make a good confession came during school hours, and bishops expected teachers to make time before major holy days for students to give their confession to the curé. At the very least, then, bishops advocated that schoolteachers spend between eight and ten hours a week (out of the twenty or thirty hours that school was in session) on religious and moral instruction. These rules applied to girls' schools run by schoolmistresses as well. Religious learning was considered crucial for both sexes, and regulations issued to school-mistresses outlining the curriculum and order of the school day were nearly identical to those given to schoolmasters.

Besides this formal religious education, bishops wanted Catholic morals, doctrines, and practices to permeate nearly every minute a child spent in school. Students learning to read were only allowed to be taught from religious books that had been approved by the curé. Some bishops further specified that the catechism should be the first book that children read after they learned the alphabet.[10] Bishop Vialart even gave advice on the best method for teaching children to read aloud: "Schoolmasters will take particular care to accustom their students to read with distinct pronunciation, and to articulate especially well the words in the recitation of their prayers; have them say their lessons with care and without hurrying; they must always begin and finish their lessons with the sign of the cross."[11] Clearly, the most important thing for the students to learn was how to say their prayers properly. In other words, in the eyes of the clergy the utility of learning to read lay in the fact that those reading skills could then be used for religious purposes. Students learning to write also found religious messages woven into their curriculum, as they copied out "sentences de piété" and "maximes Chrétiennes" to improve their penmanship.

Bishops also expected schoolmasters and schoolmistresses to find "teaching moments" during their lessons, when they could expound on some relevant moral principle. Bishop Vialart recommended that schoolteachers "remind their students often of the horror that they should have of mortal sin, since a single sin could be the cause of their damnation, and try to inspire in them the fear of God, the honor that they owe to their parents, and other important virtues."[12] Teach-ers were supposed to warn of the dangers of playing cards and dice and dancing; encourage modesty in thought and action; and urge stu-dents to bathe and dress in privacy, away from members of the oppo-site sex.

Besides fostering a general sense of modesty in their students, bishops wanted schoolteachers to maintain a strict separation of the sexes at all times. Members of the upper clergy emphasized this moral issue repeatedly in their instructions to curés and teachers. They believed that all learning, from catechism to reading and writing, should take place in a sex-segregated environment. If a village had both a schoolmaster and a schoolmistress, the schoolmaster was absolutely forbidden to teach girls in his school, and the schoolmistress could not teach any boys older than five or six. If the village had only a schoolmaster, bishops usually specified that boys and girls should meet in separate rooms or at different times of the day. If this could not be arranged, boys and girls were to be seated on opposite sides of the room and forbidden to speak with or even look at members of the opposite sex. Boys and girls were also dismissed separately, to prevent even the slightest contact between the sexes.

During parish visits, if bishops or their representatives had something to say about schools, it usually had to do with separating boys and girls. For example, the schoolmaster of Venoy (Auxerre) was told in 1785 to teach boys and girls on separate days of the week until funds for a schoolmistress could be found.[13] In 1736 the people of Coulanges-la-Vineuse (Auxerre) were told to hire a schoolmistress: "because in a large parish it is nearly impossible that there will not be great inconveniences when boys and girls are found together in the same school under the control of the same master, we ordain that a schoolmistress capable of instructing the girls be procured immediately."[14] If a bishop issued formal approval of a schoolmaster during a visit, the approbation often included an exhortation for girls to be taught separately. In many cases, visitors simply reported on whether schoolmasters taught boys and girls together.[15] The formula for visits made in the diocese of Reims in the last few decades of the seventeenth century included two questions about schools: whether the schoolmaster and schoolmistress maintained good moral standards in their personal and public lives, and whether they taught boys and girls together.[16] The 1774 questionnaire asked the curés to respond to the same questions. These records show that more often than not, at the end of the seventeenth century as well as in 1774, the *petites écoles* accommodated students of both sexes. Curés in at least three-quarters of the parishes in 1774 reported that their community employed only one schoolmaster, who taught both boys and girls.

The repeated injunctions against teaching boys and girls together demonstrate that in fact schoolteachers did not maintain the strict segregation of the sexes that their clerical superiors advocated, yet bishops continued to insist on it. In the regulations for schoolteachers published in Reims just one year before the Revolution, the archbishop still held firm in his desire for segregated classrooms:

> Knowing from sad experience how dangerous it is for children of different sexes to be taught in the same school and by the same masters, we exhort with all our powers the curés, lords, parishes, and residents, to ensure, by all the methods that charity inspires, that there are, even in small parishes, two schools, one held by a master for the boys, and the other by a mistress for the girls. We forbid, in this case, under pain of interdict, schoolmasters and schoolmistresses to teach in their schools persons not of their sex. In the parishes where it is impossible to provide for the salaries of a master and a mistress, we forbid very expressly and under pain of interdict to teach boys and girls in the same class at the same time, under any pretext whatsoever.[17]

This was evidently an issue that the upper clergy felt very strongly about, since they emphasized it so often. Even though most schoolteachers broke the rules, bishops still hoped that one day they would be able to separate boys and girls completely.

The moral lessons that bishops expected schoolteachers to provide took place not only during school hours but outside of class as well. Schoolmasters and schoolmistresses supervised the children during almost the entirety of the Sunday church meetings—at parish Mass in the morning, in the catechism class taught by the curé, and at vespers in the afternoon. Bishop Vialart recommended that teachers visit students and their parents in the students' homes at least once a month; unlike modern-day parent-teacher conferences at which teachers report on students' progress and behavior at school, schoolmasters and schoolmistresses in seventeenth- and eighteenth-century Châlons were supposed to use these visits to find out how their pupils behaved at home and then apply any appropriate punishments at school:

> [Schoolmasters] will carefully inform themselves of their students' conduct outside of school, and if they learn that their students have done something worthy of complaint they will chastise them and make the appropriate correction with the spirit of charity and prudence. To this effect, they will visit the families of the parish once a month, to learn from the fathers and mothers how their children are behaving.[18]

Evidently, the Catholic Church's vision for schoolteachers included that they not only educate the children but also serve as a kind of parole officer for all the children in the parish, making sure that students' behavior conformed to church standards for as many hours of the day as possible.

Furthermore, the bishops believed that in addition to teaching lessons on religion and morals, teachers in the *petites écoles* should provide living lessons — that is, examples of irreproachable Catholic behavior. Theoretically, the curé served as the ultimate moral figure in the parish, but bishops realized that schoolteachers could often provide even more influential examples because of their experience as lay men and women who lived in the world and had families and mundane responsibilities like everyone else in the village. Thus, the first rule that Bishop Vialart gave to his schoolmasters in 1666 concerned their responsibility toward other parishioners: "Schoolmasters will have a great esteem for their estate, and understand well that God asks more virtue of them than other laymen in order to make themselves worthy of their vocation, and thus they will be very faithful to the practice of the exercises of piety recommended to all Christians for passing the day in holiness."[19] Similarly, in 1788 Archbishop Talleyrand-Périgord of Reims recommended that schoolmasters and their whole families act as models of moral living: "They will take great care for the Christian education of their families, and to rule them so well that they serve as an example for the entire parish."[20]

The regulations for schoolmasters in Châlons and Reims included considerable detail about what it meant for them to lead by example. Archbishop Léonore d'Estampes de Valançay told schoolmasters in Reims in 1647 that they could not serve as the village *cabaretier,* or tavern-keeper, while holding the office of schoolmaster since the two occupations were morally incompatible. In 1788 Archbishop Talleyrand-Périgord forbid schoolmasters to even set foot inside a *cabaret,* let alone own and operate one. He also prohibited schoolmasters from attending *veillées* (informal gatherings held in private homes, often during winter evenings), dances, or other "public diversions" and urged them to avoid being seen in bad company. Châlons' statutes in both 1666 and 1770 included playing the violin, and other "worldly and dangerous recreations," on the list of forbidden activities, as well as speaking too liberally with young girls and women.[21]

Similarly, bishops felt that schoolmasters should exemplify good religious and moral practice by participating in both public and private devotional activities. Bishop Vialart urged schoolmasters to begin their day early, with prayers and study of religious books like *l'Imitation de Jésus Christ* or *l'Introduction à la vie devote.* They were exhorted to practice their profession "with affection, diligence, and sentiments of piety, not just out of duty, or purely for temporal profit, but to please God." In addition to attending the parish Mass with their students, schoolmasters had to confess to their curés at least once a month and always take communion on the most important feast days of the year. The church required most lay men and women to confess and take communion only once a year, at Easter, but bishops apparently believed that schoolmasters should be held to nearly the same standards as the clergy.[22]

Many of the schoolmasters' duties can be described as clerical, or at least semiclerical. In a large urban parish the curé could count on the assistance of other priests—vicaires, clerks, choirmasters, and sacristans. In the countryside, however, curés often had no other priests living nearby and either had to work alone or enlist the help of laymen. Most often, it was the schoolmaster who served as a clerical assistant. Bishops encouraged this practice and issued ordinances urging schoolmasters to perform these functions with piety, diligence, and dignity.

A schoolmaster was often referred to as a *clerc-maître d'école* in visitation records, and they performed most of the duties that clerks or sacristans would have been charged with in larger parishes.

Schoolmasters' duties for the church took a variety of forms. Most importantly, they assisted curés during many of the sacraments, including the parish Mass on Sunday mornings. Usually they acted as choirmasters, leading the music, singing along with the curé, and training the choir boys who sang during Mass. If *obits* (Masses founded to commemorate the anniversaries of parishioners' deaths) needed to be performed during the week, the schoolmaster aided the curé during those services. Whenever the curé had to take the Eucharist outside of the church, either for sick people or for processions on holy days, the schoolmaster helped him to carry it. He assisted at marriages and baptisms, helped carry the coffin during funeral processions, and, in some cases, updated the parish registers. Some schoolmasters held the position of *sonneur* and rang the church bells at specified times during the week. Finally, schoolmasters were responsible for the upkeep of the church itself, from sweeping out the sacristy to locking up the sacred ornaments after services.

In parishes in which tonsured priests were rare, schoolmasters played a vital role in regular church administration, and bishops expected that if they fulfilled some of the duties of priests, they should act like priests and even receive some clerical training. In fact, many of the rules and regulations given to schoolmasters are remarkably similar to those given to curés in their assemblies and synods, even those concerning their dress and grooming (both were to wear the surplice and square bonnet and keep their hair short). The similarity between regulations for schoolmasters and priests is evident in an institution begun by Bishop Vialart in the second half of the seventeenth century: the schoolmasters' conference. Vialart asked the schoolmasters of the diocese to meet with their rural dean and other clergymen each year. This meeting was not just a conference of professionals, however—it was a religious retreat. The daily agenda for the meeting was modeled after schedules commonly used in monastic communities and included Mass, pious readings, and lectures on "the vocation and duties of schoolmasters." No records from Vialart's retreats exist, and it is impossible to determine how many such meetings occurred; however, just the existence of this institution shows how important schoolmasters were to Bishop Vialart's program of reform.[23]

Bishops often held schoolmistresses to even more rigorous standards than schoolmasters. They expected any women involved in children's education — schoolmasters' wives, widows who taught a few children in their homes, or members of the teaching congregations — to serve as the primary example of virtuous living for both the young girls and the married women in their parishes:

> The principal care of schoolmistresses should be to invite people of their sex, by their example and by their entreaties, to the love of charity and to maintain in all their conduct a great amount of decency and modesty . . . Schoolmistresses will speak to the women often of the care that they must have to avoid occasions which could bring them to vice, like frequenting people of the opposite sex, dances, games or gambling, walks or pilgrimages with boys; schoolmistresses will show them by their example to dress modestly, and without any vanity.[24]

In order to set a good example, schoolmistresses had to conduct themselves modestly at all times. They were never to be seen in the company of men or boys, never to stop and talk with anyone in the streets, and certainly never to enter *cabarets* or other public establishments. Bishops expected all schoolmistresses to eat their meals in their homes, unless perhaps they received an invitation to dine in the home of a pious widow. So that schoolmistresses could never be accused of being lazy or idle, they had to keep some sort of handwork with them both at school and during the rest of the day, in order to occupy themselves if they ever found a free moment. Their clothing was supposed to be modest and sober — dresses of a brown color for working days and black for Sundays and feast days. They had to maintain "a grave and reserved exterior" at all times and avoid the appearance of vanity or frivolity.[25]

The most important duty of schoolmistresses outside of school was to supervise the parish *veillées,* or evening meetings. Visitation records are full of complaints about the drinking, dancing, and promiscuity involved in the nightly gatherings, and both Vialart and Le Clerc tried to reform the practice by making the *veillées* meetings for women only and by putting the village schoolmistress in charge of them: "School-mistresses will regard this occupation as one of the most important parts of their job, and try with gentleness and prudence to engage the girls and women of the parish to come and spend the evening in their homes, each working at their own tasks."[26] Bishops recommended that while the women worked, the schoolmistress should lead them in prayers, read to them from pious books, and teach lessons from the catechism. Maintaining this type of atmosphere and getting women to attend regularly would have been an extremely difficult task for the schoolmistress; judging by the constant complaints about *veillées* in Châlons' visitation records throughout the eighteenth century, they probably had very little success in carrying out the bishops' vision of pious, sex-segregated evening work parties. Yet the existence of these rules and regulations shows that bishops hoped schoolmistresses could serve as the primary example of piety, charity, and obedience for the all-important female half of the parish.

Thus, both schoolmasters and schoolmistresses were agents of reform in the eyes of seventeenth- and eighteenth-century bishops. Schoolteachers offered a useful service to bishops because they pro-vided an education in Catholic doctrine and behavior for the children of the village, as well as for their students' parents during church ser-vices and public gatherings and in everyday encounters. By assisting curés with their duties, they could compensate for a shortage of priests and ensure the proper care of church property. Reforming bishops saw schoolteachers as a crucial resource, essential in the drive to increase the level of piety in their dioceses and in carrying out the work of the Catholic Reformation.

The Village Schoolmaster: The Curés' View

Although the regulations issued by bishops for schoolteachers are instructive for understanding the church's goals for the ideal village school, they cannot tell the whole story. Parish priests also had a signifi-cant role to play in the supervision of schoolteachers. The upper clergy actually had very little contact with schoolteachers on a regular basis; the majority exercised their occupation without any approbation from bishops or *écolâtres*. Just as the bishops had no choice but to rely on members of the lower clergy to teach catechism, they had to instruct their curés to carefully monitor schools and schoolteachers and then hope that their regulations were followed. Teachers interacted with the lower clergy on a daily basis, and the nature of the curé-schoolmaster relationship could have a considerable impact on the education children received in the *petites écoles*. It was at the parish level that schoolmasters were approved in practice; therefore, an examination of the relationship between curés and schoolmasters can provide additional insight into their roles as agents of the Catholic Reformation.

In the parish of Nogent-l'Abbesse (Reims), the curé and the schoolmaster had an extremely combative relationship. In 1768 curé François Pothier wrote a letter to the archbishop complaining about the conduct of Jacques Bertrand, the village schoolmaster.[27] From Pothier's four-page list of complaints, it is obvious that the two men were engaged in a rather heated, albeit childish, power struggle. Pothier wrote that Bertrand often refused to assist with the Mass or tried to send his son in his place. This caused Pothier much grief, since he did not think the boy behaved with the proper decorum needed for the sacraments. On the days when Bertrand *père* did appear at the church in time for Mass, Pothier still faced considerable challenges. Bertrand apparently refused to follow the correct rite for the Mass and gave responses at inappropriate times, confusing the curé and the congregation. Sometimes he sang much more loudly than the curé, distracting people from the service.

Pothier also accused his schoolmaster of failing to perform other important duties for the church and of causing disruptions at parish services. Bertrand was supposed to launder the church linens, but Pothier often found himself without the necessary materials. On one occasion Pothier confronted Betrand about the missing linens, but the schoolmaster refused to provide any explanation and told the curé to go and find them himself. Another of Bertrand's responsibilities included supplying a candle for certain Masses. One particular Sunday Bertrand refused to light the candle—for no other reason than to be disobedient, according to Pothier. This interrupted the service, and the parishioners began to make so much noise as they whispered to each other about Bertrand's behavior that the curé had to cut short his reading. The next time a candle was required, the curé furnished it himself in hopes of avoiding more problems with the schoolmaster, but Bertrand again refused to light it and then ordered the choir boys not to do it either. The boys were apparently more afraid of Bertrand than they were of Pothier, because the curé eventually had to light it himself before he could continue. All of this took place during the middle of the service, causing a tremendous scandal in the parish.

According to the curé, Bertrand did not fulfill his duties at school any better than at church. Pothier wrote that he often went hunting instead of opening the school. He refused to bring his students to Mass on working days and did not supervise them during parish services on Sundays. He would not teach the children to respect the catechism (presumably this means that he either refused to teach catechism at all or did not teach it properly) and never attended the curé's Sunday catechism classes. Perhaps worst of all, Pothier complained,

> He doesn't ever send his own children to catechism class, and teaches them to look down upon the curé. If his oldest son is there by chance at the end of class, when he comes to bring back the surplice, he laughs and incites the others to laugh and to commit other immodesties that the curé cannot prevent. And if the curé warns pastorally the said Bertrand to keep his children in line, he responds in front of them: Monsieur, go away, I am better than you, and my children are too.

Bertrand apparently often made disparaging remarks about his curé, accusing him of being without charity and of working only for money and threatening to mistreat Pothier if he ever came upon him alone.

The letter is the only information available about this case, so we do not know the schoolmaster's response to the curé's complaints. Perhaps Bertrand would have argued that it was the curé who said the Mass incorrectly, or that it was the curé's responsibility to provide the candles and linens for services. He might have accused Pothier of mistreating his children during catechism class, or of making unreasonable demands on his time. The only hint we have of the conclusion of this dispute is that in 1774, when Pothier filled out a questionnaire for the archbishop, he made no complaints about the village's (unnamed) schoolmaster. Either Pothier and Bertrand were able to work out some sort of truce, or Bertrand's misbehavior was disturbing enough to force the archbishop or the village notables to dismiss him. Regardless of the outcome of the affair, the case shows how disruptive a feud between schoolmaster and curé could be to parish life. The two men together performed all of the significant clerical functions in the parish—if one failed to fulfill his duties according to the standards of the other, the consequences could range from simple resentment, arguments, and disobedience to outright scandals, threats, and even violence.

Much of the potential for conflict resulted from the different groups who claimed to have authority over schoolmasters. The *écolâtre*-archbishop dispute described above had few repercussions at the parish level, but schoolmasters still had to answer to either the curé or the village notables—or both. Individual personalities and motivations could make all the difference. Some schoolmasters might submit to the authority of a strong-willed curé, while others allied themselves with influential community members. Still others, like Bertrand, might insist on enforcing their own rules in defiance of any local or diocesan authorities. Bishops tried to mediate disputes when they could, but if they could not rely on their curés to enforce their regulations and ordinances, their interference would remain ineffective.

According to the bishops, the curés held the primary responsibility for the administration of the village schools and for the behavior of the schoolmasters. Bishops' ordinances directed toward the curés are full of exhortations to secure good schoolmasters and reminders to visit the schools often to make certain that schoolmasters followed the rules and taught good Catholic doctrine to their students. For example, in 1671 Bishop Vialart ordered that his curés "visit the school at least once a week, to see in what manner the children are being raised, to see if the master takes all the necessary precautions so that the girls and boys are taught separately, to see if he teaches the catechism at least three times a week, and if he gives his students a good education."[28] Vialart also issued a regulation requiring schoolmasters to treat their curés with the proper respect: "Schoolmasters will have, for their curés and vicaires, all the affection, submission, and respect that they owe them, and take care to never do anything in public which contradicts them."[29] These rules were designed to keep disputes like the one between Pothier and Bertrand from taking place; according to the bishops, any disagreement should be settled by deferring to the curé in his capacity as the official clerical representative in the parish. Bishops also reminded curés that they could use their power to withhold sacraments as leverage against unruly schoolmasters.

Although bishops gave curés a certain amount of supervisory authority over the *petites écoles,* they still did not have complete control and at times found themselves powerless to effect meaningful change in the schools. Curés could neither hire nor fire schoolmasters without the approval of the parish, and they rarely had any say in how the schoolmaster was paid. This limited the real power that curés could wield over the village schools: curés could "warn pastorally," but if they did not have the support of parents and village authorities (who collectively provided the bulk of the schoolmasters' salaries) or the bishop himself, they could do little to officially dismiss schoolmasters they did not like.[30]

On the other hand, a vindictive curé could make life miserable for an unwanted schoolmaster and bully him into leaving. If a curé treated his schoolmaster badly enough—forced him to do tasks not included in his contract, slandered him or his family, or ridiculed his teaching—the schoolmaster might be tempted to look for a position elsewhere. Apparently, a situation such as this occurred in the parish of Serzy-Maupas (Reims) in the early eighteenth century. The village notables wrote a letter to the archbishop complaining about the misbehavior of their curé; besides calling the women of the parish "sluts" and "whores" in his sermons and *prônes* and using the confessional to get revenge on parishioners he did not like, the curé had irritated the four previous schoolmasters so badly that they left the parish. The villagers themselves had found the schoolmasters' work satisfactory, but they had been unable to convince any of them to stay.[31] Clearly, this system of shared authority over schoolmasters and the similarities in their responsibilities could easily provide opportunities for significant disagreements between curés and schoolmasters at the parish level.

Despite this potential for conflict, visitation records indicate that the tempestuous relationship between Pothier and Bertrand may have been the exception rather than the rule.[32] Pastoral visits provided an ideal opportunity for curés to air their grievances about schoolmasters who did not fulfill their responsibilities or who led scandalous lives. If the curé and the people of the parish were divided over the activities or qualifications of their schoolmaster—if, for example, the curé thought he should be fired but the people wanted him to stay—the dispute would certainly be raised during the bishop's visit. Similarly, curés could also voice their dissatisfaction with their schoolmasters when completing their bishops' questionnaires. Remarkably, both of these types of records are generally free from such complaints. Out of the 558 schoolmasters mentioned in the deans' visits for the parishes of Reims in the late seventeenth and early eighteenth centuries, visitors made note of complaints against only twenty-eight of them, and for nine of these the sole grievance was that the schoolmaster was either too young or too old. Instead of complaining about their schoolmasters, most villagers reported to the visitor that the schoolmaster led a "good life" and had "good morals" and that he fulfilled his duties satisfactorily. In Sévigny in 1692 the curé told the dean that his schoolmaster was "of good morals and sound doctrine" and that everyone was content with him. The curé had one complaint related to educational matters, but it did not involve the schoolmaster; instead, he lamented the fact that some of the poor people in the parish neglected to send their children to school in spite of the schoolmaster's offer to teach them for free.[33]

The Reims questionnaire of 1774 also lacks information about any conflict between curés and schoolmasters. Although the curés usually had no problem reporting the vices and scandals of their parishioners, only a few mentioned their schoolmasters' deficiencies. The curé of La Neuville-en-Tourne-à-Fuy complained that his schoolmaster's behavior was neither modest, decent, proper, nor vigilant and that the people of the parish refused to send their children to school because of these shortcomings. The curé of Brécy lamented that the thirty students taught in the schoolmaster's home received a very poor education because of the constant interruptions from his wife and children. Yet even these sorts of complaints are scarce in the questionnaires. The vast majority of curés most likely agreed with Adam Remy François, curé of Ville-sur-Retourne and its annex Bignicourt, who said of his two schoolmasters: "I have no reason to complain of their life and morals, because they approach the sacraments from time to time and don't cause any trouble in the parish."[34] The early eighteenth-century questionnaires for Châlons-sur-Marne are similar to the Reims questionnaire in this respect: curés freely offer their complaints about their parishioners' faults and moral lapses but rarely make note of anything negative about the schoolmasters. They were much more likely to report that the people of the parish neglected their children's education than that the schoolmaster did not hold up his end of the bargain.

In the diocese of Auxerre in the late seventeenth and early eighteenth centuries, curés occasionally included complaints about their schoolmasters in reports submitted to the bishop. Bishops asked curés if their schoolmasters set good examples and if they taught both piety and reading to their students. This question certainly provided the perfect opportunity for curés to complain about unruly schoolmasters, and a few did take advantage of it. One curé of Briare noted that "the schoolmaster instructs his students very badly in every way, neither giving them a good example nor assisting at catechism classes nor conducting them to the church on any day of the week, and he is a man very subject to wine." The curé of Ouanne reported that his schoolmaster was perfectly capable of teaching well but that he neglected both the schools and his duties at the church because he preferred to spend his time pursuing his other (unnamed) occupations.[35]

Despite these sporadic difficulties, major disputes between curés and schoolmasters were few and far between. Why would curés refrain from complaining to their bishops or pastoral visitors about their schoolmasters, when they obviously had opportunities to do so?[36] The simplest answer might be that they had nothing to complain about, but to take this view seems rather naive and unrealistic. There were too many situations in which curés and schoolmasters might find themselves at odds. In addition, the records of clerical synods in Châlons show that bishops continually lamented the difficulties involved in securing a good schoolmaster, and curés complained that those whom they had employed frequently neglected their duties. Both bishops and curés also expressed concern during synod meetings that villagers often wanted to keep "libertine" schoolmasters, even after ecclesiastical authorities asked for their removal.[37] But this picture conflicts entirely with the one provided by visitation records and curés' questionnaires. Did curés refrain from mentioning their schoolmasters' shortcomings because they feared doing so would only draw attention to their own weaknesses and negligence of their own duties? This could certainly be the case for a number of curés, but in general curés in the late seventeenth and early eighteenth centuries cared for the souls in their parishes with much greater diligence than they had previously. Catholic Reformation clergy encouraged better conformity to Catholic doctrine in both word and by example in this period. This increasing strictness did not, however, apply to schoolmasters, at least according to a cursory reading of visitation records.

The solution to this conundrum lies in the fact that curés *wanted* to have schoolmasters in their parishes; thus, they had to accept the teachers' shortcomings. If a schoolmaster committed a few minor indiscretions—if he had a tendency to be a bit less strict than the curé might like, dismissed school early so that he could work in his fields, or spent evenings at the *cabaret* getting drunk with the rest of the parish— the curé probably refrained from complaining because he did not want to lose the only assistant he had. Like bishops, curés knew that the lack of a good Catholic education in doctrine and behavior for the children of the parish would only lead to increased licentiousness when those young people became adults. Perhaps many of them would have agreed with the curé of Liny (Reims), who remarked in 1772 that "the people in general are of good character, but they are plunged in ignorance so deep in matters of religion that there is no other hope than to reform them by dedication to the instruction of the children."[38]

Curés often expressed to bishops their desire for a schoolmaster, and some even proposed on their own initiative to contribute to teachers' salaries. The story of Estienne Lefebvre, curé of Dampierre-sous-Bouhy (Auxerre), shows just how far a curé might go to procure a schoolmaster for his parish. He reported to the bishop in 1679 that a certain woman had decided to leave a significant amount of money to the church in her will, but he had convinced her to stipulate that the money be used to hire a schoolmaster instead. After she changed her will and the inhabitants of the parish found out, their ire against both the woman and the curé became so strong that she reverted to her original will. Whereas the curé had been teaching for years for free, the villagers knew that they would have to contribute to the upkeep of the schoolmaster themselves after the benefactress's money ran out (donations rarely covered all of the expenses needed to maintain a *petite école* for more than a few years). Thus, they objected to hiring a schoolmaster whom they would one day have to support. Lefebvre risked his relationship with his parishioners in an attempt to hire a schoolmaster and was wholly unsuccessful—Dampierre still had no official schoolmaster in 1683 when Lefebvre sent another report to the bishop, nor had the parish acquired one in 1711, 1735, or 1762, as reported in visitation records for those years.[39]

In fact, in parishes that did not have schoolmasters, both bishops and parishioners often expected curés to hold unofficial schools. This was a common practice throughout the diocese of Auxerre, and it demonstrates why curés in the dioceses of Reims and Châlons, where approximately 90 percent of the parishes had at least one official *petite école,* complained only infrequently about their schoolmasters: if their complaints led to the schoolmaster's dismissal, they might be called upon to teach in the schools themselves. Teaching the parish children to read and write was not a responsibility that most curés wanted to be saddled with.

As noted above, schoolmasters also served as clerical assistants in parishes that had no resident priests other than the curé. Bishops recommended that rural schoolmasters serve as choirmasters, sacristans, and clerks, and both curés and parishioners insisted rather emphatically that schoolmasters follow this particular regulation. Some of the larger parishes had vicaires, but curés often preferred to have schoolmasters rather than vicaires assist them in their duties since they did not have to pay schoolmasters. Unless curés voluntarily left the schools a legacy in their wills, the villagers paid for schoolteachers. Even the pay that schoolmasters received for their work in the parish came from the parish fabric or from tithes rather than from the curé himself. As a result, rural communities universally employed their schoolmasters as clerical assistants. Schoolmasters were the most obvious choice for this position; they could (theoretically) read and write better than most of the other people in the parish, and they needed the extra income. A teaching salary alone rarely provided sufficient income for a schoolmaster and his family, so combining the small amount of money available for a clerical assistant and the funds that the community could contribute for their children's education was often the only way to ensure that a school-master would stay in the parish. Essentially, communities combined the two part-time positions of schoolmaster and parish clerk into one full-time position—an arrangement that worked well for curés, villagers, and the schoolmaster himself.

The extent to which curés relied on their schoolmasters for help in their clerical functions is evident from bishops' complaints about curés who shirked their duties and then required schoolmasters to perform them. Judging from the types of guidelines given at synods, various schoolmasters in Châlons performed almost every nonsacramental function possible. They taught the Sunday catechism class in many parishes, especially in annexes. Curés who had to travel back and forth between two different villages to say Mass often did not have time to teach catechism, so schoolmasters, who already taught catechism in school, were called upon for help. They also led vespers and evening prayers in both the principal parish churches and in the annexes. They performed the most important functions at funerals as well, by carrying the coffin to the church, where the curé said the customary prayers, and then bringing it back to the cemetery to supervise the burial. Bishops' regulations show that schoolmasters were allowed to perform these duties in cases of necessity, but apparently some curés took advantage of the situation. Bishop Choiseul-Beaupré reported the following at his 1736 synod:

> We have learned that several curés leave their parishes on Sundays and feast days to go visiting, and leave the schoolmaster to chant vespers; this conduct is very reprehensible and very contrary to the spirit of the Church, which means for these days to be sanctified by prayer and good works. What example is this, for the people to see their guides please themselves on days which should be entirely consecrated to the Lord?[40]

Clearly, curés had no problem allowing their schoolmasters to take over their own clerical duties when it suited their needs.

Some curés seemed to think of schoolmasters as members of the clergy, even though most were in fact laymen with wives and families.

In the section of the Reims 1774 questionnaire about ecclesiastics, curés provided information on any people "attached to the service of the parish," and in a large number of questionnaires the curé listed the *maître d'école* in this space, despite the fact that an entirely separate section of the questionnaire asked for information about the *petites écoles*. The schoolmasters listed in this section were not tonsured, celibate clergymen, yet the curés viewed them as they would other clerics. For example, the curé of Nanteuil-sur-Aisne wrote the following in the space for information about other ecclesiastics in the parish: "there is no one attached to the service of the parish except those who are indispensably necessary to the divine service, like the schoolmaster." Two other curés literally referred to their schoolmasters as clergy: Pierre Celien of Saint-Pierremont wrote "only a schoolmaster assisted by five or six children that he is teaching to sing, make all the clergy," and Nicolas Masson entered "a clerk-schoolmaster, three vicaire-choir masters, four choir boys, a sacristan. That is all the clergy [*clergé*] of the church of Beine." Elsewhere in the document Masson noted that these individuals were also *laics*—lay men who were not tonsured and most likely married. The dichotomy between clerical and lay, normally taken for granted by historians, did not exist for Masson.[41] The boundary between the clergy and the laity maintained a certain fluidity in rural parishes where, due to the lack of priests, work for the church had to be carried out by a variety of people.

Schoolmasters were therefore the most common laymen chosen to fulfill clerical duties that curés could not perform themselves, and this situation created an interesting relationship between the two individuals. Curés, who often needed a significant amount of help in order to perform all of the duties required of them, did everything in their power to obtain schoolmasters for their parishes and to keep them there for as long as possible. Although disagreements might arise between curés and schoolmasters, the advantages of having a schoolmaster far outweighed the disadvantages, leading curés to overlook their shortcomings and try to keep conflicts to a minimum. Bishops may have expected curés to maintain a solid position of authority over their schoolmasters and mold them into agents of reform, but in reality curés had to make significant compromises if they expected to keep the schools open. Curés were in no position to enforce all of the bishops' regulations for the *petites écoles*, so schoolmasters usually did not have to conform to the ecclesiastical standards of behavior that bishops outlined. Instead, schoolmasters had to answer to a much less distant authority—the village notables.

The Village Schoolmaster: The Layman's View

At the request of one of his former pupils, nineteenth-century schoolmaster François Lebon wrote a memoir about his teaching experiences that provides a general outline of his career.[42] Lebon began teaching in the village of Raidy in 1825, several months after the community's previous schoolmaster died. It was the first of four towns in which he would teach throughout his life as a schoolmaster. Although Lebon lived and taught in the early nineteenth century, his experience was not unlike that of an *ancien régime* schoolmaster—documents dealing with the pre-Revolution *petites écoles* show that seventeenth- and eighteenth-century schoolmasters went through the same hiring procedures and followed similar career patterns.

In the fall of 1825 the town council of Raidy began their search for a new schoolmaster. The mayor advertised the position in the surrounding region, and five men applied for the job—two who had been schoolmasters in other towns, a shoemaker, Lebon (who had been working as a mason), and one other with an unspecified occupation. In November the five candidates met with the town council, the mayor, and the curé for interviews. These village notables asked each applicant to read aloud a page from the New Testament and from the psalter, as well as "dans les parchemins"—a handwritten document. Each gave a writing sample in the four standard styles of the day: *cursive, ronde, bâtarde,* and *gothique.* Finally, the candidates sang *In exitu Israël* and *O salutaris hostia* to demonstrate the quality of their voices. Lebon performed well in the interview, had several cousins on the town council, and was a favorite of the curé, so he was chosen for the job.[43] He began teaching on the second of December. Lebon remained employed as schoolmaster in Raidy until 1829, and he then moved on to teach in three other towns. Although he continued to work as a mason for several years during the summers, for most of his life he made his living as a village schoolmaster.

The events of Lebon's life previous to his employment in Raidy give no indication that he had planned to become a schoolmaster. He was born in 1795 in Courteau, the son of a shepherd. His father sent him to the *petite école* in Courteau until the age of eleven, when he began to practice his father's profession. Lebon claimed that he left school able to read both handwritten and printed material, write in all four standard scripts, and with knowledge of the four rules of arithmetic. He also knew the small catechism word for word and some of Bossuet's *Histoire sainte*. Despite the fact that he was first in his class, Lebon *père* left young François no choice regarding his profession: he tended sheep until 1813, when he was conscripted to fight in the Napoleonic wars. After an absence of eight years, Lebon returned to Courteau to find that his father had died. He settled with an uncle, a mason, in Raidy.

Lebon learned his uncle's trade and practiced it until 1825, when the schoolmaster's job became available. His family and friends urged him to apply for the position, knowing that he had done very well in school himself and had a good voice. They knew that his years in the army would have prepared him to discipline rowdy young children as well. Lebon worried that he would not make enough money as a school-teacher, but his uncle told him that he could work as a mason in the summers to supplement his income. This is, in fact, what Lebon did; he wrote that until 1837 he was both mason and schoolmaster: "From the month of April or May, my thirty or forty kids took off for the fields, and as for me, I went back to my trowel."[44]

In his memoir Lebon included his contract with the town of Raidy, which details his responsibilities as schoolmaster and as assistant to the curé. First, the contract specified that Lebon would assist the curé at all Masses and other services on Sundays and feast days and at vespers every Friday, Saturday, and feast day. Second, he was required to ring the Ave Maria three times a day. Third, he cleaned the church—the contract stated that he should sweep out the church whenever neces-sary, air it out during good weather, and care for the parish's books and ornaments. Fourth, he was asked to teach catechism at the church on Wednesdays during the months school was in session, and on Sun-days during the vacation period. Finally, the last item in the contract specified that Lebon should teach school. On working days class was in session from Toussaint (November 1) until Pentecost (fifty days after

Easter), and Lebon had to teach at no charge any students designated as "indigents" by the town council on Sundays and feast days. The contract also indicated what and how Lebon was to be paid—cash and grain payments from all members of the community, fees from parents of his students, and fees for additional parish services he performed.[45] Lebon also had the use of a house owned by the community, and the stable attached to the home served as a classroom. He noted that he set up benches near the window, that the students brought wood to heat the room in the winter, and that there was enough space for his students and for his cow. The first year that he taught in Raidy he had about forty students of both sexes; fifteen of them were ages twelve to sixteen and the rest were younger than twelve.

Seventeenth- and eighteenth-century schoolmasters probably followed a similar career path as Lebon did in the early nineteenth century—certainly very little about the way villages advertised for and hired schoolmasters changed over this period. In most cases, schoolmasters were chosen by town councils, made up of village notables (including at times *seigneurs,* mayors, magistrates, or influential *laboureurs*) and the curé.[46] The curé usually advertised for a schoolmaster when the position became available, and he likely personally encouraged those whom he considered to be best for the job to apply. As in Lebon's case, candidates for a schoolmaster's job were tested on their basic skills in reading, writing, and singing, and then the council made its choice. The amount of influence that individual council members had over the final choice most likely depended on local politics and personalities. In many parishes the curé's preferred candidate was probably hired, especially if he had been the one to push for hiring a schoolmaster in the first place. The curé usually had more interest in the choice of schoolmaster than anyone else on the council since the two men would have to work together closely in order to fulfill the spiritual and educational needs of the parish. If no candidates applied for the job (a likely scenario in small villages, where the schoolmaster's salary was unlikely to attract much attention) the position usually remained vacant until someone did turn up, or until the curé or an interested village notable searched for and found someone the council would accept.[47] For the actual hiring decision, the council had the last word—whoever paid for the schoolmaster had the legal right to hire and fire, and since in most cases the villagers paid for the schools themselves, they alone had the authority to make the final decision.

Most schoolmasters came from a peasant background and had no other education than what could be obtained in the *petites écoles*. Boys who attended *collèges,* or secondary schools, had open to them more illustrious professions than village *maître d'école*. However, the fact that Lebon's father worked as a simple shepherd is somewhat unusual; schoolmasters usually came from the upper levels of the peasantry — the *laboureurs*. The relatively wealthy peasant schoolmasters often passed on their profession to their sons, in fact, and some may even have found opportunities to increase their social standing.

For example, the position of schoolmaster in Bussy-le-Château (Châlons-sur-Marne) remained in the hands of a peasant family named Gaultier from at least 1674 until the French Revolution. Jacques Gaultier, age twenty-two, is found in the parish records as a godfather in 1674, and his occupation is listed as "recteur des escolles." Jacques was married to Françoise Coullemy, the daughter of one of the town's magistrates. They had three children who lived to adulthood. Their two daughters married "cultivateurs," and their son Charles, born in 1691, succeeded his father as the village schoolmaster. Jacques did well by his son, leaving him a bit of land in his will as well as securing for him the job as schoolmaster. Charles and his wife had only two children who lived past the age of eight: a daughter, who married a *laboureur,* and a son, Jean-Claude, born in 1731, who became schoolmaster at the age of sixteen when his father gave up the job. Seven years later, Jean-Claude married the daughter of a *laboureur* and together they had at least four adult children, including two daughters who married *laboureurs,* a son whose occupation is unknown, and Jean-Denis-François Gaultier, who became schoolmaster after his father.

Judging by the spouses chosen for the daughters of the family, the Gaultiers were on a par with the *laboureurs,* who were usually the most wealthy of the peasantry. Although the Gaultiers who served as schoolmasters were never *laboureurs* themselves, they did acquire other forms of property, including land. The example of the Gaultier family and others from the Champagne region show that the position of schoolmaster could provide a significant amount of stability for a seventeenth-

or eighteenth-century peasant family and that it could be quite lucrative as well.[48]

There is other evidence that provides a conflicting view, however, and shows that many peasant schoolmasters probably lived much more unsettled and mobile lives than the Gaultiers, as they struggled to support themselves and their families. Lebon himself is a good example—he worked in four different towns during his career as a schoolmaster, and the longest period of time that he ever stayed in one place was sixteen years. He does not explain why he moved so often, but it is likely that he was continually looking for a position that paid better. Several curés in the smaller parishes in both Champagne and Burgundy complained that their schoolmasters did not stay long because of their inadequate salaries. In 1774 a curé in Reims wrote in his questionnaire that "the living of the schoolmaster of L'Héry is so modest, that we often lack a schoolmaster, and it is necessary to take them as we find them." In a visit to Châteauneuf (Auxerre) in 1680, the curé told the visitor that their schoolmaster had recently left because the people of the town had not paid him a full salary. The same situation arose in Novy (Reims) in 1689—the people had reduced the pay of their schoolmaster so much that they had been forced to hire a *garçon* of fifteen because he was the only person willing to do the job for such a meager salary.[49] It is difficult to determine just how long schoolmasters remained in one particular village, but most likely a select few stayed in one school for most of their lives and then handed the position over to one of their sons (who had probably been working as an assistant schoolmaster for some time), while most other schoolmasters moved fairly often.

This pattern is borne out in two sets of visitation records that list the length of service for schoolmasters in residence at the time of the visit.[50] In the deanery of Cernay-en-Dormois (Reims) in 1679, the visitor noted that thirty-two parishes employed a schoolmaster (see table 4.1). He gave no information about eight of the schoolmasters, but of the remaining twenty-four, ten had been working in their parishes for two years or less, and seven for between three and five years. Seven others had been working for more than five years. The statistics are similar to those for the deanery of Vesle in 1683: of twenty-three

Table 4.1. Length of Service for Schoolmasters in the Deaneries
of Cernay-en-Dormois and Vesle

	Number of Schoolmasters	
Length of Service	*Cernay-en-Dormois*	*Vesle*
15+ years	2	2
11–15 years	3	0
6–10 years	2	5
3–5 years	7	6
1–2 years	4	4
Less than 1 year	6	6

Source: AD Marne, 2 G 277, 285.

schoolmasters whose length of service is given, ten had worked for
two years or less, six for between three and five years, four for between
six and ten years, and three for ten years or more. In the two deaneries
together, only one parish in seven had a schoolmaster who had worked
there for more than ten years, and nearly half were only in their first or
second year of service. Thus, the majority of men working as schoolmasters did not establish dynasties in their parishes but rather moved
on to new positions every few years.

Lebon's description of the conditions in his early nineteenth-
century school probably applied to the *petites écoles* of the seventeenth and
eighteenth centuries as well. Communities rarely had a fixed school—
schoolmasters usually taught in their homes, whether the village provided it for them or not. Of the 580 communities that had *petites écoles* in
the diocese of Reims in 1774, only forty-three had set aside a building
specifically for use as a school.[51] Five of these buildings had been built
in the church cemetery, and in two other parishes, schoolteachers taught
in the church itself. For the vast majority of schools, however, schoolmasters simply set up shop in their kitchens or stables. Students learning
to read sat on benches and held their books in their laps; benches and a
table were set up for those learning to write. As in Lebon's school, stu-

dents not only had to compete with each other for space but with farm animals and the schoolmaster's wife and children as well.

Like Lebon, schoolmasters in the seventeenth and eighteenth centuries held other jobs in addition to teaching. Lebon tells of six colleagues who worked as schoolmasters during the winter and at other occupations during the summer, including two shoemakers, a carpenter, a weaver, a groom, and a *manouvrier*. Because they possessed more writing skills than most rural peasants, schoolmasters might also work as notaries or *greffiers* (court clerks). Some may have farmed land of their own, like the Gaultiers, and certainly most schoolmasters worked as day laborers during harvest time.

Some schoolmasters worked at other occupations during the months that school was in session as well, leading to complaints from curés and villagers alike.[52] A number of parishioners from Sugny (Reims) told the archbishop in 1716 that their schoolmaster also worked as a *greffier* and that his court duties kept him from teaching regularly. The majority of the people in the parish wanted to keep him as schoolmaster, however, and the archbishop gave him permission to stay. Jean-Pierre Goisot of Saint-Bris (Auxerre) was not so lucky: in 1770 he was fired for exercising the professions of *notaire* and *greffier* in addition to schoolmaster. In Gespunsart (Reims) the curé wrote a letter to the archbishop about the schoolmaster in his parish, who also owned and operated the local tavern—this occupation kept him from teaching and the curé felt it unseemly for a schoolmaster to engage in such a questionable activity.[53] These schoolmasters who plied other trades besides teaching almost certainly did so because the pay they received for running the schools did not cover their living expenses. Communities had to pay their schoolmasters at least 150 livres according to a royal ordinance of 1698, but this law proved impossible to enforce. In reality, schoolmasters' incomes varied from parish to parish and from year to year, depending on the price of grain and the size of the parish.

Schoolmasters' salaries came from at least four sources. First, each household in the village, no matter if it contained school-age children or not, paid a certain amount in grain, wine, or cash. *Laboureurs* contributed the most, *manouvriers* slightly less, and widows about half of whatever the *manouvriers* paid. Then the parents of each student paid monthly fees, ranging from three to twelve sous per child. The parish fabric, or money donated to the church in wills and foundations, usually contributed a small amount to the schoolmaster each year, and he was entitled to the fees known as *casuel*—paid by parishioners—for other services he performed at weddings, funerals, and holiday services. All of this could amount to the required 150 livres in large parishes. For example, in 1774 in Sorbon (Reims), the curé estimated that his schoolmaster received grain worth 180 livres from household contributions, 19 livres for assisting at founded Masses, 10 livres for taking care of the village clock, 24 livres as a housing allowance, 25 livres in *casuel,* and 65 livres in fees. In total, he earned quite a tidy sum: 323 livres a year.[54]

Sorbon's case is hardly typical, however; schoolmasters in smaller parishes who collected fewer fees and had fewer opportunities to earn extra money from Masses and services received significantly smaller salaries. For example, the schoolmaster of Prez (Reims) in 1774 received grain worth about 96 livres from the households in the village. The fabric gave him 6 livres, and each student paid 3 sous in monthly fees. The schoolmaster in Prez had twenty students for five months of the year, and his income from fees amounted to only 15 livres. Even with the *casuel,* the schoolmaster earned no more than 130 livres.[55] It is also possible that not every parent was able to pay their fees in full, and in lean years some households may not have contributed their full share of grain. Thus, the majority of schoolmasters who had their own families to support would have had to find other sources of income throughout the year to make ends meet.

Despite the fact that some villages could not afford to pay their schoolmasters very well, it is extremely significant that the lay community accepted the entire financial responsibility for primary education. Schoolmasters received only a minimal amount of money from the parish fabric, and only a handful of parishes had the right to collect money from the tithes to be used for schools. In 1774 only twelve curés noted in the Reims questionnaire that their schoolmasters received money from tithes, and none of the schoolmasters' contracts for Auxerre suggest that the church provided any income for schoolmasters.[56] Bishops and curés certainly wanted their parishes to have schools, but they were either unwilling or unable to pay for them with church funds.

Since neither the church nor the state allocated any money for primary education, there would have been no system of *petites écoles* in Auxerre, Châlons, or Reims if the laity had not paid their schoolmasters' salaries. Village notables, farmers, and peasants were all ruled by their pocketbooks in the seventeenth and eighteenth centuries, and the fact that they contributed even a few livres a year for schools is remarkable. No outside authority, either secular or religious, forced these communities to pay for schools. Bishops and curés encouraged the establishment of schools, but if the laity had not believed in the importance of primary education, they simply would not have paid for them. Just the existence of the *petites écoles,* therefore, demonstrates that the schoolmaster played an integral role in parish life and that parents wanted their children to have access to a moral and religious education.

Finally, there is one other way in which Lebon was a typical schoolmaster: he was a layman. The religious orders may have taken over the majority of the *collèges* in France,[57] but at the parish level priests who served as schoolmasters were rare exceptions. In the thirty-year period that Jacques Thuret served as *écolâtre* of Reims (1641–1670), he approved 206 schoolteachers and identified only three of them as priests.[58] In the 1774 questionnaire, curés reported that the only clerical schoolteachers consisted of a handful of vicaires who served as schoolmasters, some Latin masters in the larger urban parishes, and a relatively small number of religious men and women who held free schools for the poor. Out of the 740 parishes in the diocese, including the 218 annexes, only nine houses of *petits frères* (the major male religious teaching order in France, founded by Jean-Baptiste de La Salle) provided education in the diocese of Reims, and five of those were located in the city of Reims and its suburbs. Twenty parishes had members of the female religious orders teaching girls: Providenciennes, Soeurs du Saint-Enfant-Jésus, and Ursulines. Secular schoolmasters and schoolmistresses taught in these towns as well, but the overwhelming majority of the *petites écoles* were run by laymen who had wives and families and who had no intention of ever taking holy orders. Schoolmasters may have been responsible for a large part of the religious education that took place at the parish level, but they were not clergymen and had received no training as such.

Nevertheless, the contracts made between a village community and a schoolmaster show that village notables expected their schoolmaster to act as a substitute cleric when necessary. François Robert's contract with the village of Irancy (Auxerre) provides evidence of this. The contract is dated March 20, 1774, but Robert had actually been serving as schoolmaster since 1766. The notables of Irancy renewed his contract in 1774, and in the process of making this renewal, the village council also agreed to change the way that they paid Robert. Instead of requiring each individual family in the parish to contribute a certain amount of grain and/or wine to the schoolmaster directly (a practice that would significantly reduce Robert's earnings if some households either could not or would not pay), the council itself would collect the villagers' contributions and then guarantee the schoolmaster a salary of 150 livres in cash, paid on the first of October every year. The contract states that the villagers made this change because of "the great advantages that the parish has gained from having always had a schoolmaster, and that it is thus very much in the parish's best interests to have one and at the same time to assure him a living." The council emphasized "the utility and necessity of a schoolmaster in the parish as much to instruct and teach the children as to assist at the divine office and accompany the curé in the administration of the sacraments."[59]

The contract included a detailed list of the schoolmaster's duties, which fell into two categories: running the village school and assisting the church. The contract required Robert to

1. Hold classes every day of the week except Sundays, feast days, and one day of vacation.[60]
2. Be present at school every day (absences could only be authorized by the curé).
3. Refrain from taking any other job or practicing any other profession that would distract him or keep him from fulfilling his duties as schoolmaster.
4. Teach the catechism diligently on the days indicated by the curé.
5. Teach reading (of both printed and handwritten scripts), writing, and arithmetic to all the children of the parish, including any poor children chosen by the curé and the town magistrates.

6. Assist the curé in the administration of the sacraments, at parish services, and during processions.
7. Train several young boys to be choir boys and to assist at Mass.

Although many schoolmasters did not have official, written contracts with their parishes, they would have been informed of their duties by the curé and the town council, and those duties would have been similar to those listed for Robert.

Working for the church was not a secondary occupation, like Lebon's work as a mason, but rather an integral part of the profession of schoolmaster. For example, in addition to holding school during the week and teaching catechism for an hour on Sundays, the schoolmaster in Douzy (Reims) received forty-six livres from the fabric to assist at founded Masses, take care of the vessels used during Mass, ring the church bells, and launder the church linens. In the parish of Montcy-Notre-Dame (Reims), the requirements of the schoolmaster were "that he hold school regularly, that he assist at all the masses which are said or sung in the church, that he keep the altar, the choir, and the ornaments clean, sweep or have swept the church, ring the angelus in the evenings, mornings, and at noon, and ring for the evening prayers and the mass on working days." The town council also required the schoolmaster to teach twenty poor children in his school, without charging them the usual monthly fees.[61]

In addition to serving as an assistant to the curé, village notables specified that schoolmasters should teach religion by both word and example. Both Lebon's and Robert's contracts included the provision that catechism was to be taught in school on a regular basis; this duty is specified nearly universally in other contracts. Some contracts provided even more detail about religious teaching in schools and indicated that schoolmasters' behavior should equal that of the most upstanding members of the parish, in order to set an example for their students of how a good Catholic should live. Before any schoolmaster could be given a position, the village council had to be assured that he was *de bonne vie et moeurs*, a phrase repeated often in contracts and in visitors' notes about schoolmasters. Anyone who wanted to exercise the position of schoolmaster outside of his home parish had to bring a certificate proving that his conduct and morals had been acceptable in the past. Village notables might also require schoolmasters to officially profess their adherence to the Catholic faith in front of the village council, especially in areas with high concentrations of Protestants.

The requirement to set a good example was often explicit in schoolmasters' contracts as well. Edme Desfoux was obliged, according to his 1783 contract with the parish of Fontenoy (Auxerre), to teach religion to his students, both through catechism on Wednesdays and Saturdays and "especially to give them a good example." The community of Andryes (Auxerre) expected their schoolmaster, a Monsieur Brechat, to "be a good example to his students and to all the parish in his behavior, virtue, and in frequenting the sacraments." Brechat had to avoid going to taverns and show proper respect for the curé as well, to further serve as a good example for his students. Brechat's contract further indicated that he should teach his students obedience to and deference for parents and other authorities: he was supposed to "express to them at an early age the obedience owed to them."[62] Prayer, catechism, and virtue were integral aspects of education at the parish level, and communities expected their schoolmasters to provide this education along with their lessons in reading, writing, and arithmetic.

For the villagers who negotiated their schoolmasters' contracts, the Catholic religion was not simply a list of duties imposed upon them by curés and bishops but rather a set of moral guidelines and a way of life that they willingly chose to pass on to the children of the parish. They hired schoolmasters, at considerable expense, to help them do this. The fact that villagers paid for these clerical assistants and educators out of their own pockets indicates that they felt the presence of a schoolmaster provided an important source of order and stability for the parish. Although parents and village notables may not have felt schoolmasters had to follow all of the bishops' regulations exactly, they still wanted their children to have a religious education. Primary education should thus be considered as virtually inseparable from religion in the seventeenth and eighteenth centuries because a good education had religion and morality at its center.

Seventeenth- and eighteenth-century schoolmasters played many roles in the parishes in which they lived and worked. For bishops, good Catholic schoolmasters could help bring Catholic reform to the parish level. For curés, schoolmasters were valuable clerical assistants on whom they could rely just as they would members of the clergy. Village notables needed schoolmasters to teach reading, writing, and catechism and to help maintain religious and moral order in the parish. In parishes that were often without a spiritual and liturgical presence, they acted as representatives of the clergy and performed many clerical duties. They were agents of the Catholic Reformation, employed to teach proper Catholic behavior by word and, perhaps most importantly, by example.

For all three groups, the religious education of the next generation of Catholic believers was of paramount importance. Both the laity and the clergy wanted to secure schoolmasters for their parishes, and they worked together to open parish schools, to keep them open, and to regulate schoolmasters' conduct. The employment of schoolmasters "both for the instruction of the youth and for the divine office"[63] illustrates a crucial aspect of the Catholic Reformation: the cooperation of the laity and the clergy to improve Catholic piety and behavior at the parish level. The clergy and the laity rarely found themselves at odds with each other over education in rural communities—people from all levels of society realized the value of children's education as well as the importance of the religious services schoolmasters could provide. More often than not, in matters of primary and religious education the goals of bishops, curés, and rural village notables intersected. Thus, the schools and the type of education they provided reflect the combined vision of both laity and clergy and reveal the inner workings of the early modern Catholic reform movement, centered around the religious education of each new generation of Catholic believers.

CHAPTER FIVE

Boys and Girls at School
The Growth of the Petites Écoles

As part of his effort to combat Protestantism after the revocation of the Edict of Nantes, Louis XIV issued an edict requiring every parish in the kingdom to establish primary schools where all French boys and girls could learn to read, write, and recite their catechism:

> We ordain that as soon as possible masters and
> mistresses shall be appointed in all parishes where at
> present there are none, to instruct all the children,
> especially those whose parents have made profession
> of the so-called reformed religion, in catechism and
> prayers, and to take them to the Mass on working days,
> and give them any necessary instruction on the subject,

and to ensure that, during the time that children are in school, they also attend parish services on Sundays and feast days; in addition they will teach reading and even writing to those who need to learn.[1]

The 1698 edict specified further that each community should raise funds (between 100 and 150 livres) to hire both a schoolmaster to teach the boys of the parish and a schoolmistress to teach the girls. The king and the administrators of the French state in the seventeenth century believed in the utility of primary education for peasant children, and they expected local communities to pay for it.

Although Louis XIV certainly had the authority to ask his subjects to open schools, the early modern French state did not have the ability to enforce the edict. The king did not create an administrative system to ensure that villages hired schoolteachers, so village notables could choose to either comply with or ignore the king's request. As might be expected, adherence to the edict was less than perfect. In fact, Louis XV's government felt compelled to issue the same edict again, in 1724.[2] Despite the fact that the royal government believed in primary education in the early modern period, it was not until the nineteenth century that the state began to exert a significant amount of authority over the schools and the teachers themselves.

As a result, most historians of literacy and primary schooling in France focus on the nineteenth century, when the state began the process of taking control of education from the church. Other themes in this literature include the relationship between the growth of schooling and nineteenth-century nationalism, the numerous political debates over the purpose of and control over primary education, and the effects of the compartmentalization of elite and popular schooling.[3] These historians thus emphasize the importance of schools administered by either the state or state bureaucratic institutions, overlooking the fact that local communities often followed the king's edict and, on their own initiative, established primary schools in the seventeenth and eighteenth centuries—without the aid of the state.

For example, Sarah Curtis's work on nineteenth-century primary education demonstrates that church-run schools were present in one-third of the parishes in the suburbs of Lyon in the eighteenth century, as well as in a good number of other parishes throughout the diocese. During the Revolution, Curtis argues, these schools disappeared, leaving children with few opportunities to learn to read and write. Curtis and others conclude that the *petites écoles*—primary schools run by lay schoolmasters and schoolmistresses—were so few and so poor that they could never match the contributions of either the church or the state to primary education in the nineteenth century. Yet Lyon had one of the most centralized systems of *petites écoles* in seventeenth- and eighteenth-century France.[4] Curtis rightly rehabilitates the image of the religious orders' schools in the nineteenth century, but in doing so she neglects their ties to the *petites écoles* of the two previous centuries— ties that were only stretched during the Revolution, not broken. The availability of primary schooling did rise dramatically in the nineteenth century, but the roots of France's primary educational system are to be found in the seventeenth and eighteenth centuries.[5]

This chapter examines the growth of the *petites écoles* in the dioceses of Auxerre, Reims, and Châlons-sur-Marne. It first demonstrates that by the end of the eighteenth century, at least nine out of ten parishes in all three dioceses had schools that offered children a basic education in reading, writing, and catechism. In addition, the influence of the *petites écoles* was not limited to urban areas—in fact, schools run by the religious orders dominated urban primary education, while children in rural areas were firmly in the hands of lay schoolmasters and schoolmistresses who taught in independent, village-supported primary schools. The *petites écoles* may not have had official buildings or well-trained teachers, but they still played an important role in society by providing a religious and moral education for children in the rural parishes of the three dioceses.

Furthermore, the *petites écoles* were coeducational, despite regulations issued by both church and state against the mixing of the sexes in schools. Most historians of early modern primary education assume that regulations regarding the separation of boys and girls were generally followed and, as a result, girls had even fewer opportunities to learn to read and write than boys did.[6] According to this view, the only schools available for either urban or rural girls were those run by the religious orders—convent schools for the daughters of the wealthy, and schools for poor girls administered by teaching congregations like the Filles de Notre Dame or the Soeurs du Saint-Enfant-Jésus.[7] These schools were usually located in larger towns and villages, leaving most peasant girls with few options for formal schooling. Thus, historians have argued that if parents in early modern France spent any of their hard-earned livres on schooling, they made sure their sons learned to read and write rather than their daughters.

In reality, a close examination of visitation records and bishops' questionnaires from Reims, Châlons-sur-Marne, and Auxerre demonstrates that outside of France's larger towns, communities failed to follow the king's edict and the bishops' ordinances about the separation of boys and girls in the *petites écoles*. During the seventeenth and eighteenth centuries fewer than 25 percent of the communities in any of the dioceses established a separate school for girls. Elite ideas about the necessity of sex-segregated primary schools, as manifested in the king's edict and in the writings of both lay and religious authors, simply did not apply to peasant girls. If rural parishes opened and administered a school, they usually opened just one, and boys and girls attended together. Even if girls had to attend school with their brothers, they did have the opportunity to obtain a basic primary education. Sitting side by side on the benches of the *petites écoles,* boys and girls together received the core elements of an early modern education: reading, catechism, and the practices of the Catholic faith.

The Petites Écoles *of Champagne*

Because the teachers and administrators of the *petites écoles* left very few records of their activities, the number of schools in existence can be rather difficult to establish.[8] Schoolteachers were hardly professionalized—in many cases a "school" can only be defined as a group of villagers who decided to provide a lay man or woman, who only then became known as a "schoolmaster" or "schoolmistress," with a bit of grain and/or wine in exchange for teaching. These sorts of schools rarely leave traces in the archives. The only authority figures in rural French society who attempted to keep track of schoolteachers—other

than the village notables themselves—were churchmen, primarily bishops and curés; it is in their records, then, that we find the most information about primary education in the villages. Yet even church records are incomplete, especially those from the seventeenth century. In
some cases the evidence is only anecdotal and far from comprehensive,
but one major trend does stand out: more villages had *petites écoles* in
the eighteenth century than in the seventeenth. More and more official
schoolmasters and even some schoolmistresses appear in the records
that we do have, and by the end of the eighteenth century the presence of a paid, lay schoolmaster was commonplace in most villages of
Champagne.

Communities in Reims and Châlons began establishing *petites écoles*
early in the seventeenth century. Between 1611 and 1673 the *écolâtres* of
Reims approved 438 schoolmasters and 15 schoolmistresses. Furthermore, since a large number of teachers never formalized their appointments with the *écolâtre,* we can assume that there were easily over
1,000 people employed as schoolteachers during the first two-thirds of
the seventeenth century.[9] Information about the diocese of Châlons
in the seventeenth century also demonstrates that primary education
was available in a significant number of communities there: 54 out
of 110 parishes (49 percent) visited between 1626 and 1629 had *petites
écoles.*[10] While the exact percentage of parishes with educational institutions is impossible to determine using the available evidence for this
period, it is clear that the *petites écoles* were already widespread in both
Reims and Châlons several decades before Louis XIV made his 1698
proclamation.

Visitation records from the end of the seventeenth century provide a much more complete picture of the state of primary education
in both dioceses. When the rural deans of Reims visited the parishes
under their jurisdiction, they were required to gather information on
schools. Between 1676 and 1716, 420 out of 490 communities visited
(86 percent) had at least one primary school.[11] Furthermore, 52 of the
communities without schools were annexes attached to parishes that
did have schools. Since it was common for children who lived in the
annex to attend school in the parish (or vice versa), it can be inferred
that a phenomenal 96 percent of the children in the diocese had access

Table 5.1. Number of Parishes in Châlons-sur-Marne and Reims with Schools, Seventeenth and Eighteenth Centuries

Diocese	Date of Visitation or Inquiry	Total Number of Parishes Visited	Number of Schools	%
Châlons-sur-Marne	1626–1629	110	54	49.0
	1697–1698	216	191	88.0
	1728–1732	242	223	92.0
	1748–1752	293	274	93.5
Reims	1672–1716	490	420	86.0
	1774	694	663	95.5

Source: AD Marne, G 105–27; 2 G 253–87.

to a basic education in reading, writing, and catechism by the year 1700. Similarly, 191 out of 216 communities (88 percent) in Châlons visited in 1697–1698 had a *petite école*.[12] In addition, 2 of these parishes had annexes that had their own schoolmasters, and 10 of the annexes were attached to parishes with a school. Thus, 94 percent of the children had relatively easy access to a school by 1698—a much greater number than in the 1620s, and similar to the percentage for the diocese of Reims. These percentages remained fairly constant in the next five decades (see table 5.1). By the year 1750, any children in the Champagne region who were willing to walk one or two miles (at most) to school, and whose parents could afford to spare them from full-time work as well as provide a few sous a month in fees, could attend a *petite école*.

Unfortunately, there are no surviving visitation records for the diocese of Châlons-sur-Marne after the mid-eighteenth century, but the 1774 questionnaire for Reims provides a tremendous amount of information about primary education in the last few decades of the *ancien régime*. Because parish curés rather than the bishop's secretaries (who were usually in a hurry and probably rather tired of paperwork) filled out the questionnaires, they are much more detailed than visitation records and the information given is usually more complete. In addition, over seven hundred questionnaires have survived—nearly every community in this vast diocese is represented in this set of records. The information in these questionnaires reveals that the system of *petites écoles* was as strong as ever on the eve of the Revolution.

The 1774 questionnaires demonstrate that the city of Reims itself contained several primary schools for the children of the lower classes. In the nineteen parishes of the deanery of La Chrétienté—the urban parishes of Reims and its immediate suburbs—there were at least five separate houses of *petits frères* (the major male teaching order in France, founded by Jean-Baptiste de La Salle) for the boys, and children from all over the city received instruction there. At least five female teaching orders administered schools in Reims as well.[13] Four parishes had lay schoolmasters, supported financially by heads of households and student fees. Although only one of the questionnaires mentions any unofficial teachers (in Saint-Martin two widows taught the youngest children of both sexes in their homes), there were almost certainly a large number of widows, itinerant schoolmasters, Latin masters, and writing masters who ran their own small schools in the city. Unfortunately, since they were not official teachers, there is no way to establish their numbers, or the numbers of students in their schools.

Schoolmasters were also well established in the parishes and annexes outside of the city of Reims. Out of the 694 communities for which information about schools exists, 663 had schoolmasters—that is, over 95 percent of the communities in Reims had at least one primary school of their own (see table 5.1). Twenty-seven of the communities without schools were annexes that had access to the school in the parish, and only 5 of them had more than one hundred communicants (13 had fewer than fifty). Only 4 regular parishes had no schoolmaster of their own, and they were among the smallest parishes in the diocese: Corbon (fifteen communicants), Melzicourt (eighty communicants), Montmarin (two households), and Moronvilliers (forty communicants). Each of these parishes had an annex with a much larger population and a school. The presence of a schoolmaster in each parish of the diocese was thus practically universal in 1774: every community with a total population of at least 150 somehow found the means to maintain a *petite école*.

For the dioceses of Reims and Châlons-sur-Marne, therefore, the *petites écoles* were already flourishing when Louis XIV issued his 1698 proclamation, and their numbers continued to grow throughout the eighteenth century. Perhaps the king and his advisors thought of the Champagne-Ardennes region as proof that it was indeed possible for every parish to have a school.[14] Other parts of the kingdom had not been quite so compliant, however: in the diocese of Auxerre, where official schools had been established in only about one-third of its parishes by 1699, village notables, curés, and parents obviously had some work to do before their children had as many opportunities to attend school as their northern neighbors.

The Petites Écoles of Auxerre

After Louis XIV's 1698 edict, the Intendant of Orléans sent a message to the bishop of Auxerre asking him to investigate the state of the schools in his diocese. The following year, Bishop André Colbert sent out a brief questionnaire to all of his curés to find out exactly how many teachers were working in the diocese. Each curé was supposed to note if his village had a schoolmaster or mistress and if there was a specific fund from which they were paid. If no teacher existed, the curé was to estimate how much money the community would need to hire one, and then determine whether there were any funds in the parish that could be used for this purpose. Seventy-two questionnaires, filled out in varying detail by parish priests, have survived.[15] While this means that only slightly more than one-third of the parishes in the diocese are represented, these questionnaires give a snapshot of the state of education in the Auxerre region in 1699.

Of the seventy-two parishes, only thirty-two had schoolmasters. Of those thirty-two, four parishes had women from various religious teaching orders available to teach the girls, and four others had secular schoolmistresses.[16] In two parishes, Appoigny and Coulanges-la-Vineuse, the schoolmaster's wife taught the girls of the parish. Thus, at most 44 percent of the parishes had *petites écoles* for the boys of the parish, 14 percent had sex-segregated schools, and 56 percent had no official schoolteachers at all. For these forty parishes without teachers, the curés noted that they would need between 100 and 150 livres to provide a living for a schoolmaster and about half that for a schoolmistress.

Only a handful of curés gave any indication that sufficient funds could be raised to pay for schoolteachers. Several parishes reported that they would like to have a schoolmaster for the good of the parish but that a schoolmistress was not necessary—presumably because it was routine for schoolmasters to teach boys and girls, despite being forbidden to do so by the bishop. For example, the curé of Ouzouer mentioned that his parish had employed a schoolmaster since 1678 who had been teaching boys and girls "against your ordinances." Others said that they did not need a schoolmaster because the number of children in the parish was too small, or because the people of the parish felt that the curé himself was a suitable schoolmaster. The curé of Ronchères expressed this idea in a note attached to the questionnaire that he returned to Bishop Colbert: "There is no need for a schoolmaster in my parish; when any of the inhabitants want their children to learn to read and write, I teach them." Drastic changes were needed if the parishes of Auxerre were to obey the king and employ a schoolmaster as well as a schoolmistress in every parish in the diocese.

The results of Bishop Colbert's 1699 questionnaire on the state of education in Auxerre are somewhat misleading, however, since there are so few surviving responses. Fortunately, other sources provide additional information about the number of schools in the diocese and demonstrate that although some schoolmasters did provide primary education in seventeenth-century Auxerre, they were much less widespread than in Champagne, and rural parents were more likely to send their children to their curé for instruction than pay for a schoolmaster. For example, Bishop Colbert periodically asked for reports about the state of affairs in the parishes, and curés used this opportunity to report whether or not they taught children themselves or if the parish had a schoolmaster. Financial and notarial records can also indicate the existence of schoolteachers in a parish. Using these records,[17] we find that only 77 of the 202 parishes had their own schoolmasters at some time between 1670 and 1700, meaning just 38 percent of the villages in the diocese had established *petites écoles* by the time of the 1698 proclamation.[18]

Despite the fact that the number of official schools was much lower than that in either Reims or Châlons for the same time period, other opportunities for education did exist in the diocese of Auxerre.

Table 5.2. Number of Parishes in Auxerre with Schools, Eighteenth Century

Date	Number of Parishes Visited	Type of Parish	Number of Schools	%
ca. 1700	202	With a school	77	38.0
	202	With access to a school	116	57.0
ca. 1740	202	With a school	109	54.0
	202	With access to a school	148	73.0
ca. 1789	128	Parishes with a school	114	89.0

Source: AD Yonne, G 1649, 1651–68; Quantin, "Histoire de l'instruction primaire."

Because Bishop Colbert did not ask his curés to use a standardized, printed form for their reports, they were not limited by space in their responses and often gave quite extensive answers to the bishop's questions. The curés in twenty-eight of the parishes without schoolmasters responded that they themselves (or their vicaires) ran their own schools. The curé of Accolay was one of these, and he also reported that an unofficial schoolmistress taught some children in his parish as well: "There is no schoolmaster due to the poverty of the village but I have never failed to instruct the children that are sent to me. There is a good widow who teaches some children to read, and Christian doctrine is taught often."[19] In addition to unofficial teachers, a schoolmistress provided all of the education in two parishes—for the boys as well as the girls. Fourteen other curés noted that the village had no school of its own but that the children went to a schoolmaster in a neighboring parish on a regular basis. Thus, the availability of primary education was actually much greater than the number of *petites écoles* suggests; it is likely that the children in at least 116 parishes (57 percent) had access to some kind of teacher, either official or unofficial, clerical or secular (see table 5.2).

Furthermore, the number of *petites écoles* in the diocese increased dramatically early in the eighteenth century. Inhabitants of parishes who claimed they had no need for schools at the end of the seventeenth century hired schoolmasters just a few decades later. The curé of Escolives lamented in 1679 that he would be willing to teach any children of the parish who wanted to learn to read or write but that parents would not send their children because they had too much work to do, and the curé who filled out a questionnaire in 1699 declared that "the people say that they have no need for a schoolmaster." A few years later, however, the situation had changed completely: the community of Escolives employed a schoolmaster every year between 1740 and 1789. The curé of Leugny stated in 1699 that the people of his parish felt they had no need for either a schoolmaster or a schoolmistress, but by 1712 they had both and continued to employ schoolteachers throughout the eighteenth century. In Saint-Sauveur in 1699, the curé reported that a schoolmaster was needed but "a schoolmistress is not necessary in this parish, because there are so few people who want their daughters to learn to read and write." By 1720, the parish had hired a schoolmaster, and by 1762 they had brought in two members of one of the female teaching congregations to instruct the girls.[20]

When Bishop Charles de Caylus conducted a series of visits throughout the diocese in the first few decades of the eighteenth century, he found that parishes that had established schools by 1699 generally kept them, while other parishes had hired schoolmasters in the interim.[21] Of the 80 parishes that had no schools in 1699, 22 had their own schoolteachers by the mid-1730s, and 10 more had a *petite école* by the mid-1740s. Nine of the parishes in which the curé had been teaching the children himself had established schools run by lay schoolmasters at this time as well. Although there are fewer visitation records for the diocese after 1740, those that do exist, combined with information from notarial records, show that the number of *petites écoles* continued to increase in the second half of the eighteenth century.[22] By 1789, of the 128 parishes for which there is information about schools (excluding the city of Auxerre itself), 114 (89 percent) had schoolmasters. The ratio of schools-to-parishes for Auxerre was still not quite as high as in Reims or Châlons, but the number of schools had more than doubled by the end of the eighteenth century. Overall, the system of *petites écoles* spread extensively in the seventeenth and eighteenth centuries in all three dioceses, so that in 1789 the vast majority of children from all social levels—girls as well as boys—had access to primary education.

Education for Girls in Reims, Châlons-sur-Marne, and Auxerre

As discussed above, one of the most important aspects of the reforming bishops' program of religious education was their staunch belief that boys and girls should be educated separately. Since the core curriculum for girls and boys was largely the same—both sexes learned the same catechism and learned to read from the same religious books—the bishops' main reasoning for this separation was their fear that letting girls and boys mingle together too much would lead to immorality. Thus, in their ordinances and regulations they insisted that communities find funds for a schoolmaster to teach the boys and a schoolmistress for the girls, and in their pastoral letters they encouraged separating boys and girls in both schools and catechism classes and made inquiries as to how well curés and village authorities followed regulations during pastoral visits.

At the same time, both religious and lay educational theorists argued that boys and girls ought to be educated separately so that they could concentrate on the skills that would be most useful to them later in life. Fénelon, the future archbishop of Cambrai and tutor to Louis XIV's grandchildren, insisted in his 1687 treatise on girls' education that girls should be educated for their roles as wives, mothers, and household managers but there was no need to instruct them beyond their innate capacity. He recommended that girls be taught reading, writing, and the four rules of arithmetic (so they would be able to keep household accounts), as well as how to deal with servants, negotiate legal contracts, and educate their children in religion and morals.[23]

Other religious and lay writers on education made similar arguments. Madame de Maintenon, the mistress and later wife of Louis XIV, founded and maintained an academy for daughters of the poor nobility. Her school at Saint-Cyr taught reading, religion, and morals as well as handwork, comportment, domestic and household tasks, and other maternal and marital duties. The overarching goal of the institution was to teach the *demoiselles* the requirements of their two primary positions in society—as women and as members of the French nobility.[24] Cardinal Fleury, who succeeded Fénelon as royal tutor and maintained a significant influence over his pupil Louis XV throughout his life, argued that girls could bypass subjects like Latin, history, mathematics, poetry, and other "curiosities" in favor of lessons on remedies for common ailments and how to properly compose a letter or a memoir.[25]

The Enlightenment did little to change ideas about elite female pedagogy; in fact, the belief that boys and girls should be educated separately, with an eye toward their vastly different roles in society, gained strength throughout the eighteenth century. Locke's *Some Thoughts Concerning Education* had a great deal of influence in France, and his emphasis on providing a moral and civic education for children provided ammunition for those opposed to convent schools. Enlightenment thinkers argued that since cloistered nuns knew little about raising a family or running a household, they were ill-suited to teach daughters of the nobility, who would spend their lives in the home rather than the convent.[26] Rousseau also distrusted schools run by the religious orders, and while his method of education for his fictional pupil Émile was seen as somewhat extreme, his plan for the education of Sophie, Émile's future wife, found a significant number of followers.[27] Throughout book 5 of *Émile,* Rousseau emphasized that because the nature and constitution of men and women were so different, their education should also be different. Like Fénelon, Rousseau argued that girls had to be prepared for their lives as wives and mothers from a young age but could forgo subjects that were suitable only for men's natures: "To cultivate man's qualities in women and to neglect those which are proper to them is obviously to work to their detriment."[28]

Debates on education during the revolutionary period echoed Rousseau's insistence on a domestic education for girls. Educational theorists of the late eighteenth century believed that the primary purpose of all education was to serve the larger needs of society and the state, and since women's role in the state was to provide an environment in which loyal and productive citizens could thrive, they should be educated specifically for that role. Girls were to be taught to read, write, and count, but a significant part of their education was to be dedicated to handwork, household tasks, and, most importantly, religious and ethical morality.[29] Rousseau also believed in the necessity of an education in both religion and morality for all girls, as he makes clear when he describes Émile's future wife: "Sophie is religious, but her religion is reasonable and simple, with little dogma and less in the way of devout practices—or rather, she knows no essential practice other than morality, and she devotes her entire life to serving God by doing good."[30]

These educational theorists' emphasis on separate and gender-specific education for both boys and girls had a good deal of influence in the seventeenth and eighteenth centuries, but that influence was primarily limited to the daughters of the nobility and the urban bourgeoisie. Fénelon, Fleury, and Madame de Maintenon wrote to and for parents at the highest levels of French society—their lengthy discussions of governesses, responsibilities toward servants, and the dangers of spoiling daughters with novels and expensive dresses would have been completely useless to all but the wealthiest parents. As Harvey Chisick has pointed out, Enlightenment thinkers rarely advocated a comprehensive system of education for peasant children. They argued for reform in the *collège* and university systems but generally left the *petites écoles* alone.[31] Schools for peasants were limited to teaching reading, religion, and a little bit of writing, and the only further education that Enlightenment thinkers encouraged was technical training in farming and the mechanical arts. Thus, ideas about the education of the vast majority of girls in the early modern period were completely untouched by the debates of *philosophes* and educational theorists, who were far removed from the realities of rural life.

Parents and village notables, rather than elite educational theorists, bishops, or even the king, had the most direct influence over girls' education in the seventeenth and eighteenth centuries. Local authorities—those who decided what the boys and girls in their communities would learn and how they would learn it—paid little attention to the pedagogical debates over feminine education. Furthermore, they were free to disregard much of what the king and the bishops dictated about separating boys and girls in schools. When Louis XIV issued his 1698 edict requiring parishes to establish *petites écoles,* he indicated that girls should have their own schools, with their own schoolmistresses. The costs involved in supporting both a schoolmaster and a schoolmistress generally proved prohibitive, however, and parishes had to find other ways to make sure that their daughters received an education.

Judging solely by the number of girls' schools in Reims, Châlons, and Auxerre in the seventeenth and eighteenth centuries, the availability of primary education for girls appears to have been limited to the more

Table 5.3. Number of Parishes with Sex-Segregated Schools, Eighteenth Century

Diocese	Date of Visitation or Inquiry	Number of Parishes Visited	Number of Schools	%
Châlons-sur-Marne	1697–1698	216	7	3.0
	1728–1732	242	10	4.0
	1748–1752	293	33	11.0
Reims	1672–1716	490	11	2.0
	1774	694	38	5.5
Auxerre	ca. 1700	202	16	8.0
	ca. 1789	128	32	25.0

Source: AD Marne, G 105–27 and 2 G 253–87; AD Yonne, G 1649, 1651–68; Quantin, "Histoire de l'instruction primaire."

heavily populated towns and cities. Only thirty-eight (5.5 percent) of the Reims curés who filled out the 1774 questionnaire mention the presence of a girls' school in their parishes (not including the parishes of Reims itself), either those run by the religious orders or by secular mistresses. By 1750, thirty-three parishes (11 percent) in Châlons had sex-segregated education, and by 1789, 25 percent of Auxerre's parishes had girls' schools (see table 5.3). These schools were most often located in the largest towns and cities. Reims itself had five houses of female teaching orders and several official and unofficial secular mistresses. There were schools for girls in all but one of the other large towns (with more than one thousand communicants) in the diocese as well. Châlons had six houses of *religieuses* entrusted with education, including four schools run by the Ursulines. Auxerre had three girls' schools, run by the Ursulines, the Providenciennes, and the Religieuses de la Visitation. Like Reims, Châlons and Auxerre also employed a varying number of secular schoolmistresses in addition to the religious orders.[32]

Historians have frequently emphasized the role played by the religious teaching congregations in augmenting the schooling available for girls in the seventeenth and eighteenth centuries. Elizabeth Rapley and others have described the congregations as a lay manifestation of both Catholic Reformation piety and an increasing interest in girls' education and emphasized that the Ursulines and other teaching orders took it upon themselves to improve educational opportunities for girls long before Fénelon wrote his famous treatise.[33] The larger towns and cities in the dioceses of Reims, Châlons, and Auxerre made use of the religious orders when they opened a school for girls, and they usually became a significant social and religious asset to the parish. Their schools were often of better quality than the free boys' schools, at least in the judgment of several curés. The curé of Saint-Denis, one of the nineteen parishes in the city of Reims, for instance, complained that students who attended the schools run by the *petits frères* in the city remained ignorant, while the curé of Saint-André of Reims noted that his parishioners held the well-attended schools of the Soeurs du Saint-Enfant-Jésus in high regard.[34] Despite the success and overall importance of these girls' schools in the larger cities and towns, however, they could not reach even a significant minority of school-age girls in rural areas, where schools run by the female religious orders simply did not exist. As noted above, at least 75 percent of the parishes in Auxerre, and 90 percent of the parishes in Reims and Châlons, did not establish sex-segregated schools.

This by no means indicates that girls in rural parishes did not have access to education, however; rather, communities identified other teachers when the female religious orders were unavailable. Unlike schoolmasters, the majority of *official* schoolmistresses may have been members of religious orders, but *unofficial* lay schoolmistresses were likely much more prevalent than the Ursulines or the Providenciennes.[35] Like most female labor in the early modern period, schoolmistresses' work, if not unnoticed, was usually unrecorded.[36] I have found no surviving contracts for schoolmistresses, although there are records of foundations made to benefit women who would teach the young girls of the parish. For example, Jeanne Darc, the wife of the *seigneur* of Foissy (Auxerre), left one hundred livres of rent for a schoolmistress. Her heirs were required to choose "a girl who reads and writes well, who is at least forty years old, and who is sensible and pious; she will be obliged to hold school every morning and every afternoon for all the girls of the parish of Foissy, and to teach catechism on Sundays and feast days."[37] Similar records are hard to find, however; schoolmistresses were simply less permanent than schoolmasters. For example, a young unmarried girl might teach for a few years, until she got married or until the parish could no longer afford to pay her. Widows held small classes in their homes for girls whose parents wanted their daughters to learn their prayers, the catechism, a bit of reading, and some sewing skills, but they had no official contracts, and they were paid only by the parents of their students.

Statistical evidence for these kinds of educators is nearly impossible to obtain, but church records do provide a significant amount of anecdotal evidence, suggesting that a variety of teachers for girls did exist. In Bourgogne (Reims) in 1697, the curé's sister taught the girls in the parish for free—most likely her brother supported her financially and he enlisted her as an unofficial schoolmistress for the parish. In 1767 in the town of La Charité (Auxerre), a widow named Marie Germain taught girls to read and recite the catechism, for "a very small fee." Another widow, Jeanne Marie Tallard of Clamecy (Auxerre), wrote a petition to the bishop in 1702 for permission to teach girls in order to support her own young daughters, ages seven and twelve. She promised to lead her students in devotional activities and teach reading, writing, and even arithmetic; once the bishop was assured that she was of "good life and morals," he gave his approbation.[38]

The most common unofficial schoolmistresses were not widows or relatives of the curé, however; perhaps unsurprisingly, communities often expected schoolmasters' wives to teach the girls of the parish if no separate school could be established for them. Just like the baker's wife who took care of the shop while her husband baked, the schoolmaster's wife shared teaching responsibilities so that more students could be accommodated and the couple could collect more fees. The curé of Olizy (Reims) reported that in his parish "there is no schoolmistress other than the wife of the schoolmaster." Students of both sexes were taught in the same school, but in different rooms. In Voncq (Reims) the *petite école* had a total of 180 students in the wintertime, and the schoolmaster employed both a *sous-maître* and his wife, who taught the girls. In Auxerre twelve parishes had schoolmasters' wives acting as unofficial schoolmistresses at some point between 1679 and 1789, and in Ouanne (Auxerre) in 1708, the schoolmaster enlisted the help of his daughter, who taught the girls in a room separate from that of the main school.[39]

It is impossible to know just how many women taught girls in their communities, either in official or unofficial settings. Yet women were not the only ones who taught girls. Despite prohibitions from bishops and other clergymen against teaching boys and girls together, visitation records from all three dioceses make it clear that schoolmasters taught both sexes on a regular basis. Over and over again, visitors and curés reported that girls were taught alongside their brothers in the *petites écoles*.[40] If rural parishes opened and administered a school, they usually opened just one, and boys and girls attended together—or as one curé put it, "boys and girls are all mixed together in the school."[41]

Even in parishes with sex-segregated schools, schoolmasters might still accept girls as students. In 1774 the parish of Buzancy (Reims) had a schoolmistress with a foundation of forty *écus* and free lodging with the *dame* of the parish, but she and the schoolmaster each taught both boys and girls despite the efforts of the curé to separate them. The dean of Épernay reported in 1672 that since the schoolmistress of Auvilliers (Reims) was unable to write, some parents sent their daughters to the parish schoolmaster instead. Similarly, the curé of Renwez complained in his questionnaire that some parents sent their daughters to the schoolmaster because they disagreed with the religious mistresses' methods and because the boys' school was better heated.[42]

Parents, schoolmasters, and village notables evidently had few difficulties with boys and girls being taught in the same schools by male teachers, primarily due to financial considerations. They may have shared in principle the clergy's belief that coeducational schools would negatively affect the morals of the youth, but in practice they recognized that educating boys and girls together was preferable to not educating them at all. Most rural parishes simply could not afford to have both a schoolmaster and a schoolmistress, especially since separate lodgings had to be found for both. Unless a wealthy patron made a foundation for a girls' school—which happened rarely—only the largest and wealthiest parishes established sex-segregated schools. Even in cases in which foundations for girls' schools did exist, the funds were often too meager to support a schoolmistress. In Pouilly (Reims) in 1774, one hundred livres was available for a schoolmistress, but since the curé had not found anyone willing (or able) to live on this amount, the schoolmaster taught both boys and girls and added the schoolmistress' funds to his own paltry salary.[43]

Furthermore, many schoolmasters would have been out of a job if they had not been able to accept girls as students. Even if they were not able to draw from foundations that rightfully belonged to schoolmistresses, they needed the extra fees that the girls' parents provided. In a visit to the parish of Pouilly (Auxerre) in 1688, villagers told Bishop André Colbert that schoolmaster René Bouchet taught boys and girls in the same school. When the bishop confronted the curé about this, he tried to justify the situation by pointing out that the schoolmaster's wife taught the girls separately. This answer apparently did not satisfy Colbert, and he asked the curé why he had not corrected Bouchet. The curé finally replied that the schoolmaster and his family had no choice but to accept girls into the school—they would have been unable to maintain themselves financially without the extra income. Bishop Colbert issued an ordinance at the end of his visit, stating that the schoolmaster should under no circumstances accept girls into his school. The records do not indicate if Bouchet actually followed the bishop's order, but nearly a century later when Bishop Champion de Cicé visited the parish in 1782, boys and girls still attended school together in the *petite école* run by Jean Baptiste Raquiat and his wife. The bishop made no comment about this in the ordinances that he issued after the latter visit.[44] It appears, then, that separation of girls and boys in schools was another aspect of their program of religious education on which bishops were forced to compromise.

School Attendance

In theory, the system of *petites écoles* in seventeenth- and eighteenth-century Auxerre, Reims, and Châlons-sur-Marne provided both boys and girls with a basic primary education. There is perhaps more to this story, however; just because any child could attend school does not mean that every child did. On the one hand, we know that schools were not empty. As demonstrated in the previous chapter, villages financed the *petites écoles,* and if people did not feel these schools were necessary they would not have dedicated their scant surplus resources to them, royal proclamations and clerical sermons notwithstanding. Therefore, just the existence of the schools indicates that enough students attended to justify the expense and to keep schoolmasters employed. The seventeenth- and eighteenth-century state did not support local schools, so they could not remain open if schoolmasters could not fill their benches—or at least the majority of them. On the other hand, curés and bishops often complained that parents failed to provide their children with the education they needed. Many parents needed their children's labor either inside or outside of the household in order to keep their families afloat, and they simply could not afford to send them to school. So how many children actually did take advantage of the *petites écoles?* How many children learned to read, write, and recite their catechism from the village schoolmaster?

The exact number of children educated in the *petites écoles* is impossible to calculate, but because some curés reported on the number of children in their schools in the Reims questionnaire, a rough estimate of the level of attendance can be determined. In addition, supplemental questionnaires exist for several of the Reims deaneries that provide not only the number of communicants in the parish but also the number of "souls"—the number of communicants plus the number of children who had not yet taken their first communion. Table 5.4 shows the number of children in each parish for the deanery of Bétheniville in 1773, the number of students in each school, and the percentage of children who were attending school that year. For the deanery as a whole, over 53 percent of the children were attending school in 1773–1774. Supplemental questionnaires reporting the number of souls in the parish as well as the number of communicants exist for three other Reims deaneries: Cernay-en-Dormois, Dun, and Varennes. The percentages of children attending school there are similar (see table 5.5).

The numbers reported in the supplemental questionnaires can be somewhat misleading, however, and should only be viewed as rough approximations. Curés, who usually reported the exact number of communicants in their parishes quite conscientiously, most likely estimated the number of souls, so we cannot know the exact number of children. In addition, the number of school-age children was certainly lower

Table 5.4. School Attendance in the Deanery of Bétheniville, 1773–1774

Parish	Souls	Communicants	Children	Students	%
Bétheniville	400	260	140	40	29
Contreuve	300	223	77	40	52
Dontrien[a]	200	170	30	30	100
Junchery-sur-Suippe	400	260	140	50–60	36–43
L'Elfinville	250	170	80	40	50
Liry	500	326	174	30–35	17–20
Machault[b]	500	330	170	100	59
Pauvre	200	130	70	30	43
Dricourt (annex)	150	108	42	10	24
Saint-Clément	130	80	50	40–50	80–100
Auviné (annex)	500	300	200	60–80	30–40
Sainte-Marie-à-Py	500	378	122	100	82
Saint-Étienne-à-Arnes	600	450	150	100	67
Saint-Hilaire-le-Grand	600	460	140	80–110	57–78
Saint-Hilaire-le-Petit	600	400	200	40	20
Saint-Pierre-à-Arnes	150	100	50	15	30
Saint-Souplet	430	300	130	70	54
Semide	500	337	163	80	49
Sommepy	1,200	750	450	160–200	36–44
Somme-Suippe	600	400	200	100	50
Suippes	2,000	1,500	500	400–420	80–84
Ville-sur-Retourne	200	130	70	30	43
Bignicourt (annex)	150	100	50	30	60

Source: AD Marne, 2 G 283–84.

Note: Only parishes for which the number of children and the number of students can be calculated are included.

[a] Includes the annex of Saint-Martin-l'Heureux.

[b] Includes the annex of Mont-Saint-Remi.

Table 5.5. School Attendance in Reims by Deanery, 1773–1774

Deanery	Children	Students	%
Bétheniville	3,398	1,810	53.3
Cernay-en-Dormois	1,422	768	54.0
Dun	2,163	1,165	53.9
Varennes	1,803	1,001	55.5

Source: AD Marne, 2 G 277–78 for Cernay, 2 G 272–73 for Dun, and 2 G 274–75 for Varennes.
Note: Only parishes for which the number of children and the number of students can be calculated are included.

than the total number of children in the parish—the number of souls included infants and toddlers who did not yet belong in the *petites écoles.* There may have been some students attending school who were older than twelve or thirteen and had already taken first communion as well (and would thus be counted as adults in the parish), but their numbers were probably much smaller than the number of children under age five or six. Therefore, although impossible to determine definitively, the percentages in table 5.5 may be lower than they would be if we knew the exact number of school-age children in each of the parishes.

Another factor that makes calculating the level of attendance difficult is the fact that students did not always attend the *petite école* in their own village. A child who lived far away from the schoolmaster of his parish might choose to attend the school of a neighboring parish if it was closer. A student living in a parish with an annex might also choose to attend the annex school for the same reason, or perhaps because his or her parents thought the annex schoolmaster was superior to the one in the parish. For example, the *petite école* of Saint-Clément had between forty and fifty students in a parish with only eighty communicants, while its annex had only eighty students out of three hundred communicants.[45] This does not indicate that the people of the parish sent their children to school more diligently than those of the annex; rather, we can assume that some of the annex children probably attended the parish *petite école.* Inevitably, some schoolmasters were more well liked than others and attracted students from other parishes, which accounts for the large differences in the percentages of children attending school from parish to parish. Finally, just because a child did not attend the parish's official *petite école* did not mean that he or she had no opportunity for primary education—curés usually did not report the number of students being taught by unofficial masters or mistresses.

Yet even with these caveats in mind, a significant number of eligible children—as many as one-fourth to one-half—did not attend the *petites écoles* at all, or only for a short amount of time. The curés who filled out the 1774 questionnaire did so in January—the month when attendance was likely to be at its highest. Schools that remained open all year (except for harvest time) were few and far between: of 169 Reims schools for which information about the length of the school year is available, only 38 (22.5 percent) were open for nine months of the year or longer. Another 38 remained open for between six and eight months, from October until Easter. Attendance usually dropped off in the spring and summer, even if the school stayed open. For example, the curé of Chamery noted that his parish school housed between seventy and eighty students in the winter but only twelve to twenty in the summer. The curé of Cauroy reported that there were between sixty and eighty students attending school between December and March, but from April to July only twenty to thirty students went to school.[46] In most of the smaller villages, attendance fell so drastically in the spring and summer that schools had to close as soon as the weather warmed up: ninety-three curés (55 percent) reported that schoolmasters taught only during the winter, or for between three and five months of the year.

Curés often complained about lackluster school attendance in visitation records and questionnaires. While poverty prevented many parishes in the diocese of Auxerre from employing a schoolmaster, even those that did have a *petite école* often had difficulty ensuring that all eligible children attended. The curé of Courson said in 1699 that his parish's schoolmaster was paid only by the students' parents, but this was never enough because there were so few students. The parish had four hundred communicants, but about one-third of the families lived in a hamlet far from the center of the parish and did not send their children to school as a result. Complaints about poor school attendance continued in Auxerre throughout the eighteenth century. When the bishop visited Étais in 1735, he found the children to be so ignorant of Christian doctrine that he refused to confirm any of them. He was told that both schools and catechism classes were poorly attended; in response, he issued an ordinance exhorting parents to send their children to school and the schoolmaster to teach catechism in the school at least three times a week. The bishop returned to Étais one year later, found the children to be "passably instructed," and confirmed those children who were presented to him.[47]

Even in the dioceses of Châlons-sur-Marne and Reims, where village schools were nearly universal by the end of the seventeenth century, the number of children attending was not as high as it could have been. Attendance was high enough for schools to remain open, but schools were rarely filled to capacity. The best evidence of absenteeism in the *petites écoles* in Châlons is found in a questionnaire filled out by curés sometime before their parishes were visited between 1728 and 1732. Out of 242 parishes and annexes, twenty-eight curés complained about parents neglecting to send their children to school. When the curé of Mathons was asked to identify the common vices in his parish, he responded: "the negligence of the parents to send their children to school, preferring to send them to guard their animals." The curé of Boussemont complained that parents did not send their children to school even though the parish itself paid the monthly fees. Fewer curés made complaints about absenteeism in the 1748–1752 visits, but the problem had not been resolved. Several curés complained that even if parents did send their children to school in the winter, they removed them early in the spring to work. The curé of Robert-Magny noted that the children's responsibility for taking care of their families' animals kept them from attending both school and his catechism classes: "It seems as though they were made for guarding the animals and nothing more. This negligence for their salvation is responsible for their lack of religion."[48]

In the minds of the curés, there were two basic reasons why parents did not send their children to school: neglect and poverty. This was true in Reims as well as in Châlons and Auxerre. The curé of Écly, a parish of two hundred communicants, reported in 1774 that thirty students attended the village school but that there could be twice that number "if the parents had more zeal for the education of their children." In Iges, where the majority of the four hundred communicants were poor workers at a cloth manufacturer in nearby Sedan, the curé noted that "the fathers and mothers here are very ignorant, [they] completely ignore the utility of an education for their children." The curé of Prouilly recognized that poverty and negligence usually went hand in hand: "either too much self-interest, or too much misery makes them neglect the instruction of their children; they send them to school for only two or three months of the year."[49]

Perhaps ignorance and neglect did prevent some children from taking advantage of the *petites écoles,* but most curés realized that poverty was the real reason behind absenteeism. Even if communities paid for the schoolmaster's salary and exempted poor children from paying monthly fees, parents often felt their children would be of more use to them at home or at work. In Floing (Reims) the schools held very few children in 1774 because "the children are employed from their most tender youth at the cloth manufacturer's." In Pouru-Saint-Remy (Reims), which, except for twenty-two households of *laboureurs,* was composed entirely of impoverished workers in the cloth industry, the curé lamented the fact that poverty and the need for children to work to supplement their parents' income kept the schools emptier than they should have been: "There are around sixty students, although there could be many more; poverty prevents the majority of the fathers and mothers from sending their children . . . they are sent to work as soon as they reach the age of seven or eight."[50]

Curés in several other parishes made similar complaints; it seems that the families of the middle classes were in a position to send their children to school while the poorer families—the day laborers and the factory workers—needed the income generated by sending their children to work. The situation in all three dioceses was likely similar to that described by the bishop of Auxerre when he visited Clamecy in 1733. He noted that "the schoolmasters and schoolmistresses do their duty, and the bourgeois send their children assiduously, but not the humble folk." Another visitor to the town said that the situation was much the same in 1774.[51] Although the *petites écoles* were theoretically open to children of all social classes, and in many cases village notables and curés did everything they could to pay the monthly fees for students whose families could not afford them, in reality the village schools could not reach the poorest children of the parish. More often than not, the harsh realities of eighteenth-century life prevented children at the bottom of the social ladder from learning to read, write, and recite.

  ℰ—   Despite the fact that the children of the poor often slipped through the cracks in the early modern educational system, the large number of *petites écoles* in existence on the eve of the Revolution suggests that primary education had become a significant part of the childhood experience for a majority of children and young adults in Reims, Châlons, and Auxerre. The fact that parents and village notables paid for these schools and administered them locally was no small feat. With little assistance from either church or state, at least nine out of ten communities in all three dioceses hired schoolmasters to teach parish children their letters and the catechism. Parents and community leaders felt strongly about primary education for girls as well as for boys—if they had no funds to hire a lay schoolmistress or bring in members of a female religious order or teaching congregation, they simply sent their daughters to the schoolmaster's home along with their sons.

  Far from being neglected or ignored, primary education became an important social and moral issue in the seventeenth and eighteenth centuries—an issue that even parents and village notables in rural areas cared about. No longer the preserve of elites and clergy alone, schooling became such a significant priority to many rural peasants that they were willing to pay for it themselves. Although the *petites écoles* might seem rudimentary from a twenty-first-century perspective, and eighteenth-century schoolteachers certainly could not achieve all that their counterparts did in the 1880s and 1890s, they still accomplished a great deal. Despite the fact that the children of the lowest classes in the dioceses of Auxerre, Châlons-sur-Marne, and Reims may never have set foot inside a school, it is clear, from the very existence of the schools themselves, that the majority of middle-class children did attend school for at least several months of the year.

CHAPTER SIX

Learning to Read, Write, and Recite
The Petites Écoles *and the Catholic Reformation*

Students in the *petites écoles* were expected to learn to read, write, and recite their catechism and to practice Christian morals and behavior. These are the skills that Louis XIV emphasized in his 1698 edict, and the bishops and village notables who hired schoolmasters for their communities had similar aims as well. The potential for the existence of a considerable gap between prescription and practice leaves the historian with several questions, however. How effective were these schools in reality? Did the children who attended school actually learn and retain what their schoolmasters and schoolmistresses taught? Traditionally, the effectiveness of most premodern educational systems has been evaluated through studies of literacy.[1] Literacy in early modern France is usually calculated by counting signatures on marriage records, since both men and women from all social classes had a chance to sign their names when they married. Signature rates in Auxerre, Châlons-sur-Marne, and Reims increased significantly during the seventeenth and eighteenth centuries—in one case by as much as 170 percent.[2]

Yet determining literacy rates based on signatures alone cannot provide a complete picture of the effectiveness of the *petites écoles*. Signature rates, as traditionally calculated, have a significant number of flaws that need to be addressed in order to gain a true picture of the *petites écoles* as an educational system. Most importantly, signature rates cannot measure the two most important skills taught in the schools—reading and religion. Historians have a tendency to assume that the issues that concern today's educators—proficiency in reading, writing, and arithmetic—were the same issues that led early modern parents and authorities to establish and maintain primary schools. Increasing literacy was, in fact, a by-product of the *petites écoles:* their primary purpose was to teach children how to be good French villagers, and good French villagers were also good Catholics.

In challenging the widely held view that an effective school always produced children who could both read and write—and thus sign their names on an *acte de mariage*—this chapter reveals how well Catholic Reformation principles, as taught in the *petites écoles,* had spread throughout rural parishes by the end of the eighteenth century. In fact, Catholics in Auxerre, Châlons, and Reims were better educated in Catholic doctrine than perhaps they had ever been. They participated in the sacraments and church services willingly and with regularity. They attended Mass, they sent their children to catechism, and they generally got along well with their curés. They even desired a greater clerical presence in their parishes, to ensure that they would be able to practice their religion as they wished. Although the laity did not conform to every rule that their bishops and curés laid down for them, the clergy and the laity found ways to compromise on many issues and bring about a great deal of reform at the parish level. From both clerical and lay perspectives, many of the goals of the Catholic Reformation had been achieved by the end of the eighteenth century, and the *petites écoles* deserve a great amount of credit for those achievements.

The Petites Écoles *and Literacy*

Although communities employed schoolteachers to provide instruction in reading, writing, and arithmetic, they did not in fact teach these subjects with equal frequency.[3] In modern primary schools children usually learn to read and write their letters simultaneously, and they begin learning basic math long before they are competent readers and writers. In contrast, in the early modern period students always learned each skill separately and in a specific order—only after a child had mastered reading could he or she move on to writing.[4] Jean-Baptiste de La Salle, the founder of the Brothers of the Christian Schools, or *petits frères,* articulated strict rules for teaching writing in his *Conduite des Écoles chrétiennes*; the first paragraph of a chapter on writing begins, "It is necessary that the students know how to read perfectly both in French and in Latin, before teaching them to write."[5]

In the seventeenth century children always learned to read in Latin before their native language, and this was accomplished in seven stages, or classes. Students in the first class learned the names and sounds of each letter. In the second class students memorized the pronunciation of dozens of syllables. Unlike modern kindergartners, who begin sounding out words even before they have learned all of the letters of the alphabet, early modern children memorized dozens of possible syllables that they might later encounter before they tried reading words. The emphasis on memorization and pronunciation continued in the third and fourth classes, when students learned to put syllables together as Latin words. Not until the fifth class did students learn to read in French, from works of piety. In the sixth and seventh classes schoolmasters introduced their students to a variety of different texts, including handwritten documents.[6]

In the eighteenth century a significant pedagogical change took place in primary education, but it does not seem to have made the process of learning to read any less tedious. Under the influence of La Salle, teachers began to use French rather than Latin texts to teach beginning readers. La Salle advocated a six-stage method for teaching children to read in French, and each stage had beginner, intermediate, and advanced substages. In the first three stages children learned letters and syllables by studying alphabet charts posted on the walls of the schoolroom, and in the third stage they were finally introduced to an actual book. The fourth stage consisted of sounding out syllables in basic readers and learning correct pronunciation and spelling. Not until the advanced level of the fifth stage did students begin to learn to read words rather than syllables. The final stage, before moving on to reading in Latin and then writing, was spent reading for practice as well as instruction in inserting appropriate pauses, punctuation, and accent marks.[7]

Although not every child would have followed La Salle's exact method, learning to read was a complex process in the early modern period nonetheless. No matter which method their instructor used, students always followed the same order in their studies: letters, syllables, and finally words. A great deal of memorization was required, and although learning to read in French rather than Latin must have been much easier, many students would have struggled to accomplish the tasks required of them. Only the most dedicated would have been able to move on to writing—an even more difficult subject.

In his *Conduite des Écoles chrétiennes,* La Salle first enumerates instructions on the practical side of writing and writing equipment. He provides detailed information about the types of pens, ink, and paper that should be used and how writing instruments should be cared for. The text includes an extended discussion on posture, as well as on the way the pen should be held and the correct positions of the arm and wrist. Writing was essentially calligraphy—an art as well as a skill. Thus, it was important to train the body as well as the mind. In their work on early modern literacy, François Furet and Jacques Ozouf remind us that "for a long time writing was really a technical exercise, involving instruments, muscular gymnastics and a knack."[8]

After a student had learned how to hold his pen and sit up straight, he began copying letters. La Salle recommended that students start with the letters *C, O, I, F,* and *M* and begin by filling an entire page with each letter.[9] In an incredibly painstaking process, students learned how to write one pen stroke at a time, until they could copy out all the letters of the alphabet and then entire words. Instructors had to make sure that students paid attention to many other elements besides the letters themselves, including spacing, the connections made between letters, and whether or not their handwriting was bold, firm, and smooth. Students then spent hours copying out sentences from books and were graded on accuracy and penmanship. Schoolmasters did not encourage creativity. If any student learned composition and grammar in the *petites écoles* or in any of the free schools run by the religious orders, it was an extremely rare occurrence. Only at a *collège* or with a private tutor could children receive formal instruction in how to compose a text of their own.

The great amount of time and effort required to learn to write limited the number of students who undertook the task. Furthermore, the pedagogical reasons for teaching reading and writing separately were reinforced by the fees parents paid—schoolmasters based their fees on the skill a child learned rather than age or year in school. Usually, the fees for students learning to write amounted to approximately twice the fee paid by those learning to read. For example, in the parish of Druyes, schoolmaster Jean Baptiste Chevereau earned 5 sous a month from his readers, 10 sous from his writers, and 15 sous from those learning arithmetic. From an analysis of thirty-two contracts, the average monthly fee for reading was 4.7 sous; for writing 9 sous; and for arithmetic 13 sous.[10] Because of the added difficulty and expense required to learn to write, many children may have left school before ever taking up a pen.

The fact that children learned to read before they learned to write has a significant impact on the way we understand and evaluate literacy. In traditional calculations of literacy rates for this period, using analyses of signatures on notarial and church documents, a person who signed their name is considered literate, and a person who could only make a mark is considered illiterate. But if, for financial and/or pedagogical reasons, children did not learn to write, they may not have been able to sign their names. This is just one of many difficulties that can result when equating signature rates with literacy.

Eighteenth-century literacy rates for France are largely based on the signatures of spouses on marriage records, as collected by Louis Maggiolo, a nineteenth-century schoolmaster. Maggiolo sent out requests to schoolmasters in every department in France, asking them to count the signatures of both men and women on marriage records during four different five-year periods: 1686–1690, 1786–1790, 1816–1820, and 1872–1876. Nearly sixteen thousand schoolmasters followed Maggi-

Table 6.1. Percentage of Men Able to Sign an *acte de mariage*

Department	1686–1690	1786–1790	% increase from 1686 to 1786–1790	1816–1820	% increase from 1686 to 1816–1820
Marne	61.39	79.80	29.99	83.76	36.44
Ardennes	54.73	75.68	38.28	96.28	75.92
Yonne	32.99	48.49	46.98	56.75	72.02
France	29.06	47.05	61.91	54.35	87.03

Source: Ministère de l'Instruction Publique et des Beaux-Arts, *Statistique de l'enseignement primaire* (the Maggiolo report).

olo's instructions and sent statistics to him; the resulting "Maggiolo report" shows that, by 1820, 54 percent of the men and 34 percent of the women in France could sign their *acte de mariage,* thus qualifying them as literate. Maggiolo published his results by department, thus implying that literacy could be predicted by geographical region.[11]

A comparison of Maggiolo's signature rates with the growth of schooling in the dioceses of Auxerre, Châlons, and Reims reveals a predictable pattern: as the number of schools increased over the course of the eighteenth century, so did the signature rates. While the department of the Yonne, which included the diocese of Auxerre, had signature rates comparable to those of France as a whole, the departments of the Marne and the Ardennes, which included both of the dioceses of Châlons-sur-Marne and Reims, had significantly higher rates (see tables 6.1 and 6.2). In 1790 only eight departments had a higher percentage of men who could sign their names.[12] In Champagne, where a system of schools had been established as early as the mid-seventeenth century, signature rates were the highest. In contrast, Auxerre, which had schools in only about one-third of its parishes at the beginning of the eighteenth century, had substantially lower rates, although both literacy and schools did increase significantly throughout the century.

The Maggiolo report was first analyzed by twentieth-century historians in a 1957 article by Michel Fleury and Pierre Valmary, who, after imposing the data onto a map of France, divided the country into

Table 6.2. Percentage of Women Able to Sign an *acte de mariage*

Department	1686–1690	1786–1790	% increase from 1686 to 1786–1790	1816–1820	% increase from 1686 to 1816–1820
Marne	24.93	46.73	87.44	67.24	169.72
Ardennes	28.99	48.88	68.61	55.53	91.55
Yonne	15.06	22.37	48.54	30.51	102.59
France	13.97	26.87	92.34	34.74	148.68

Source: Ministère de l'Instruction Publique et des Beaux-Arts, *Statistique de l'enseignement primaire* (the Maggiolo report).

the literate and modern northeast and the illiterate and backward south and southwest. Fleury and Valmary noted that Maggiolo's statistics were somewhat uneven (the response rates in some departments were poor, making it impossible to come to any generalizable conclusions), as well as biased toward rural rather than urban areas (more schoolmasters from rural areas reported data than their urban counterparts, most likely due to difficulties in collecting information). Despite these drawbacks, their Saint-Malo-to-Geneva line, dividing literate and nonliterate France, became the standard interpretation of signature rates for the eighteenth century.[13]

Two teams of historians challenged these findings in the 1970s, noting that examining the statistics in terms of provinces and regions obscured other types of differences in signature rates. Chartier, Julia, and Compère in 1976, and Furet and Ozouf in 1977, cite other factors that seemed much more determinative of the ability to sign than geographical region. Besides the obvious fact that men tended to be more literate than women all over France, urbanites had higher signature rates than those who lived in the countryside. Social class was also important—even in the highly illiterate countryside, landowners most likely could sign their names while peasants could not. Similarly, urban merchants and artisans whose professions required reading and writing skills had very high rates of literacy, but urban laborers remained overwhelmingly illiterate. The location of villages could also be a determining factor: villages connected by major roads and trade routes were more likely to have a higher percentage of signatures than more isolated villages, especially those in mountainous regions. In general, the primary determining factors of literacy were sex and profession, not geographical region. If individuals or communities spent time and money on an education for either themselves or their children, they had to be sure it would pay off in the long term.[14]

Another serious problem with Maggiolo's data is the fact that he organized his statistics by departments—artificially created administrative districts that often did not coincide with the cultural, religious, or economic regions that were historically more significant.[15] In Champagne Maggiolo's organization of the data is unproblematic—except for a few districts, the dioceses of Reims and Châlons-sur-Marne became the departments of the Marne and the Ardennes[16]—but the modern department of the Yonne, which includes the city of Auxerre, was cobbled together from four different dioceses. Each of these dioceses contributed one or more districts to the department when it was created during the French Revolution: the Senonais came from the diocese of Sens, the Auxerrois and the Puisaye from Auxerre, the Avallonais from Autun, and the Tonnerrois from Langres.

Signature rates at the end of the eighteenth century varied significantly in each of these regions. The Senonais had the highest rates (64 percent for men and 35 percent for women), while the Puisaye— about half of the diocese of Auxerre—had the lowest: only 29 percent of men and 10 percent of women could sign their *acte de mariage*. The rates for the Auxerrois were higher than those for the Puisaye but nowhere near those of the Senonais: 40 percent of men signed, and 21 percent of women. Thus, the figures for the whole department of the Yonne (48 percent for men and 22 percent for women) represent only an average of these very disparate regions; signature rates in many parts of the diocese of Auxerre were actually much lower than both the departmental and the national averages.[17]

Furet and Ozouf recognized the limitations inherent in literacy rates calculated through signatures, as well as the possibility of significant variations within departments; therefore, they decided to test the data Maggiolo collected for the nineteenth century. Using different types of military and school records that measure both reading and writing ability, they calculated literacy rates and then compared them to Maggiolo's signature rates from the same time period. They found that the two sets of data produced similar results and argued that what Maggiolo reported for the eighteenth century could be used to accurately gauge literacy during that time period as well.[18]

There may have been significant differences, however, between the educational systems and methods of the eighteenth century and those of the nineteenth that could make signature rates from the earlier time period a poor indicator of literacy, or at least reading ability. In the eighteenth century a person's inability to provide a signature did not necessarily mean that person was illiterate—he or she may have been able to read but not write. For example, it is entirely possible that more children stayed in school longer in the nineteenth century and thus had more opportunities to learn to write, while the majority of the children in the eighteenth century learned reading only and could not sign their names. As noted above, learning to write was a very complicated and expensive task in the early modern period. The subject required significant time from a student, especially since he or she had to master reading before moving on to writing.

Perhaps most importantly, even if students had the time and the money, rural schoolmasters could only teach a few students to write at a time since they held classes in their homes. Students learning to read could be crammed onto benches in every corner of the schoolroom, but students learning to write had to have desks—a luxury in terms of money and space that most *petites écoles* could not afford.[19] Some writing masters in towns and villages taught writing only and thus had more space, but schoolmasters in rural areas simply did not have enough room or equipment to teach all of their students to write. It was not until the advent of the modern school building in the nineteenth century that most students would have had the chance to learn to write as a part of their primary school experience.

The fact that the *petites écoles* were equipped to teach primarily reading and religion rather than writing may help us to understand another puzzling aspect of eighteenth-century signature rates: the fact that males who signed their names always significantly outnumbered female signers. At best, for every two men in Auxerre, Châlons, or Reims who signed their marriage records, only one woman could do the same

Table 6.3. Comparison of Male and Female Signature Rates (by Percentage)

Department	1686–1690		1786–1790	
	Men	Women	Men	Women
Marne	61.39	24.93	79.80	46.73
Ardennes	54.73	28.99	75.68	48.88
Yonne	32.99	15.06	48.49	22.37
France	29.06	13.97	47.05	26.87

Source: Ministère de l'Instruction Publique et des Beaux-Arts, *Statistique de l'enseignement primaire* (the Maggiolo report).

(see table 6.3). Female signature rates did improve in the eighteenth century—by 1786, the number of women who could sign their marriage records increased by 87.4 percent in the department of the Marne, 68.6 percent in the Ardennes, and 48.5 percent in the Yonne (see table 6.2). Although female literacy rates in the Yonne still lagged slightly behind national rates, the percentages of literate women in the Marne (46.7 percent) and the Ardennes (48.9 percent) were nearly double those of France as a whole (26.9 percent). Yet their signature rates still remained lower than men's.

How do we account for this difference? A lack of schooling cannot explain the fact that girls were unable to sign their names, since we have seen that girls had just as many educational opportunities as boys. Twenty-eight curés in the diocese of Reims listed both the number of boys and the number of girls attending schools in their parishes in 1774; only five parishes had more boys attending schools than girls (table 6.4). Eleven parishes had equal numbers, and twelve others had more girls than boys. Since the number of girls is thus significantly higher than the number of boys (in total, 1,400 boys and 1,594 girls were in school in these twenty-eight parishes), we can assume that girls were either more likely to attend school in the first place or that they stayed in school longer than their brothers, who might have had more opportunities for occupations outside of school.[20] While this is admittedly a rather small sample, it does show that girls probably had just as many opportunities for schooling as boys did, even in rural areas.

Table 6.4. Male and Female Students Attending Schools in Reims, 1774

Parish	Communicants	Boys	Girls
Beaumont	160	15	25
Beaumont-en-Argonne	700	82	48
Braux	800	60	100
Cernay-en-Dormois	360	50	50
Cormicy	800	70	90
Cumières	600	80	80
Donchery	1,000	70	70
Grandpré	590	40	50
Hauteville	200	15	15
Jonchery	219	31	42
La Romagne	203	40	50
Le Chesne	750	70	70
Louvois	250	30	30
Mareuil	400	30	75
Mourmelon-le-Grand	220	30	30
Renwez	700	110	110
Rocroy	1,500	80	120
Romain	184	26	14
Rumigny	500	45	50
Saint-Souplet	300	30	40
Saint-Thierry	300	30	30
Sapogne	284	18	16
Son	180	24	13
Suippes	1,400	120	200
Thugny	500	30	30
Vandeuil	134	24	26
Varennes	1,100	80	80
Vendresse	821	70	40

Source: AD Marne, 2 G 253–87.

If girls attended the *petites écoles* with just as much frequency as their brothers, the discrepancy between male and female literacy rates must be accounted for in other ways—specifically by examining both the methods used to determine literacy and the gendered nature of reading and writing. What does the fact that a man or a woman signed his or her name on a marriage record actually mean? Can we consider a person who was able to sign as being truly literate? And, in contrast, can we be sure that a person who could not sign was truly illiterate? It is entirely possible, for instance, that a person who could neither read nor write could learn to copy out his or her name. On the other hand, because children always learned to read before they learned to write, it is even more likely that some of the nonsigners could read but not write.

Thus, the inability to sign an *acte de mariage* cannot be equated with complete illiteracy. Instead of dividing people into the binary categories of literate and illiterate, we need to look at literacy as a wide spectrum of skills. In his study of European literacy, R. A. Houston suggests several categories of literacy: basic reading, advanced reading, basic writing (can copy or sign one's name), advanced writing, basic counting, and numeracy.[21] Signatures only test one of these categories—basic writing—and cannot provide a complete picture of the total package of skills that both signers and nonsigners may have possessed.

Because reading and writing were not taught simultaneously, and because parents had to pay higher fees if they wanted their children to learn to write, boys were more likely to learn to write than girls in the early modern period. Since reading religious texts and prayers was a central feature of Catholic Reformation practice, reading became the most important aspect of primary education. Community leaders and church authorities viewed writing as supplementary, rather than central, to a good education in the *petites écoles*. Parents did not see the extra time and expense required to teach a daughter to write as a necessity since she would be unlikely to need that skill as an adult. Writing was a practical skill, used primarily by scholars and record keepers, and women were usually neither of these. Therefore, most girls who attended schools spent their time learning to read their prayers and other religious texts and never took writing lessons, even if they might have had enough time to do so. Even sex-segregated girls' schools focused on teaching catechism, prayers, reading, and other practical skills that women would use as adults.

A number of examples from local communities confirm this attitude toward girls' schools. When the curé of Murvaux (Reims) drew up a list of rules for the annual election of the most virtuous girl in the parish (called La Rosière), he noted that any candidate had to be able to read: "This rule is necessary to encourage parents to make sure that their children are instructed, in order to banish ignorance—the usual origin of nearly every vice."[22] Significantly, however, the rules did not require La Rosière to be able to write. The Ursulines of Cravant (Auxerre), whose charter states that they were founded to teach young girls piety and the Christian religion, had forty students in 1682 when the bishop visited their convent, but not a single girl was learning to write.[23] Lay schoolmistresses probably rarely taught writing either; one mistress for the parish of Auvilliers (Reims) did not even know how to write herself.[24] Instead of spending their time learning to write, girls (especially those taught by female teachers) learned sewing and other handwork.[25] Writing—and the ability to sign one's name—was primarily a male skill. Women, who may have been able to read just as well as their brothers and husbands, never bothered to learn to sign their names, while men, who would have found basic writing skills useful and even necessary in adult life, did learn how to sign even if they could not write well and could not be described as fully literate in the modern sense of the word.

It is also possible that many of the men who signed their marriage records had not learned this skill in the *petites écoles* at all. These schools simply did not have the capacity to teach more than a handful of students to write. If writing skills had been acquired solely in the *petites écoles,* then Reims' schoolmasters would have had to teach writing to eight out of every ten boys, and five out of every ten girls, in order to match the signature rate of the Maggiolo report for the department of the Marne. In reality, most rural schoolmasters could only teach a few children of either sex how to write. Schoolmasters often had nearly one hundred students in their schools, which meant that even with the help of their wives or assistant masters, students would have had very little of the individual attention that children learning to write required. Many students must have learned writing skills elsewhere, outside of the official *petites écoles,* where students learning to read significantly outnumbered those learning to write. It is likely that children and adolescents learned to write from a parent or other relative, or from a writing master. Individuals who found writing skills necessary for their profession may have also learned to write on the job, from their peers and coworkers. In any case, writing skills were acquired piecemeal, with many learning only enough to sign their names and perhaps keep basic records and whatever else was necessary for their work.

In fact, in the early modern period writing abilities and schooling may not have been closely related at all. Houston emphasizes that formal schooling was only the first step in acquiring literacy; most of the skills that we would consider crucial for total literacy came later in life.[26] Near-complete literacy could be achieved without any sort of public educational system, as demonstrated by Egil Johansson in a study of Swedish visitation records. This study shows that when Protestant authorities tested children on their catechism during their visits, they also tested reading abilities. By the end of the eighteenth century, between 80 and 95 percent of those tested could read, despite the fact that Sweden had almost no public or private primary schools. The responsibility for teaching children to read rested squarely with parents, for whom it was seen as a crucial religious and civic duty. But in Sweden the ability to write was not nearly as common: Johansson estimates that only between 10 and 25 percent of the population could write in 1800. If literacy rates in Sweden had been calculated in the traditional manner, using signatures and the number of schools, those rates would have appeared extremely low. In reality, the country probably had one of the highest percentages of people who could read in all of Europe.[27]

Measuring the effectiveness of the early modern *petites écoles* through increases in signature rates alone is therefore quite problematic. Signature rates cannot measure the ability to read with enough accuracy, as many individuals who may have been able to read could not sign their names. It is especially difficult to gauge the literacy skills that girls may have acquired in the *petites écoles* since they were less likely to learn to write than boys. But perhaps even more importantly, we must remember that the primary purpose of the *petites écoles* was not to teach writing, or even reading in some cases; rather, primary education meant religious education in the early modern period. Louis XIV's 1698 edict makes this quite clear—he begins by emphasizing the importance of teaching religion to all children and only notes that the schools might teach reading and writing at the end of his proclamation, almost as an afterthought: "in addition [schoolteachers] will teach reading and even writing to those who need to learn."[28] Because the *petites écoles* primarily taught reading and religion, which cannot be tested by signatures alone, they should not be judged by signature rates or even by an evaluation of literacy.[29]

Catechism and Schools: Primary Education for a Lifetime

In his seminal work *Peasants into Frenchmen,* Eugen Weber described primary schools before the 1880s as "dark, humid, crowded, unventilated, unfurnished, unlit, unheated or smelly and smoky when a fire or stove was lit, drafty, unwelcoming, and ugly." He noted that schoolmasters' wives did housework and prepared meals in the schoolroom while students huddled together on benches or even the floor, and he portrayed schoolmasters as unprofessional, untrained, negligent of their duties, and barely capable of reading and writing themselves.[30] Yet Weber's larger argument is that when the state did finally provide adequate primary schooling in the 1880s, those schools succeeded largely because by that time peasants could see the economic and social value in learning to read and write and thus chose to send their children to school. The primary schools that villages established for their children in the seventeenth and eighteenth centuries may have fallen far short of the standards set by administrators and politicians at the end of the nineteenth century, but, as Weber argues, they must have fulfilled a need or no children would have attended. And, unlike the state-supported schools of the 1880s, which would have continued to receive state funding even if no children enrolled, the *petites écoles* would not have existed if parents had been unwilling to send their children along with their monthly fees.

Parents' primary motive for sending their children to school in the eighteenth century was generally not economic. In fact, many early modern parents—especially in rural areas—did not believe that the ability to read and write would give their children any financial advantage whatsoever. As late as the 1820s in Limousin, both Léonard Nadaud's wife and his father vehemently objected to Léonard's decision to send his son Martin to their local schoolmaster on the grounds that no one in their family had ever starved because they were illiterate. No one in his extended family believed that education in reading and writing would do anything except keep Martin from his duties as the primary caretaker of the family's livestock. However, both of Martin's parents did react with joy and pride when he earned a prize of two religious books at the end of the school year; in his memoir Martin notes that they wept and complimented him profusely.[31]

Instead of concentrating only on the acquisition of literacy in the *petites écoles,* we must place them in their proper historical context and examine their effectiveness in teaching the subjects that parents and authorities found to be the most important: Catholic doctrines and practices. When placed in the context of the Catholic Reformation, the *petites écoles* can be seen as a way to bring about increased conformity to Catholic practices among even the most uneducated peasants. In combination with the curés' Sunday catechism classes, schools were supposed to inculcate Catholic doctrine into the minds and souls of their Catholic students and teach them proper Catholic behavior.

As discussed in chapter 1 of this volume, one of the most important purposes of primary and catechetical instruction was to prepare children for their first communion; therefore, bishops devoted large sections of their catechisms to the doctrines behind the important sacraments of confession and communion. Closely tied to these two sacraments was the Mass itself, whether one took communion during the ceremony or not. Catechism classes repeatedly stressed the importance of regular Mass attendance, and schoolteachers reinforced the curés' teachings by taking their students to Mass on weekdays and by regulating their behavior at Mass on Sundays and feast days. Both catechisms and schools were designed to prepare children for their first communion and then a lifetime of attendance at Mass and regular confession and communion; thus, a study of these practices can serve as a revealing indicator of the effectiveness of early modern primary education.

Catholic Church leaders expected all adults and children over the age of twelve or thirteen to attend the Mass conducted by their curé every Sunday. By the end of the eighteenth century, the vast majority of

Catholics faithfully fulfilled this requirement, and people in the diocese of Auxerre were no exception.[32] Records of pastoral visits in Auxerre at the end of the eighteenth century include printed forms with a section on Mass attendance and Easter communion.[33] Although only thirty-eight of these visitation records have survived, they still provide a glimpse into how well the Catholics of Auxerre fulfilled their basic religious duties. Mass attendance, according to these records, was very high. In only two parishes did the visitors note that significant numbers of people failed to attend Mass regularly. One rural curé serving in Surgy, a parish of five hundred communicants, did complain that some of his parishioners neglected to attend the parish Mass, but he noted that they did not miss services entirely— they just preferred the more centrally located church of a neighboring village. The majority of the records indicate that the Sunday Mass was generally well attended and that many people attended other offices and services throughout the day.

With a few significant exceptions, visitors in Auxerre noted that most people fulfilled their "Easter duty" faithfully as well. The church required every Catholic to take communion at least once a year, generally at Easter, and most curés in small, rural parishes had little difficulty in persuading their parishioners to fulfill this duty.[34] In Saint-Privé, a parish of five hundred communicants, the curé reported to the bishop that the majority of his parishioners had taken communion at Easter that year (1785) and that people attended Mass with exactitude. That same year in Bleigny only twelve individuals had not done their Easter duty (out of three hundred communicants), including one fifty-year-old man who had never taken communion. In general, the curé felt that his parishioners attended services "regularly enough." In several parishes, however, curés reported that large numbers of people neglected their Easter duty: in Clamecy it seems that at least one-third of the parishioners had not taken communion in 1782, when a visit was made. In total, the visitors noted that significant numbers of individuals had failed to complete their Easter duty in 13 of the 38 parishes. However, all but 2 of the 13 communities had a population of more than one thousand communicants. In large parishes, noncommunicants could easily slip through the cracks since a single curé could not keep track of so many people. In the smaller- and average-sized parishes, however, only a handful of people neglected to do their Easter duty.[35]

A similar pattern existed in the diocese of Châlons. Questionnaires filled out by curés in Châlons either immediately before or during the bishop's visits around 1730, and twenty years later around 1750, asked curés to give the number of individuals in their parishes who had not completed their Easter duty that year. Some curés only reported "few" or "some" noncommunicants, so exact percentages of those who had taken communion cannot be calculated; however, the number of people who had refused to confess to the curé in order to take communion was very small. Because Châlons had more clergymen working in the diocese and had much smaller parishes than Auxerre, only a few individuals in each parish did not take communion each year. Of 247 curés who gave precise numbers of noncommunicants, 122 said that all of their parishioners had done their Easter duty, and 99 listed fewer than ten noncommunicants. Only 26 parishes had more than ten, and these were always the larger parishes: in only four cases was the percentage of noncommunicants greater than 10 percent of the total number of adults in the parish.

The numbers of noncommunicants in Châlons did not change significantly during the next twenty years—in 1750 31 parishes (out of 228) had more than ten noncommunicants, 117 had fewer than ten, and 80 had a completion rate of 100 percent. Thus, all but a handful of individuals in the rural parishes faithfully fulfilled their Easter duty each year. Noncommunicants got away with missing their Easter communion more easily in the larger towns, but by and large the situation was probably much as the curé of L'Épine described it in 1727: "They approach the sacraments with enough exactitude, and for a long time there hasn't been anyone in the parish who has not done their Easter duty . . . There is nothing scandalous in the parish, it appears to be well regulated; during the week people are busy with their work, and on Sundays there is great assiduousness for the offices of the parish."[36]

The Châlons questionnaires do reveal another difficulty in measuring the numbers of communicants and noncommunicants, however. Several curés complained that although their parishioners came to them for confession in the weeks before Easter, they could not actually take communion because they did not complete the penance that the curé had prescribed for them. The curé of Larzicourt, a parish of 450 communicants, listed only one member of his parish as a noncommunicant, but he noted that about one-third of his parishioners had not returned to do their Easter duty after having been deferred in the confessional.[37] The curé also said that his parish was one of the most difficult to govern in the entire diocese, and since no visitation record or questionnaire for either Auxerre or Reims indicates that these halfhearted communicants were an issue in those dioceses, it is difficult to know if this had become a serious problem elsewhere as well.[38]

Even if some parishioners only confessed and did not actually complete their Easter duty, it is still significant that they visited the confessional in the first place. If they had no fundamental faith or belief in the Catholic Church at all, why would they have bothered to confess, knowing that they would be turned away? One of the most common reasons that curés turned parishioners away from the altar was involvement in a lawsuit or a longstanding argument with neighbors or relatives. Perhaps many of those who were deferred simply accepted that they would not be able to do their Easter duty for one or two years but then could return to the fold once their disputes had been resolved. The catechism stressed sincere repentance before taking communion, so abstaining from the sacrament might actually be a testament to true belief. Perhaps some individuals did not want to take communion with unresolved sins on their consciences, and they needed more time to reach the correct state of mind.[39] Certainly, of course, some of the noncommunicants were simply recalcitrant and cared very little about their exclusion from the altar at Easter, but the overall tone of the curés in the visitation records indicates that most people did their best to take communion at least once a year, if not more often.

Records for Reims, although lacking precise numbers of communicants and noncommunicants, also show that Catholics in the diocese completed their Easter duty regularly and attended Mass faithfully. The questionnaire of 1774 includes a section in which curés were supposed to report on the character of their parishioners; this section is replete with praise for the exactitude with which people in the diocese of Reims attended services and fulfilled their Easter duty. It seems that very few parishioners failed to take communion at Easter, and many went beyond the minimum requirement and confessed and approached the altar for the Eucharist at other times of the year as well.

Many of the curés in Reims also noted that the women in their parishes participated in the sacraments with greater frequency than the men. In Heutrégiville the curé reported that while the men fulfilled the letter of the law and confessed and communed exactly once a year, at Easter, the women approached the sacraments at least twice a year. A vicaire who filled out a questionnaire for the annex of Vaux noticed a difference in male and female religious practices as well: "the masculine sex is as negligent to approach the sacraments as the feminine is exact and edifying, but one can see with pleasure in both sexes honesty and decency in their morals, and a great attachment to religion, assiduousness at instructions and hearts sensitive to the word of God."[40] Whether this indicates a trend toward the feminization of Catholicism is difficult to say, but the dedication of these women to the Eucharist confirms that the teachings of the Catholic Reformation had taken root at the parish level.

Of course, both sexes received a religious education at catechism classes and in school, and the Reims questionnaires demonstrate that in many parishes, people of both sexes faithfully fulfilled their religious duties. The curé of Épinonville reported that his parishioners were very poor but "tranquil and docile enough"; they approached the sacraments two or three times a year. The curé of Marvaux wrote that while three of his four hundred communicants had not done their Easter duty in several years, the rest attended services faithfully and "there are scarcely any Sundays when there is not someone who approaches the sacraments." In Vraux the curé gave a long list of problems in his parish— too much drinking at the *cabaret,* obstinacy, and quarrels—but he was not stingy with his praise for their good qualities either: "They are vigilant, hardworking, exact in attending all of the offices of the church with much respect and modesty . . . they approach the sacraments at least once a year besides at Easter-time, and attend the Mass willingly on working days as often as they can."[41]

Unfortunately, not every parishioner was as diligent as those of Marvaux or Vraux at attending services and taking communion at the appropriate times. Many curés made note of a variety of excuses their parishioners gave for their failure to attend Mass. Most commonly, people who lived a significant distance from the church complained of the transportation time required and of the condition of the roads in bad weather. In Pouru-Saint-Remy the curé complained that thefts at worshipers' homes had been committed during services so many times that people were afraid to go to Mass and leave their homes unattended. In some parishes children and servants regularly skipped Mass in the summer because they had to take the animals out to pasture. Other curés complained that their parishioners attended Mass in other parishes rather than their own—either because the neighboring parish's church was closer or because the time was more convenient. The people of Saint-Lambert wrote a letter to the bishop in 1722 asking that their parish Mass be said at four in the morning in the summer and six-thirty in the winter because they had to travel to a nearby city on Sundays in order to pick up materials for the next week's work. The curé of Saint-Lambert protested this time change and wrote his own letter to the bishop, explaining that in reality his parishioners wanted to get Mass out of the way as early as possible on Sundays so that they could have the rest of the day to spend in *cabarets*.[42]

Even if the curé's side of the story was correct, it is still significant that the people of Saint-Lambert wrote their letter at all. They apparently felt that attending Mass was important, they just wanted to do it according to their own schedule. Attendance at Mass was never perfect, but the visitation records show that in most parishes, the vast majority of the population attended at least one church service every Sunday, whether it was their own parish Mass or not. Perhaps not every curé could claim, like the curé of Perthes, that his parishioners "love the ceremonies of the church, and attend willingly and exactly,"[43] but Mass attendance was deeply woven into the fabric of village life, so much so that parishioners preferred to attend a 4:00 a.m. Mass rather than live with the stigma of not attending at all.

In addition to information about Mass and communion, the Reims questionnaire provides valuable information about religious belief and behavior, including parishioners' common sins and shortcomings. Some curés had several negative things to say about their parishioners and wrote long lists of vices and defaults. Jean-Baptiste Hoste, curé of Serzy-Maupas, complained that the people in his parish were self-interested, dangerous, liars, and drunks; the curé of Tramery described his parishioners as having "extreme greed for the goods of the earth, which makes them litigious, untrustworthy, and negligent to work for their salvation." In Villedemanche people were so stubborn and moneygrubbing that a dispute over two sous could cause enough division and rancor that those involved had to be excluded from the altar at Easter. The curé of Dreize reported that people fought so much in his parish that they would tear each other apart over a potato.[44] In general, the most common problems seemed to have been *cabarets,* dances and drunkenness, quarrels and lawsuits, dishonesty, gossip, slander, and swearing. These vices were not confined to the diocese of Reims—the Châlons questionnaires in the 1730s and 1750s reveal the same problems in that diocese.

These lists of vices and defaults are hardly surprising. It seems that the education children received in catechism classes and schools did not prevent them from frequenting *cabarets,* or from fighting over their commercial, financial, or personal interests once they became adults. Yet none of these vices were strictly antireligious or anti-Catholic in nature, and curés did not report any of the more serious problems their sixteenth- and seventeenth-century counterparts had faced regularly. No curé complained about superstitions or heresy. This was one of the standard questions for rural deans when they made their visits at the end of the seventeenth century, but curés were not asked to report on superstitious behaviors or heretical beliefs in the eighteenth-century questionnaire. A few visitation records from the seventeenth century complain about people who tried to use charms and prayers to heal their animals, and a few reports on individuals suspected of witchcraft do exist, but curés mentioned none of this in the 1774 questionnaire. Complaints about the laity turning holy days into profane celebrations were noticeably absent from the curés' comments—not a single one included anything about misbehavior during Carnival. Curés might complain that some people had not taken care to receive as much instruction as they should, but they did not mention that ignorance of true Catholic doctrines was leading to suspicious or heretical beliefs and behavior.

In addition, there were more curés who praised the character and behavior of their parishioners than those who complained about their

vices. Even though the curé of Villedemanche complained about the
constant financial disputes in his parish, he had good things to say as
well: "They are all vine growers, but they are not drunks; they are attached to their curé and listen ever more willingly to the word of God;
they are very regular in attending the offices and observe them with
modesty." In Évigny the curé noted that "the parishioners are very well
behaved, very religious, very docile to the voice of the curé, and very
godfearing; there is no notable vice, even among the young people."
The curé of Prix had a long list of positive things to say about his parishioners: "Their dominant character is gentleness; I can testify that
they have no great vice and that they have many good qualities, like
peace, compassion for the poor, the fear of God, attachment to the essential duties of a Christian, a great trust in God, and assiduousness at
the offices." The curé assured the bishop that the people of Belval, the
annex of Prix, had just as many good qualities, even if they did sometimes work on Sundays and feast days without permission.[45]

In general, curés portrayed their parishioners as hardworking,
pious, charitable toward the poor, and, like the people of Vaux, in pos-
session of "hearts sensitive to the word of God." Perhaps most importantly, they attended services and participated in the sacraments—
the two aspects of early modern Catholicism that upper and lower clergy
alike emphasized repeatedly. Curés like François Barbert of Courta-
gnon recognized that their parishioners were "all children of Adam; they
all, with no exception, have to earn their bread with the sweat of their
bodies" and that this could lead to a few vices—such as a tendency to
drink, swear, and argue; overall, however, they lived at peace with their
neighbors and took communion every year.[46] Sacraments and services
were the first step toward a more Christian life, and by the end of the
eighteenth century the vast majority of Catholics, at least according to
the curés of Reims, had already taken that step. Curés and bishops understood this and believed that vices and defaults would be corrected
with time and the confessional.

Another sign that religious education was working—and consequently producing better educated and better behaved Catholics—was
that curés and their parishioners, for the most part, got along fairly
well. Philip Hoffman has argued that in Lyon the Tridentine reforms

caused a rift between curés and lay men and women. Using court records, he demonstrates that curés became so exacting about reform that they could no longer identify with their parishioners, leading to increased friction and the eventual isolation of members of the clergy from the larger community.[47] Hoffman's argument does not seem to apply in Reims, however. The archbishop's 1774 questionnaire provided a perfect opportunity for curés to complain about people who refused to respect their authority, and yet they rarely did so. In fact, curés often expressed a great deal of sympathy for their parishioners. For example, when asked about the character of the people in his parish, Jean Baptiste Lambin responded: "To be badly nourished, badly housed, poorly clothed, exposed in the fields and roads to either the wind or the heat of the sun: these are the praiseworthy virtues practiced every day by the inhabitants of Cauroy."[48] Lambin recognized the difficulties that peasants faced, but he believed that a certain virtue existed in the struggle for survival itself.

Only a handful of curés' responses indicated overt tension between themselves and their parishioners. A few curés reported that people did not respond well to attempts at reform. The curé of Vantelet complained of "insubordination" in his parish, while in Saint-Fergeux people showed no respect for the curé or anything he said. In Tahure the curé wrote at length about the village officials' lack of support for his attempts to convince people to stop working on Sundays and feast days. But curés were more likely to report that their parishioners listened to them and respected their authority: "My parishioners are honest and attached to their pastor; I don't know of any great defaults, and that's the truth," wrote the curé of Aigny in his questionnaire.[49]

Of course, it is entirely possible that the laity saw their relationship with the clergy in a completely different way; after all, bishops' questionnaires can only tell one side of the story. Yet other sources show that people recognized the crucial role curés played in the parish and reveal the lengths that the laity might go to in order to ensure that qualified priests were readily available. Bishops' archives contain a number of letters from village notables asking that more members of the clergy be sent to their parishes to perform the sacraments and meet the spiritual needs of the people. Catechisms emphasized the clergy's sacramental function and their importance as spiritual guides, and based on the desire expressed in these letters for a greater clerical presence in their parishes, it seems this teaching was quite influential.

Requests for additional clergymen generally took two forms: parishioners asked for either a vicaire who would help an existing curé with his duties, or for a change in parish boundaries that would require the church to appoint another curé.[50] The people of Guignicourt told the archbishop in 1724 that the community would pay one hundred livres toward a vicaire's salary so that there could be more than one Mass said on Sundays and feast days in their parish. Their request was granted, and in 1774 the parish still had a vicaire. Other communities wanted an upgrade in their status, from annex to parish, and to have their own curé. In 1716 the people of Feuchères, a hamlet of Sapogne, requested that they be allowed to rebuild—at their own expense—a war-damaged chapel. The "bourgeois" who wrote the letter to the archbishop argued that the seventy adults in the parish wanted to be able to hear Mass and attend services every Sunday, instead of only those Sundays when the weather cooperated and the roads were passable. They mentioned that a number of elderly people had been missing the Mass entirely because of the distance to the church. They also wanted to establish a school, run by a schoolmaster they planned to compensate themselves, and who would "teach their children the religion of Jesus Christ, and Christian doctrines."[51] The archbishop refused to grant the hamlet's request, perhaps because the curé of Sapogne did not like the idea of having to share his income with another priest, even though the inhabitants had offered to supplement the curés' salaries if necessary.

Requests for curés continued through the latter part of the eighteenth century. In 1782 the inhabitants of two other hamlets, Champis and La Fontaine, wrote a four-page list, signed by thirty men and women, of reasons why they believed they should have their own curé.[52] Besides the fact that they had 180 communicants in the two hamlets, a population larger than many other parishes in the diocese, they argued that the great distance between the hamlets and the parish church at Nouart caused significant problems for the inhabitants. They wanted to build their own church, with their own funds, so that they could have services in their village. The church in Nouart was not large enough to hold all of the people of the parish (Nouart had 580 communicants in

1774) and people were forced to stand in the cemetery in all kinds of weather. They complained of the danger of dying without the sacraments that their distance from the church exposed them to—it was nearly impossible for the curé to reach someone who had suddenly fallen ill. This was a common complaint in many of the requests for curés: the thought of dying with unconfessed sins struck fear into the hearts of many individuals.

Residents of Champis and La Fontaine found many additional reasons to complain about the lack of a priest in their hamlets. They worried about children dying without baptism, but also that the baptism itself could cause infants to become sick due to the exposure to the cold when they were taken to church. The hamlets' inhabitants also complained that they had difficulty in getting to the confessional, especially at Easter, because the curé was so busy confessing the residents of Nouart. They described long lines of people waiting to meet with the curé and arguments breaking out over places in the line. Finally, the people voiced concern over the education of their children. They argued that parents were afraid to send their children to catechism alone due to the dangerousness of the road. The letter indicates that these two hamlets had been trying to secure their own curé for over twenty years; unfortunately, it seems that once again the archbishop turned down their appeal. Clearly, these individuals were desperate for their own curé. They may have exaggerated some of the difficulties they had in getting to Nouart in order to strengthen their case, but they obviously wanted to have a priest nearby. The sacraments and the Mass were extremely important to them, and they were willing to go to great lengths to ensure that clergymen were available to perform those sacraments.

The desire for a greater clerical presence is evident in Auxerre as well. The people of Arquian wrote a letter to the bishop asking for a vicaire because their curé was either unable or unwilling to perform his duties—specifically, the sacraments and catechism instruction. The people of Coulangeron, an annex of Chery, asked to have their own curé because the great distance between their hamlet and the church prevented a good number of people from attending the Mass and from receiving the sacraments. People worried about dying without confession, and they complained that their children lacked instruction. The efforts of the people of Coulangeron eventually had the desired effect:

the bishop granted them the status of parish in 1740. The inhabitants of another annex, Beaumont, wanted their own curé so badly that they pledged to supply his income themselves, with no help from the tithes. They argued that they had a large parish church, a house for a curé, all of the ornaments necessary to celebrate the Mass, and funds from some land that the parish owned. If the church did not provide the curé's income, they vowed that "the inhabitants of the village would supplement [his salary], rather than suffer from being deprived of all spiritual aid, especially the very holy mass." They included in their 1678 letter a list of people in the parish and the amount of money that they could contribute.[53]

The importance of a strong clerical presence is also evident in the lists of grievances, or *cahiers de doléances,* that parishes submitted for the meeting of the Estates General in 1789.[54] The people of La Neuvillette (Reims) included the following statement in their *cahier:*

> We groan to see how, for so long, ecclesiastical goods have been distributed unfairly; we see both secular and regular priests carry their opulence and uselessness here and there, while we have no resident priests in our village to provide spiritual aid, and also while many curés do not have what they need; the bishops and tithe-holders want to keep everything for themselves, leaving curés in misery and parishioners with a dearth of priests.[55]

Many historians have emphasized the anticlericalism of the French Revolution, but the *cahiers* show that the laity directed any negative feelings toward clergymen at members of the religious orders rather than the curés. *Cahiers* from the Third Estates of Auxerre, Châlons, and Reims all express frustration with the unequal distribution of tithes and other church funds. Many communities wished that the religious orders either be dissolved or given some task that made them useful to society, either in education or in caring for the poor and the sick. They felt that more money could then be made available for the curés, who were the most useful members of the clergy. Many annexes and hamlets complained in their *cahiers* that they deserved to have their own curés, while communities that already had their own curés asked for additional priests to reside in their parishes as well, recommending that any village with more than two hundred households have a vicaire available to administer the sacraments and say Mass.

In addition, the *cahiers* demonstrate a nearly universal desire for existing curés and vicaires to be better paid. People wanted their curés to have enough income from the tithes so that they would not have to charge fees for their services at baptisms, marriages, and funerals. They recommended that curés be paid at least twelve hundred livres and vicaires at least six hundred livres—twice the amount that most curés received at the time.[56] Again, this indicates a recognition of the fact that the laity believed the majority of church funds should go toward those clergymen who had care of souls rather than the religious orders or the already extravagantly wealthy bishops and cardinals. Because the laity found the services their curés and vicaires provided useful and even critical to their everyday activities, they paid their tithes in order to ensure that those services would continue.

Thus, on the eve of the Revolution, the desire for a greater clerical presence at the parish level was as strong as it had ever been in the early modern period. The laity, now better educated through catechisms and the *petites écoles,* recognized the importance of the clergy in their lives and demanded that the church supply curés and vicaires to administer the sacraments, lead church services, and educate their children in the Catholic faith.

☞— When asked about the character of his parishioners, the curé of Écly (Reims) quoted Matthew 13:47: "The kingdom of heaven is like unto a net, that was cast into the sea, and gathered of every kind."[57] Curés recognized that the people in their parishes did not comply perfectly with the church's rules and regulations regarding religious and moral behavior. Their evenings (and sometimes early mornings) at the *cabarets* and their petty squabbles were often annoying and worrisome vices, but the laity attended Sunday morning Mass with regularity and listened to the gospel with piety and devotion. By the end of the eighteenth century, Catholics were better instructed in the doctrines of their faith than most of their ancestors had been. The *petites écoles,* which taught religion and catechism above all other skills, were plentiful and generally well attended. Students may not have achieved complete literacy in the months and years that they attended these schools, but what they did learn was considered to be much more important at the time. Students learned to go to Mass, sit quietly, and listen to the counsel of their curés, both in his sermons and in the confessional. They learned that the sacraments were the pathway to heaven and to respect the clergymen who administered them. The goal of the *petites écoles* was to produce the next generation of French Catholic villagers, who would be regular in their religious thought and moral behavior. They were supposed to provide the foundation for a lifetime of Catholic faith and worship with other members of the village community. Judging by the practices of the Catholic laity, as seen through visitation records and curés' questionnaires, these schools were an overwhelming success.

Conclusion

In 1695 a peasant boy named Valentin Jamerey-Duval was born and baptized in the village of Arthonnay, in what is today the department of the Yonne. Valentin spent the early years of his life in abject poverty—his mother, a widow, could barely eke out a living for her family, and when she remarried, her new husband mistreated Valentin so badly that he left home at the age of thirteen. Despite his difficult beginning, Valentin eventually managed to get an education, and he became a popular example used by the *philosophes* to demonstrate the fact that peasants could indeed learn to read and write. As an adult Jamerey-Duval wrote a memoir of his experiences, in which he described the education he had received in his earliest years:

My education consisted of learning the Our Father, in Latin and in bad French, along with some other prayers that were explained to me in various elegant translations *en patois*. The catechism was taught in the same way, by repeating bits of it to me, I came, in a fashion, to know that there was a God, a Church and sacraments. I also learned that there was a pope, the visible head of the Church, priests and monks; I was taught to respect them and even to fear them, and that's what I do still.[1]

Even this boy, from the very poorest level of society, learned at least part of his catechism. One of the most important tasks of the Catholic Reformation was to educate the laity, and if a poor boy like Valentin Jamerey-Duval learned about God and the sacraments, church reformers were doing something right.

By the eighteenth century in France, catechism had become a routine part of childhood. For the majority of Catholic children, catechism was the first and most essential part of an entire program of religious education espoused by bishops and curés but generally accepted by parents and most members of the village community. The Catholic Reformation was not a one-sided affair, carried out on an unwilling lay population; both clergymen and the laity worked together to carry out religious reforms in the eighteenth century. Historians of the Catholic Reformation era often assume that the clergy and the laity were on opposite sides of every issue, but on the subject of primary education, they generally agreed. Parish priests, village notables, and parents alike wanted children to spend a few seasons in a schoolroom, learning to behave like proper French Catholics instead of like the animals that they had to tend when they were not in school. Catholicism was not just about doctrines; it was an entire way of living—a code of behavior that had to be maintained in order to keep society running. Thus, children learned their catechism at church from their curés, as well as from schoolmasters and schoolmistresses in the *petites écoles*. They were instructed in all of the Catholic Church's basic doctrines: the existence of God and Jesus Christ, the importance of the institutional church, and the necessity of prayer and the sacraments. At the same time, they learned proper respect for the church and its priests, how to participate in the sacraments, and codes of moral and ethical behavior that applied in both religious and secular settings.

As a result of this education, Catholics in the dioceses of Reims, Châlons-sur-Marne, and Auxerre did conform, for the most part, to the standards of religious behavior that their curés and bishops expected. They attended Mass every Sunday and feast day. They satisfied their "Easter duty" faithfully, taking communion at least once during the two-week Easter period. They participated in all of the sacraments regularly and often went to great lengths to make sure that they had qualified priests in their villages to perform those sacraments for them. Of course, just because people went to church and took part in the sacraments does not mean that they did everything right. One of the main goals of the Catholic Reformation was the separation of the sacred and the profane. The clergy believed that they could eventually stamp out all of the profane aspects of the laity's lives, leaving only the sacred. The laity, however, took the injunction literally; they often only separated the profane from the sacred and continued with behavior that the clergy did not like — they just made sure that this behavior did not spill over into the church's territory.

For example, complaints about working on Sundays were nearly universal. People did attend Mass, and they even behaved with decency in the church, but they used the rest of the day for their own affairs. Another ubiquitous complaint of parish priests involved the disruptions caused by unruly patrons of *cabarets*. Priests disliked the gambling and carousing that took place in *cabarets* whenever the cost of wine was cheap, but the laity seemed to think that once they had paid their tithes, the church should have nothing to say to them if they decided to waste their money on dice and alcohol. If they showed up to Mass on Sunday, what did it matter what they had been doing on Saturday night, especially if they confessed their sins regularly?

Thus, Catholic Reformation practices penetrated only so far into the hearts and minds of the laity in rural towns and villages. The reforming bishops simply did not have enough control over the laity to make them behave like monks and nuns; the laity interpreted the reforms of the Catholic Reformation in their own way and chose which aspects to follow and which to reject. We can see this in the way that religious education was carried out. The laity wanted their children to have both primary and religious education, so they hired schoolmasters who could teach reading, writing, and catechism. Despite bishops' ordinances requiring that boys and girls be educated separately, parents sent them to school and catechism class together, where they learned the same catechism and read from the same books. They made sure that when their children turned twelve or thirteen, they could recite their catechism backwards and forwards and take their first communion; however, parents decided that once first communion was over, the obligation to memorize the catechism was complete. Bishops still urged adults to study the catechism with their children and retain its lessons in their memory throughout their lives, but adult members of the parish, feeling that the catechetical exercise was appropriate only for children, ignored bishops' pronouncements and expected to be able to participate in the sacraments even if they could no longer recite the catechism in its entirety. Thus, the seventeenth- and eighteenth-century program of religious and primary education was the result of cooperation and compromise between bishops, curés, and parents.

My examination of both catechism and the *petites écoles* provides an example of the way in which church, state, and local authorities interacted in the early modern period and suggests relevant areas of future research. The *petites écoles* demonstrate one of the many limits to absolutism in France, as well as to the confessionalization model of Catholic reform. The state either could not or would not get involved in primary education. The state did not provide any money for schools, nor did they try to dictate what was taught or by whom. The French kings and their councilors were perfectly content to let either the church or local authorities take charge of both religious and primary education. At the same time, historians have assumed that the church was solidly in control of education in the eighteenth century, yet I have shown that the *petites écoles* were in fact administered by local and lay authorities. The church did not finance the schools, and they did not have the final say in how they were run. The dominant theme in the historical literature on post-Revolution education is that during the nineteenth century the state successfully wrested control over education from the church. But if the church had not been in control in the first place, this history of education should examine the transfer of authority from local leaders to state bureaucrats, who certainly built upon the system of *petites écoles* that had been in place for at least a century. More research is needed on this issue, but that research will perhaps show that eighteenth-century rural primary schools provide important background for the educational reforms that came about in the nineteenth century.

Future research might also shed light on the relationship between the implementation of a program of religious education and the French Revolution. In *Reclaiming the Sacred,* Suzanne Desan studied religious and political behavior in the department of the Yonne, including most of the diocese of Auxerre. She found that the vast majority of the communes in the department supported the Revolution, but they also supported a return to traditional church practices and the reinstatement of the church hierarchy. During the years that their churches were closed, Catholics organized their own services, with lay ministers (often the schoolmasters) performing a variety of devotional and sacramental functions, including Mass, vespers, feasts, and processions.[2] Was this remarkable activity the result of nearly a century of consistent religious education in Auxerre's rural parishes? It certainly seems plausible, although it would be a difficult theory to prove using the available sources.

Similarly, Timothy Tackett has postulated that the level of "clericalization" in a given region had an impact on adherence to the Ecclesiastical Oath of 1791 and might even predict the level of religiosity found in those regions in the nineteenth and twentieth centuries. Tackett argues that Auxerre, Reims, and Châlons were less affected by clericalization than other regions, but he also demonstrates the existence of a type of clerical culture that might not have been connected to lay religious culture at all. Regions of the Yonne certainly seemed to have their own religious culture, as Desan demonstrates. In the department of the Marne, 79 percent of curés took the oath, but an even greater number (89 percent) took it in the Yonne.[3] Had a different sort of religious culture been created in Burgundy and Champagne that led to support for the state's revolutionary measures initially but a backlash against them as dechristianization progressed? Was this religious culture created as parents and local leaders adapted the church's program of religious education to fit their needs throughout the eighteenth century?

Evidence presented here cannot fully answer this question, but future research might further illuminate the issue.

No matter what the Revolutionary period held for Auxerre, Reims, and Châlons, it is still significant that by the eighteenth century, religious and primary education was widely available to children of both sexes and of all social classes. Religious and secular learning were both parts of an educational program built from the ground up by parents, schoolmasters, village councils, and parish priests and designed to instill the ethical, moral, and doctrinal values of French Catholicism to the next generation of believers. This educational system was just one part of the larger Catholic Reformation movement, which could not have been successful without the cooperation of both the clergy and the laity, demonstrated so clearly in their joint championing of both catechisms and the *petites écoles*.

Notes

Introduction

1. For just two examples, see Benedict, *Rouen during the Wars of Religion,* and Davis, *Society and Culture.*

2. Talleyrand-Périgord, "Synode de Reims," 810. All translations from French are my own, unless otherwise noted.

3. In the third volume Carrière outlined topics and questions that needed to be developed by future historians, and nearly half of that volume is devoted to the question of the Protestant Reformation and the Catholic Church's reaction to it in the sixteenth century. Jansenism is the primary topic that he focuses on for the seventeenth and eighteenth centuries, however, and the only sort of education that he touches on at all is adult education, mainly through an analysis of sermons.

4. Gabriel Le Bras was a pioneer in the study of popular religious practices, beginning with his *Introduction à l'histoire de la pratique religieuse en France.* His work was followed by a number of histories that focus on one particular diocese; a sampling of these titles includes Pérouas, *Le diocèse de La Rochelle*; Sauzet, *Les visites pastorales dans le diocèse de Chartres* and *Contre-réforme et réforme catholique en bas-Languedoc*; Minois, *La Bretagne des prêtres*; Deregnaucourt, *De Fénelon à la Révolution*; and Baccrabère, *Les paroisses rurales du diocèse de Toulouse.* Éditions Beauchesne also published an extensive series of diocesan histories beginning in the 1960s, but none of these studies deals with catechism or religious education in significant detail.

5. For more on urban confraternities, see especially Barnes, *The Social Dimension of Piety*; and Galpern, *The Religions of the People,* who examines urban confraternities in the larger towns of the Reims, Châlons, and Troyes regions.

Goujard, *Un catholicisme bien tempéré,* 117–46, 337–62, provides an excellent analysis of rural confraternities in the diocese of Rouen.

6. Nalle, *God in La Mancha,* 126, also notes that catechetical education in Spain was most effective in midsize parishes.

7. Châtellier's *La religion des pauvres* was translated into English as *The Religion of the Poor,* and his discussion of the growth of rural spirituality can be found primarily in part 3. For more on the strength of rural religion and the weakening of Catholic fervor in the towns, see Desan, *Reclaiming the Sacred,* 42–47, who deals specifically with the Auxerre region.

8. Chartier, Julia, and Compère, *L'Éducation en France,* 231–32.

9. Fénelon, *De l'éducation des filles,* 1–2, 65–79.

10. I have examined 78 of these catechisms from 60 dioceses, published in the microfiche collection entitled *The Catholic Reformation.* Hézard, *Histoire du catéchisme,* 275–472, lists 103 others published between 1650 and 1800. Figures do not include reprint editions. There were approximately 137 dioceses in France during the seventeenth and eighteenth centuries (including Alsace and Lorraine, the Franche Comté, Avignon, and Cambrai). The 60 dioceses covered in the microfiche collection are the largest dioceses in France and primarily in the northern and central parts of the country. Noticeably absent in the collection are catechisms from some dioceses in Brittany, southern Languedoc, Gascony, and Provence, but Hézard demonstrates that catechisms were published in these regions of France in the seventeenth and eighteenth centuries. The diocesan catechism was clearly a statewide phenomenon in these centuries.

11. Session 24, chap. 3: "Decree concerning reform." See Schroeder, *Canons and Decrees of the Council of Trent,* 194.

12. Historians who argue for the importance of visitation records as a historical source for religious practices in the parish include Delumeau, *Catholicism between Luther and Voltaire,* 134–35; Bergin, *Church, Society and Religious Change,* 175–80; and Venard, "Les visites pastorales françaises."

13. Historians have long recognized the existence of significant cultural and, most importantly for this study, educational differences between northern and southern France. As all three of the dioceses I have examined are in northern France, the arguments I make here should not necessarily be seen as applicable to France as a whole. For more on the north-south split in education and literacy, see Fleury and Valmary, "Les progrès de l'instruction élémentaire"; and Furet and Ozouf, *Reading and Writing,* 5–47.

14. According to McManners, *Church and Society,* 1:177–78, Reims was one of twelve dioceses to have more than five hundred parishes (not including annexes) in 1789. Reims was also an archdiocese, meaning the archbishop

of Reims had some administrative authority over the eight other dioceses in the archdiocese.

15. Literacy rates in France are usually calculated using the data collected by a nineteenth-century schoolteacher, Louis Maggiolo. The results of the Maggiolo report, in a simplified form, were published by the Ministère de l'Instruction Publique et des Beaux-Arts in *Statistique de l'enseignement primaire,* 2:clxvi–clxxiii.

16. For more on ecclesiastical finances, see Bergin, *The Making of the French Episcopate,* 108–37. Revenues in Reims actually dropped in the seventeenth century, but by the early part of the eighteenth century the diocese had recovered and was reportedly worth 45,000 livres in 1723. Ecclesiastical income doubled over the seventeenth century in Châlons, to 21,000 livres in the 1670s. Bergin does not provide figures for Auxerre in the late seventeenth and eighteenth centuries, but Desan, *Reclaiming the Sacred,* 31–75, notes the extreme poverty of parts of the diocese at the time of the French Revolution.

17. This is demonstrated in the four-volume evaluation of visitation records edited by Gabriel Le Bras that provides a guide to the content of medieval and early modern visits. Information about education or catechisms is practically nonexistent in records before the end of the seventeenth century. In Reims, for example, visits done by the deans of Archbishop Charles de Guise (Cardinal of Lorraine) during his episcopate (1538–1574) are concerned with the physical condition of the church and its altars, ornaments, and bells; the finances of the fabric, the curé's income, and the tithe; and the number of priests in the parish and their duties, morals, and residence. The archbishop asked for virtually no significant information about the laity. See Le Bras, *Répertoire des visites pastorales,* 3:405–538.

18. See Le Bras, *Répertoire des visites pastorales,* 1:141–48 for Auxerre and 2:69–84 for Châlons. The only records that exist before 1673 for Auxerre are visits to four villages in 1634, 1642, 1659, and 1667; the 1667 visit mentions a schoolmaster. For Châlons there are no visitation records before a 1626 visit to the deaneries of Joinville and Perthes, which does contain information about schools but only a few brief references to catechisms.

19. Le Bras, *Répertoire des visites pastorales,* 4:69–129. For a comprehensive treatment of reform in Rouen, see Goujard, *Un catholicisme bien tempéré.*

20. Hoffman, *Church and Community,* 99–101, and Strauss, *Luther's House of Learning,* 249–63, both comment on the advantages and disadvantages of visitation records as historical sources.

21. Surprisingly, the 1774 *enquête* has rarely been used by historians. Le Bras mentions it briefly in volume 1 of his *Introduction à l'histoire de la pratique religieuse en France,* 95, and he notes that he examined at least some of the

questionnaires himself. The only other historian to make significant use of both the *enquête* and the deans' visits of the late seventeenth century is Dominique Julia, who published his findings in a series of articles, including "Le clergé paroissial"; "L'Enseignement primaire"; and "Les petites écoles rurales."

22. For example, in their study of the financial, administrative, and curricular aspects of both primary and secondary schools, Chartier, Julia, and Compère, *L'Éducation en France*, 84, recognize that primary education has to be placed in the context of religious reform and the desire on the part of local authorities to establish discipline and order in their communities, but they devote most of their time and attention to questions of literacy. In fact, their most pressing objective is to find evidence of modern pedagogical methods in pre-Revolution schools.

23. This reluctance to examine the existence and importance of local schools began in the late nineteenth century, when the leaders of the Third Republic attempted to improve their image by denigrating church- or parish-run schools and associating their own support of state-administered primary schooling with democratic progress and the battle against ignorance and superstition. Modern historians have perpetuated this trend in more recent works; Ozouf, *L'École, l'Église et la République*, examines this literature and provides a comprehensive study of education in the Third Republic. See also Weber, *Peasants into Frenchmen*, 303–38.

24. Grew and Harrigan, *School, State, and Society*, 31, and table S.1 on p. 251.

25. Huppert, *Public Schools in Renaissance France*, recognized this lack of attention to early modern schools and urged historians to look to the last decades of the fifteenth century to find the beginnings of France's public educational system with the rise of the *collège* — city-supported secondary education. Although his overall purpose is to show how the *collège* system came to be dominated by the church, Huppert still downplays the importance of religious education. His work thus continues to perpetuate a significant misconception in the history of secondary education — namely, that the instruction provided by the religious orders was automatically backward, reactionary, or of lower quality than that in schools run by lay authorities.

26. Furet and Ozouf, *Reading and Writing*, 58–82; Chartier, Julia, and Compère, *L'Éducation en France*, 27–31, 45–48; Grosperrin, *Les petites écoles*, 12–15, 30–31; Viguerie, *L'institution des enfants*, 76, 119; Allain, *L'instruction primaire*, 122–32, 242–74.

27. Maynes, *Schooling in Western Europe*, 84–102, 142–45, argues that it would have been nearly impossible to use an education in primary schools as a stepping-stone to higher education and an increase in wealth or social status in the early nineteenth century. She notes that most peasant- or working-class individuals understood this and thus must have had other reasons for sending

their children to school. Only at the end of the nineteenth century did parents begin to believe that schooling could provide their children with skills and attitudes that would lead toward social advancement.

28. AD Marne, 2 G 276, folder 15.

29. The movement for reform has been called both the "Counter Reformation" and the "Catholic Reformation"; I have used the latter term since the idea of "counter" reform implies that the Catholic Church was only reacting against the Protestant threat, when in reality many of the changes taking place during this time period had nothing to do with Protestantism at all. The first historian to clearly articulate the debate over identification of this movement was Hubert Jedin, in his 1946 article, "Catholic Reformation or Counter-Reformation?" Jedin analyzed the terms and argued that both were needed and in fact described different but intimately related aspects of Catholicism from the fifteenth through the eighteenth centuries. For a book-length treatment of the debate, see O'Malley, *Trent and All That,* who surveys the relevant issues and offers his own term: "Early Modern Catholicism." Because this term does not clearly indicate the fact that there was an active movement toward reform (even if that movement was not uniform), I have not used it here. The term "Catholic Reformation" is more appropriate in this regard and is broad enough to include reforming activities of both the clergy and the laity.

30. On Protestantism, see Benedict, *The Huguenot Population of France;* Dompnier, *Le venin de l'hérésie;* and Hanlon, *Confession and Community.* On bishops, see Bergin, *The Making of the French Episcopate;* Forrestal, *Fathers, Pastors and Kings;* Julg, *Les évêques dans l'histoire de la France;* and Peronnet, *Les Évêques de l'ancienne France.* On the religious orders, see Armstrong, *The Politics of Piety;* Harline, *The Burdens of Sister Margaret;* Leonard, *Nails in the Wall;* Nelson, *The Jesuits and the Monarchy;* O'Malley, *The First Jesuits;* and Selwyn, *A Paradise Inhabited by Devils.* On the Council of Trent, see Tallon, *La France et le Concile de Trente.* The most comprehensive treatment of the institutional church in the seventeenth century is Bergin, *Church, Society and Religious Change.* For the eighteenth century, see the two-volume work by McManners, *Church and Society.* Gallicanism, a highly influential force within the French church, has recently been examined by Parsons in *The Church in the Republic.*

31. Influential works include Bossy, *Christianity in the West;* Châtellier, *L'Europe des dévots* and *The Religion of the Poor;* Christian, *Local Religion in Sixteenth-Century Spain;* Delumeau, *Catholicism between Luther and Voltaire;* Diefendorf, *From Penitence to Charity;* Galpern, *The Religions of the People;* Goujard, *Un catholicisme bien tempéré;* Harline and Put, *A Bishop's Tale;* Hoffman, *Church and Community;* Luria, *Sacred Boundaries* and *Territories of Grace;* Nalle, *God in La Mancha;* Phillips, *Church and Culture;* and Poska, *Regulating the People.*

32. See Wolfgang Reinhard's two articles, "Gegenreformation als Modernisierung?" and "Reformation, Counter-Reformation, and the Early Modern State." Heinz Schilling's articles include "'Konfessionsbildung' und 'Konfessionalisierung'" and "Confessionalization in the Empire."

33. For Germany, see Hsia, *Social Discipline in the Reformation*; for the Low Countries, see Kaplan, *Calvinists and Libertines*; for Italy, see de Boer, "Social Discipline in Italy"; for Spain, see Poska, "Confessionalization and Social Discipline in the Iberian World"; and for Ireland, see Lotz-Heumann, "Social Control and Church Discipline in Ireland."

34. Benedict, "Confessionalization in France?" See also Farr, "Confessionalization and Social Discipline in France"; and Luria, *Sacred Boundaries,* who demonstrates how the boundaries between Catholics and Protestants in Poitou were created and then shifted, stretched, broken, reformed, and hardened over the course of the seventeenth century due to both local and state influences.

35. Bergin, *Church, Society and Religious Change,* xii.

36. Hoffman, *Church and Community*; Tackett, *Priest and Parish*; and Goujard, *Un catholicisme bien tempéré.*

37. The fact that the French state had very little influence over primary education can be seen as evidence of the weakness of the so-called absolutist state. This view coincides with other works criticizing dominance of the discourse of absolutism in French history, especially Beik, *Absolutism and Society,* and Collins, *The Fiscal Limits of Absolutism* and *The State in Early Modern France.*

38. Luria, *Sacred Boundaries*; Froeschlé-Chopard, *La religion populaire en Provence orientale*; and de Boer, *The Conquest of the Soul.*

39. See especially Foucault, *Surveiller et punir*; and Elias, *The Civilizing Process.*

40. Forster, *Catholic Revival in the Age of the Baroque.*

41. Beam, *Laughing Matters.*

42. *Catéchisme ou abrégé de la doctrine chrétienne* (Bourges, 1688), "Avertissement."

Chapter 1. *The Science of Salvation*

1. *Catéchisme du diocèse de Toul* (1736), v–vi; *Catéchisme du diocèse de Saint-Claude,* 4; *Catéchisme à l'usage du diocèse de Laon,* xv; *Catéchisme, ou Exposition de la doctrine chrétienne* (Soissons), iii–iv.

2. Ross, "Scientist: The Story of a Word."

3. For more on the bishops' role in the reform process, see Bergin, *The Making of the French Episcopate*; Forrestal, *Fathers, Pastors and Kings*; and Hayden

and Greenshields, *Six Hundred Years of Reform*. For a comprehensive treatment of the results of French Catholic reform in the seventeenth century, see Bergin, *Church, Society and Religious Change*.

4. The diocesan catechisms were published by bishops, but it is not always clear who actually wrote the text. Some bishops likely were heavily involved in the writing process, while others may have left the job to other clergymen who served in their administrations. All bishops would have approved the catechisms that they published, however; thus, catechisms can represent both the opinions and motivations of the bishops as well as the overall church hierarchy. For a further discussion of the bishops' role in issuing catechisms, see McManners, *Church and Society*, 2:10–12.

5. The most significant study of catechisms in France is Dhotel, *Les origines du Catéchisme moderne*. Dhotel does not examine the diocesan catechisms, however, and sees very little change in catechetical education after 1650. A collection of essays dealing with pre-1660 catechisms in France can be found in Colin, *Aux origines du catéchisme en France*. Two other general works on catechism include Germain, *Langages de la foi*, and Marthaler, *The Catechism Yesterday and Today*. For catechetical education elsewhere in Europe, see Green, *The Christian's ABC*; Strauss, *Luther's House of Learning*; and Bast, *Honor Your Fathers*.

6. Strauss, *Luther's House of Learning*. See Green, *The Christian's ABC*, 557–63, for a thoughtful critique of Strauss's argument.

7. In 1759 the *libraire* Jean-François Behourt of Rouen had more than 12,000 catechisms—a total of 6 percent of all of the works of piety that he had in stock. See Chartier, Julia, and Compère, *L'Éducation en France*, 9. Even as late as 1777, a bookseller in Angers had 823 catechisms in stock, constituting nearly 7 percent of his total inventory (of 12,030 volumes) and 12 percent of all religious books. See Maillard, "Le livre religieux," 387.

8. Brown, *The Cult of the Saints*, 1–22; Arnold, *Belief and Unbelief*, 11–14, 28–32; de Boer, *The Conquest of the Soul*, 323–25. Michael Carroll makes a similar, if slightly more controversial, argument in his *Veiled Threats*, 11.

9. Hézard, *Histoire du catéchisme*, 9–13.

10. For a general study of the evolution of baptism in the early church and in the medieval period, see Cramer, *Baptism and Change in the Early Middle Ages*.

11. Hézard, *Histoire du catéchisme*, 4.

12. Hézard, *Histoire du catéchisme*, 29–40, 52–58, 61–66, 137–38. Bast, *Honor Your Fathers*, discusses a number of fifteenth-century catechetical texts, but they too were used primarily by the clergy.

13. Germain, *Langages de la foi*, 27, notes that more than fifty provincial church councils in the sixteenth century recommended that Gerson's *Oeuvre tripartite* be taught by curés to their parishioners on Sundays. See also Dhotel, *Les origines du Catéchisme moderne*, 29–31, and Hézard, *Histoire du catéchisme*,

156–58. For more on Gerson, see McGuire, *Jean Gerson and the Last Medieval Reformation.*

14. Lemaitre, "Le catéchisme avant les catéchismes," 34–41. For more on medieval catechisms, see Bast, *Honor Your Fathers,* 3–32, who argues that the structure and content of catechisms began to be standardized in the fifteenth century, but the frameworks for teaching the catechism and then evaluating the effectiveness of that teaching were not built until the sixteenth century.

15. Germain, *Langages de la foi,* 32.

16. Dhotel, *Les origines du Catéchisme moderne,* 22. Dhotel provides convincing evidence that Genevan editions of Calvin's catechism were smuggled into France and distributed widely, especially after 1550.

17. Marthaler, *The Catechism Yesterday and Today,* 28. For a more complete discussion of Calvin's catechism, see Millet, "Rendre raison de la foi," and Dhotel, *Les origines du Catéchisme moderne,* 38–50.

18. Dhotel, *Les origines du Catéchisme moderne,* 51.

19. Hézard, *Histoire du catéchisme,* 328, 407, 438.

20. The *Catechism of the Council of Trent* was originally published in Latin as *Catechismus ex decreto Concilii Tridentini ad parochos Pii V jussu editus* in 1566. The original manuscript is no longer extant, but other sixteenth-century Latin editions are available, published by Paulus Manutius (Rome, 1566); De Farris (Venice, 1567); Henricus Aquensis (Cologne, 1567); Kerver (Paris, 1568); and Fabrician (Antwerp, 1587). As far as translations are concerned, the first Italian version was printed by Alexis Figliucci in 1566; French versions appeared in Bordeaux in 1567 and Paris in 1578. A German translation was made in 1568 by Paul Hoffaeus (Dillingen). The first complete English edition, translated by John Bromley, was not printed until 1687. See McHugh and Callan, *Catechism of the Council of Trent for Parish Priests,* xxiii–xxix.

21. Dhotel, *Les origines du Catéchisme moderne,* 61. His extended discussion of Auger's catechism can be found on pages 50–62.

22. Germain, *Langages de la foi,* 39–40; Châtellier, *The Religion of the Poor,* 16.

23. Dhotel, *Les origines du Catéchisme moderne,* 81. See also Marthaler, *The Catechism Yesterday and Today,* 47–48, who notes that by 1597 Canisius's catechism had been translated into fifteen different languages and had been reprinted over two hundred times across Europe. Bedouelle, "L'influence des catéchismes de Canisius en France," 67–86, links the success of Canisius's catechism to the influence of the Jesuits.

24. Germain, *Langages de la foi,* 46–52; Dhotel, *Les origines du Catéchisme moderne,* 107–8.

25. Napoleon imposed an Imperial Catechism on all of the dioceses in France during his reign, but as soon as the monarchy was restored bishops immediately redistributed their own diocesan catechisms.

26. Dhotel, *Les origines du Catéchisme moderne,* situates the origin of the modern catechism between 1541 (Calvin's catechism) and 1660. He argues that because the bishops who published their diocesan catechisms after 1660 borrowed heavily from Calvin, Auger, Canisius, and Bellarmine, among others, there were few changes in the catechetical method after this date. While the content of the catechism may have changed very little, the advent of the diocesan catechism is much more significant than Dhotel admits. Even if the catechisms were in actuality written in the early seventeenth century—and thus owe their origins to that time period, as Dhotel argues—they were taught to the greatest extent only in the eighteenth century. Thus, the eighteenth century is the most important time period for understanding the relationship between catechism and the Catholic Reformation and justifies a careful study of the diocesan catechisms. See also Armogathe, "Les catéchismes et l'enseignement populaire," for a critique of Dhotel's work.

27. *Catéchisme pour les écoles du diocèse de Lyon,* 69–96.

28. Delumeau describes the Catechism of the Three Henris as "a sign, among many others, of the new religious mentality thirsting for dogmatic clarity and doctrinal guidance." See his *Catholicism between Luther and Voltaire,* 201.

29. *Catéchisme ou doctrine chestienne* (Angers, 1679), "Mandement," n.p. The three bishops who published the catechism were Henri Arnauld (Angers, 1650–1692), Henri-Marie de Laval-Boisdaupin (La Rochelle, 1661–1693), and Henri de Barillon (Luçon, 1671–1699). For more about the Catechism of the Three Henris, and its reputation as a Jansenist catechism, see Darricau, "Les catéchismes, au XVIIIe siècle, dans les diocèses de l'Ouest," 604–8; and Dhotel, *Les origines du Catéchisme moderne,* 324–25.

30. Nantes published three catechisms in 1689; Laon in 1698; Aix in 1737–1738; and Arras in 1745.

31. Only one bishop, Armand de Béthune of Le Puy, issued a large catechism without either a small or an ordinary version. See *Catéchisme de la foi, et des moeurs chrétiennes, dressé particuliérement pour l'usage du diocèse du Puy,* vol. 1 (first edition published in 1674). The Le Puy catechism is an anomaly in more ways than one; it was so large that Bishop Béthune decided to publish it in two volumes. The first volume contains 620 pages, with seventy-nine lessons on the Apostles' Creed and forty-one lessons on prayer—a subject usually covered in two or three lessons in most ordinary catechisms. Although I have not seen the second volume, it is likely that it is at least as long as volume 1 since it has to cover the commandments and the sacraments; thus, the entire catechism is probably between 1,200 and 1,500 pages long. This is by far the longest catechism that I have encountered. Hézard, *Histoire du catéchisme,* 422, notes that Béthune's successor published an ordinary catechism, borrowed from the diocese of Sens, in 1707.

32. The four other eighteenth-century large catechisms were published in Grenoble in 1712 (427 pages), Toul in 1732 (395 pages), Aix in 1738 (790 pages), and Arras in 1745 (310 pages). The average length of the ten seventeenth-century large catechisms is 500 pages.

33. The ordinary catechism was most commonly taught to children who were preparing for their first communion; these texts were usually about twice as long as the small versions. The sixty-seven ordinary catechisms published in the eighteenth century range from the 56-page catechism published in 1770 in the diocese of Mende to the 298-page catechism issued by Étienne de Champflour when he took over the diocese of La Rochelle in 1717.

34. Small catechisms would have been used by the youngest children, and in some cases bishops indicated that children or young adults with very limited intellectual capacity could be allowed to take communion as long as they could recite the questions and answers of the small catechism. See the *mandement* of Bishop Barthélemy-Louis de Chaumont de la Galaisière of Saint-Dié, published in the small catechism of 1787. The title page is missing from this catechism, so publication details are unknown. See also the *mandement* of François-Renaud de Villeneuve of Viviers, *Catéchisme du diocèse de Viviers* (1743).

35. *Catéchisme ou Instruction chrétienne pour le diocèse de Sens,* 10–11.

36. *Catéchisme du diocèse de Sens,* "Mandement," n.p.

37. Bishops were the only members of the clergy who had the authorization to confirm; this was one of their most important activities during pastoral visits.

38. For a more extended discussion of the history and uses of feast catechisms, see Dhotel, *Les origines du Catéchisme moderne,* 190–200.

39. *Catéchisme réimprimé par ordre de Monseigneur Louis-Marie de Nicolay* (Cahors).

40. *Catéchisme du diocèse de Meaux* (1687). Other catechisms modeled after those of Canisius include catechisms published in Beauvais in 1680, Châlons-sur-Marne in 1727, Langres in 1792, Lyon in 1665 and 1730, Strasbourg in 1700, Troyes in 1705, and Valence in 1773.

41. *Catéchisme ou abrégé de la foy, et des véritez chrétiennes* (Le Mans, 1695).

42. The Rouen version is *Catéchisme ou abrégé de la foy et de la doctrine chrétienne* (1730). Goujard, *Un catholicisme bien tempéré,* 160–63, analyzes the Rouen catechism in more detail and notes that it was compiled by the archbishop's secretary, Jean Saas. See also Hézard, *Histoire du catéchisme,* 301, 322–23, 351, 440, who claims that the Cahors catechism published in 1781 was also based on the 1730 Rouen catechism.

43. *Catéchisme du diocèse de Viviers,* iv–v.

44. *Catéchisme du diocèse de Saint-Flour,* 13–14. The *mandement* is dated 1748.

45. The title page of this catechism is missing, but the *mandement* is dated 1762. Quotation found on p. 3. Hézard, *Histoire du catéchisme,* 403, lists the title as *Catéchisme du diocèse d'Orléans par l'ordre de Mgr l'illustrissime et révérendissime Louis Sextius de Jarente de la Bruyère.* Hézard also notes that the first catechism issued for the diocese of Orléans was published in 1709; it is likely that the catechism published in 1762 was based on the 1709 version.

46. *Catéchisme ou Abbrégé des véritéz, et des devoirs de la religion chrestienne* (La Rochelle), ii.

47. *Catéchisme imprimé par l'ordre du dernier concile provincial d'Avignon.* The eleven other catechisms were published in the dioceses of Agen (1665), Besançon (1756), Bourges (1688, 1699, and 1707), Grenoble (1712 and 1786), Mâcon (1765), Nîmes (1698), Saint-Malo (1770), and Verdun (1684). Sometimes the authors used different verbs to describe the parts of the catechism (a Besançon catechism used *savoir, pratiquer, recevoir,* and *demander,* for example) or presented them in a different order, but the effect was essentially the same.

48. Dhotel, *Les origines du Catéchisme moderne,* 104–6; Germain, *Langages de la foi,* 51.

49. *Catéchisme ou Instruction chrétienne pour le diocèse de Sens,* 15–18.

50. *Catéchisme ou instruction sur les principales vérités de la Religion Catholique* (Auxerre, 1751).

51. *Catéchisme ou instruction sur les principales vérités de la Religion Catholique* (Auxerre, 1751), 11–12. These questions and answers are typical of most catechisms.

52. *Catéchisme ou instruction sur les principales vérités de la Religion Catholique* (Auxerre, 1751), viii–ix.

53. *Catéchisme du diocèse de Valence,* 21.

54. *Catéchisme où les principales vérités de la doctrine chrétienne sont expliquées* (Grenoble), 79–109, 292–95.

55. *Catéchisme ou instruction sur les principales vérités de la Religion Catholique* (Auxerre, 1751), 120–24.

56. *Catéchisme du diocèse de Grenoble,* 327.

57. *Catéchisme du diocèse de Grenoble,* 332–33. This is neither the first nor the only catechism to publish a similar list of instructions for taking communion; see also *Catéchismes, ou abrégéz de la doctrine chrétienne, cy-devant intitulez, Catéchisme de Bourges,* 368–69.

58. The exceptions to this are the catechisms issued by Jansenist bishops. Jansenism was a somewhat unorthodox form of Catholicism begun by the Dutch theologian Cornelius Jansen (1585–1638), who emphasized original sin, human depravity, and the necessity of grace. Jansenism acquired a number of followers among seventeenth- and eighteenth-century bishops.

The Catechism of the Three Henris was known as a Jansenist catechism; while it does teach children that they should not take communion if they are not in a state of grace, it does not engage in any theological debates. The differences between Jansenist and orthodox catechisms are usually so minuscule that most of the laity never would have noticed. Other so-called Jansenist catechisms were published in 1734 for Auxerre and in 1669 for Sens. For more on Jansenism, see Sedgwick, *Jansenism in Seventeenth-Century France*; Van Kley, *The Jansenists and the Expulsion of the Jesuits from France*; and Doyle, *Jansenism*.

59. See, for example, the three-catechism set published in the diocese of Arras in 1745; none of the twenty-three lesson topics included in each of the three catechisms is on the doctrine of grace. *Catéchisme imprimé par ordonnance de Monseigneur François de Baglion de La Salle* (Arras).

60. *Catéchisme ou abrégé de la foi & des véritez chrestiennes* (Paris), 65–66.

61. Taken from a 1689 catechism, although the title page is missing. Quotation on pp. 360–61. The fourth edition of this catechism was published in 1718 with the title *Catéchisme du diocèse de Nantes*.

62. *L'escole chrestienne, ou l'on apprend a devenir bon chrestien* (Châlons-sur-Marne), 88–90.

63. *Catéchisme ou instruction sur les principales vérités de la Religion Catholique* (Auxerre, 1751), 84–86.

64. *Catéchisme imprimé par ordonnance de Monseigneur François de Baglion de La Salle* (Arras), 348–51.

65. *Catéchisme ou instruction sur les principales vérités de la Religion Catholique* (Auxerre, 1751), 88–90.

66. See Bast, *Honor Your Fathers,* 53–107, for an extended discussion of the fourth commandment and the strengthening of patriarchy in the household.

67. *Catéchisme où les principales vérités de la doctrine chrétienne sont expliquées* (Grenoble), 206–12.

68. *Les devoirs du chrestien dressez en forme de catéchisme* (Agen), 92.

69. Archbishop Michel Phélypeaux de la Vrillière of Bourges warned against this in an *avertissement* to his 1688 catechism, *Catéchisme ou abrégé de la doctrine chrétienne* (Bourges, 1688).

70. *Catéchisme en faveur de la jeunesse du diocèse de Besançon,* 70–71.

71. *Catéchisme du diocèse de Meaux* (1687), 83–84.

Chapter 2. **The Catechetical Method**

1. *Catéchisme du diocèse de Toul* (1736), xvii–xviii.

2. Ariès, *Centuries of Childhood,* 33–39, 128–33.

3. For a good discussion of the Ariès controversy, see Cunningham, *Children and Childhood,* 3–15. Two prominent works that have thoroughly refuted Ariès's principal thesis are Shahar, *Childhood in the Middle Ages,* and Orme, *Medieval Children.* Other general works on European childhood include Fletcher, *Growing Up in England,* and Heywood, *Growing Up in France.*

4. Shahar, *Childhood in the Middle Ages,* 99–100, also notes that until age seven children were seen as innocent and had little need for formal education.

5. Ariès, *Centuries of Childhood,* 100–19.

6. Quintilian, *The Orator's Education,* 1:73, 81, 247–48.

7. See Russell's introduction to Quintilian, *The Orator's Education,* 1:23–26, and Farrell, *The Jesuit Code of Liberal Education,* 357–59.

8. Erasmus, "De pueris," 187.

9. O'Malley, *The First Jesuits,* 226–27, 239; Huppert, *Public Schools in Renaissance France,* 104–29. For a general treatment of the Jesuits in the field of education, see Dainville, *L'Éducation des jésuits.*

10. Farrell, *The Jesuit* Ratio Studiorum *of 1599,* 62. This is the first rule under the heading "Common Rules for the Teachers of the Lower Classes."

11. See especially Rapley, *The Dévotes,* 142–66; and Martin, *Ursuline Method of Education.*

12. Lux-Sterritt, *Redefining Female Religious Life,* 22–25, 81–101.

13. Strauss, *Luther's House of Learning,* 165–75.

14. Quintilian, *The Orator's Education,* 5:59.

15. Carruthers, *The Book of Memory,* 5–12.

16. Erasmus, "De ratione studii," 177–78.

17. Carruthers, *The Book of Memory,* 156–64, 201.

18. Farrell, *The Jesuit* Ratio Studiorum *of 1599.* See especially "Common Rules of the Professors of the Higher Faculties," 25–29; "Common Rules for the Teachers of the Lower Classes," 62–72; and "Rules for Written Examinations," 57–59.

19. Ariès, *Centuries of Childhood,* 114.

20. *L'escole chrestienne, ou l'on apprend a devenir bon chrestien* (Châlons-sur-Marne), "Avertissement aux Curés," n.p. Compare to 1 Cor. 3:2, "I have fed you with milk, and not with meat: for hitherto ye were not able to bear it, neither yet now are ye able."

21. *Catéchisme du diocèse de Lyon pour l'instruction de la jeunesse,* 7–8.

22. *Catéchisme à l'usage du diocèse d'Angers* (1762), iv.

23. Sommerville, *The Discovery of Childhood in Puritan England,* 136.

24. For more on medieval memory techniques, see Carruthers, *The Book of Memory,* especially chapters 1, 3, and 4; Yates, *The Art of Memory;* and Spence, *The Memory Palace of Matteo Ricci.*

25. *Catéchisme du diocèse de Viviers,* "Mandement," n.p.

26. Erasmus, "De pueris," 180; Quintilian, *The Orator's Education*, 5:73.

27. *Catéchisme du diocèse de Nantes*, "Avis sur la maniere de faire le Cate-chisme," n.p.

28. *Catéchisme à l'usage du diocèse de Clermont*, "Mandement," n.p.; *Caté-chisme du diocèse de Belley*, 5.

29. *Catéchisme ou abrégé de la doctrine chrétienne* (Bourges, 1688), "Avertisse-ment," n.p.

30. *Catéchisme où les principales vérités de la doctrine chrétienne sont expliquées* (Grenoble), preface, n.p.

31. *Catéchisme du diocèse de Meaux* (1687), "Avertissement," n.p.

32. *Catéchisme ou abrégé de la doctrine chrétienne* (Bourges, 1688), "Avertisse-ment," n.p.

33. Erasmus, "De pueris," 209.

34. The author of this catechism is unknown, and it is unlikely that it was issued by Bishop Michel-François Couët du Vivier de Lorry, who resigned as bishop of Angers in 1801 after nearly twenty years of service. See Jean, *Les Évêques et les Archevêques de France*, 428. Instead, the author may have been one of the bishop's *grands vicaires*.

35. *Explication et développement de la première partie du catéchisme du diocèse d'Angers*, 15–16.

36. *Explication du catéchisme, sur les sacrements* (Angers), 5–6.

37. These theories are surveyed in Maynes, *Schooling in Western Europe*, 38–60.

38. Locke, *Some Thoughts Concerning Education*, 83.

39. Locke, *Some Thoughts Concerning Education*, 142–43.

40. Locke, *Some Thoughts Concerning Education*, 226–31.

41. See Yolton and Yolton's introduction to Locke, *Some Thoughts Concerning Education*, 18.

42. Locke, *Some Thoughts Concerning Education*, 195.

43. Locke, *Some Thoughts Concerning Education*, 212, 214, 233.

44. For more about educational thought in this period, see especially parts 2 and 3 of Grandière, *L'Idéal pédagogique*. See also Anderson, *Education in France*, and Gildea, *Education in Provincial France*.

45. Rousseau, *Emile*, 257.

46. Bloch, *Rousseauism and Education*, 21–29.

47. Bloch, *Rousseauism and Education*, 4, 59; Py, *Rousseau et les éducateurs*, 572. Instead, Rousseau would have a much more direct effect on ideas about infant and child care. He urged mothers to breastfeed their own children, and he spoke out against swaddling bands and other constrictive clothing. The public—especially women—were very receptive to these ideas, as well as

those about the necessity of physical activity for young children and the importance of play.

48. Chisick, *The Limits of Reform in the Enlightenment*.

49. La Chalotais, "Essay on National Education," 78, 156.

50. La Chalotais, "Essay on National Education," 60; see also Chisick, *The Limits of Reform in the Enlightenment*, 92.

51. La Chalotais, "Essay on National Education," 51–52, 162–63.

52. *Catéchisme réimprimé par ordre de Monseigneur Louis-Marie de Nicolay* (Cahors), "Mandement," n.p.

53. *Catéchisme du diocèse de Mâcon* (1765), iv.

54. Foucault, *Surveiller et punir* and *Histoire de la folie*; Elias, *The Civilizing Process*; Weber, *The Protestant Ethic*.

55. See especially Schilling, "Confessional Europe," 637–64.

56. See Gorski, *The Disciplinary Revolution*, 15–38, and Farr, "Confessionalization and Social Discipline," 276–79, for more on the influence of theories of social discipline on confessionalization history.

57. Gorski, *The Disciplinary Revolution*; Benedict, "Confessionalization in France?"; Luria, *Sacred Boundaries*. For applications of the confessional model outside of France, see Hsia, *Social Discipline in the Reformation*; Kaplan, *Calvinists and Libertines*; de Boer, *The Conquest of the Soul*; and Poska, "Confessionalization and Social Discipline in the Iberian World."

58. I have found thirteen such handbooks, in catechisms published for the following dioceses: Agen (1665), Auch (1764), Bourges (1688), Châlons-sur-Marne (1660), Clermont (1731), Lyon (1767), Montpellier (1701), Nantes (1689), Poitiers (1715), Saint-Flour (1748), Toul (1732), Troyes (1705), and Valence (1773). Some of these were published in other dioceses as well; for example, a Tarbes catechism (1785) includes the rules issued for Lyon, and the handbook first used in the diocese of Nantes in 1689 was published with catechisms in Vannes in the nineteenth century.

59. Julia, "La leçon de catéchisme," makes a similar point in his analysis of the method for both schools and catechisms found in *L'Escole Paroissiale*, a pedagogical text first published in Paris in 1654.

60. For example, the bishop of Valence recommended that catechism be taught at noon: "so that the shepherds or the children who take the animals out to pasture can attend more easily." *Catéchisme du diocèse de Valence*, x.

61. *Les devoirs du chrestien dressez en forme de catéchisme* (Agen), "Avertissement," n.p.

62. *Catéchisme du diocèse de Saint-Flour*, v.

63. *L'escole chrestienne, ou l'on apprend a devenir bon chrestien* (Châlons-sur-Marne), 69.

64. *Catéchisme pour le diocèse d'Auch,* xvii.

65. *Catéchisme du diocèse de Nantes,* "Avis sur la maniere de faire le Cate-chisme," n.p.

66. In the years following the Protestant Reformation, communities that allowed members of minority faiths to build churches often specified that those churches could not install bells. For example, a treaty made between different religious sects in 1648 in Hamburg specified that only the official Lutheran churches could have bells; see Whaley, *Religious Toleration and Social Change,* 4–5. On the other hand, the Edict of Nantes (secret article 34) did allow Protestant churches to have bells.

67. *Catéchisme pour le diocèse d'Auch,* xii.

68. Strauss, *Luther's House of Learning,* 108–31, argues that Protestant leaders in sixteenth-century Germany felt the same way, and they turned toward public, church-sponsored religious education as a result. In Protestant England, however, parents were much more involved in religious education, as the large number of privately printed catechisms can attest. See Cunning-ham, *Children and Childhood,* 45–58.

69. *Catéchisme du diocèse de Saint-Flour,* v.

70. *Catéchismes du diocèse de Montpellier* (1705), 6.

71. *Catéchisme imprimé par l'ordre du dernier concile provincial d'Avignon,* 22.

72. *Catéchisme ou abrégé de la doctrine chrétienne* (Bourges, 1688), "Avertisse-ment," n.p.

73. Both Erasmus and Locke advised against using the rod as well. Eras-mus argued that effective teachers would not need to resort to beating their charges; teachers who hit their students were only trying to cover up their in-competence. See his "De pueris," 205–9. Locke felt that beating children was counterproductive—it only provided an example of exactly the kind of be-havior that education was supposed to prevent. See his *Some Thoughts Concern-ing Education,* 113–14.

74. *Catéchisme imprimé par l'ordre du dernier concile provincial d'Avignon,* 20.

75. *Catéchisme du diocèse de Poitiers,* "Méthode pour bien faire le Caté-chisme," 14.

76. *Catéchisme imprimé par l'ordre du dernier concile provincial d'Avignon,* 26–27.

77. *Catéchisme du diocèse de Nantes,* n.p. Using a baton or hand signals to make silent signs to students was a common method used by the Christian Brothers order, founded by Jean-Baptiste de La Salle. See his *Conduite des Écoles chrétiennes,* 124–32.

78. One of the biggest debates about first communion concerned the age of discretion—theologians disagreed about how old children should be before they were allowed to approach the altar. Borromeo indicated that most

children were ready between the ages of ten and twelve, but other bishops imposed their own standards and recommended that some children wait until fifteen or sixteen. Goubet-Mahé, "Le premier rituel de la première Communion," 54–57, deals with this question, as does Robert, "Fonctionnement et enjeux d'une institution chrétienne," 94–95. For more on first communion, see Lemaitre, "Avant la Communion solennelle," 15–32; and Sauzet, "Aux origines," 33–50.

79. *Catéchisme du diocèse de Poitiers,* 23–26.

80. *Catéchisme, ou Exposition de la doctrine chrétienne* (Soissons), xxi.

Chapter 3. **The Curé and the Catechism**

1. *L'escole chrestienne, ou l'on apprend a devenir bon chrestien* (Châlons-sur-Marne), "Avertissement aux Curés," n.p.

2. For more on the education and training of priests, see especially Bergin, *Church, Society and Religious Change,* 183–207; Delumeau, *Catholicism between Luther and Voltaire,* 179–89; Hoffman, *Church and Community,* 71–97; and McManners, *Church and Society,* 1:321–83. For an international perspective, see de Boer, *The Conquest of the Soul,* 22–27, for Italy; and Parker, *Faith on the Margins,* chap. 2, for the Dutch Republic.

3. *Catéchisme ou instruction sur les principales vérités de la Religion Catholique* (Auxerre, 1751), 6.

4. Visitation records for Auxerre are found in the *Archives départementales* (AD) of the Yonne (in the city of Auxerre), primarily in series G and 1 J. Records for Châlons are in AD Marne, series G, in the city of Châlons-en-Champagne, and those for Reims are found in AD Marne, series 2 G, located in the Marne archive annex in Reims. In Auxerre there are records of a visit made by André Colbert in 1688–1689 and of two visits made by Charles de Caylus—the first between 1708 and 1712, and the second between 1733 and 1736. At the end of the eighteenth century, there are records from visits done by Jean-Baptiste-Marie Champion de Cicé throughout his tenure as bishop, from 1761 until the Revolution. In Châlons records from a visit made to at least a part of the diocese in 1626 have survived; more complete records exist for visits made in 1697 by Gaston-Jean-Baptiste-Louis de Noailles, Nicolas-Charles de Saulx-Tavannes in 1724–1732, and Claude-Antoine de Choiseul-Beaupré in 1748–1752. All of the Auxerre and Châlons visits were made by bishops, but in Reims there are also records of visits done by deans, who were required to visit all of the parishes in their deaneries (there were twenty-four deaneries, or administrative districts, in Reims) and report back to the archbishop. There

are reports for fourteen deaneries that were visited at least once and often twice between 1672 and 1716, during the episcopates of Charles-Maurice Le Tellier and François de Mailly. Records from visits made personally by Archbishop Armand-Jules de Rohan-Guémené also exist for several deaneries. Finally, visits were made by Talleyrand-Périgord at the end of the century.

5. Aston, *The End of an Élite*, 12, notes that only sixteen non-noble bishops held an episcopal office between 1682 and 1700, and only two during the reign of Louis XVI. A complicated patronage system was in place throughout the early modern period that kept bishoprics and archbishoprics firmly in the hands of the nobility. One hundred of the 130 bishops in office in 1787 came from families who claimed noble ancestry that dated back to the sixteenth century or earlier. Another 25 came from more recently ennobled families, leaving only 5 non-noble bishops. All of the bishops of Auxerre, Châlons, and Reims came from some of the most prestigious noble families of France — Colbert, Le Tellier, Champion de Cicé, Saulx-Tavannes, and Choiseul-Beaupré, to name a few.

6. Bergin, *The Making of the French Episcopate*, 275–76, 343–46.

7. For example, the first reforming bishop of Châlons-sur-Marne was Félix Vialart de Herse, the son of a *parlementaire*. He faithfully resided in his diocese, built a seminary, and dedicated much of his fortune to charity in the diocese. Coming from a family experienced in creating administrative structures at the state level, Bishop Vialart, along with his successor Louis-Antoine de Noailles (who later became the archbishop of Paris), built and supported the bureaucratic institutions that would administer the diocese through a series of largely nonresident bishops in the eighteenth century. Despite the fact that eighteenth-century bishops were not known for their exceptional piety or charity, they were considered able administrators, and they even conducted visits — by now a task considered an essential part of the episcopal position for any bishop, not just those who dedicated their time and efforts to reform. See Boulanger, "Deux siècles de réforme catholique," 84–87. See also Jean, *Les Évêques et les Archevêques de France*, 304–9, 318–22, 369–71, for more information about the bishops of Auxerre, Châlons, and Reims.

8. A parallel development occurred within the royal administration as government officials began to use printed survey forms in order to collect information about the provinces. See Rigogne, *Between State and Market*, 17–21.

9. Adam, *La vie paroissiale en France*, 141–70, 288–89.

10. Sauzet, *Les visites pastorales dans le diocèse de Chartres*, 126–34.

11. Minois, *La Bretagne des prêtres*, 194, demonstrates that it was not until after 1730 that the curés of the diocese of Tréguier in Brittany began to conform to ecclesiastical norms of behavior; he notes that out of 530 priests mentioned in visits between 1700 and 1730, 147 were classified as "ivrogne,"

and 41 were "débauché." A total of 237 clerics fell short of the mark on morals.

12. McManners, *Church and Society,* 1:358–73. Like McManners, Timothy Tackett also emphasizes the improvement in views of the curés all over France and demonstrates their improved status in the diocese of Gap. See his *Priest and Parish,* 166–69.

13. For information on the early modern *collège* system in France, see Compère and Julia, *Les collèges français,* and Huppert, *Public Schools in Renaissance France.* For the *collège* in Champagne, see Enright, "The Politics of Education."

14. Julia, "Le clergé paroissial." This pattern is true for most of the dioceses in France according to McManners, who also emphasizes that the expense of a clerical education limited the types of families who could dedicate sons to the priesthood. See his *Church and Society,* 1:326–30. Tackett, *Priest and Parish,* 56–57, gives the following statistics for the social origins of the clergy in Gap: 27 percent from the peasantry (2 percent *journaliers,* 25 percent *laboureurs*), 27 percent from the merchant class, 8.5 percent from the artisan class, and 37.5 percent from the group of "notables" (bourgeois, office holders, and the liberal professions).

15. Although a few seminaries were established in the sixteenth century, most were opened in the seventeenth: 36 between 1642 and 1660, 56 between 1660 and 1682, 25 between 1683 and 1720, and only 7 more between 1720 and 1789. See Bergin, *Church, Society and Religious Change,* 200. The basic authority on French seminaries is Degert, *Histoire des séminaires français.* See also Miller, "The French Seminary in the Eighteenth Century." In addition, Deregnaucourt provides an excellent analysis of clerical education, in seminaries and otherwise, in his study of the diocese of Cambrai, *De Fénelon à la Révolution.*

16. See Degert, *Histoire des séminaires français,* 1:58–60, 312–14 for Reims; 1:96, 219–20 for Châlons; 1:295 for Auxerre. See also Boulanger, "Deux siècles de réforme catholique," 87–89, and his *Réforme et visites pastorales,* 47–48, for more on the seminary in Châlons.

17. Tackett, *Priest and Parish,* 77–79, 139; Bergin, *Church, Society and Religious Change,* 65–67. Bergin notes that in some areas of France in the seventeenth century, the minimum amount required for the patrimonial title was as low as fifty livres, but one hundred livres was much more common in the eighteenth century.

18. Degert, *Histoire des séminaires français,* 1:5–18. Miller, "The French Seminary in the Eighteenth Century," 136–37, argues that in the eighteenth century there were even more varieties of seminaries, but as time went on all of them offered at the very least a year of practical and spiritual preparation for those who would become parish priests and a place of retreat for active clergy. Another type of seminary common in both the seventeenth and eighteenth

centuries was the *petit,* or minor, seminary. Ideally, the *petit séminaire* provided a way to begin clerical education for boys at the *collège* level, but since these institutions accepted all types of students—those who planned on a clerical career and those who did not—most were indistinguishable from any other *collège* run by religious orders. Reims, Châlons-sur-Marne, and Auxerre all had minor seminaries by the second half of the eighteenth century.

19. The following description is taken from Miller, "The French Seminary in the Eighteenth Century," 223–39, who studied rules and regulations for fourteen different eighteenth-century seminaries.

20. Comerford, "Clerical Education, Catechesis, and Catholic Confessionalism," emphasizes that the catechism was not taught in any standardized way in diocesan seminaries until the eighteenth century, although her research focuses more on Italy than France.

21. Tackett, *Priest and Parish,* 75.

22. Julia, "Le clergé paroissial," 211–12, notes the numbers of both curés and vicaires who spent time at a university and concludes that 42 percent were at the level of *gradué* or higher. Unfortunately, none of the visitation records from either Auxerre or Châlons consistently indicates how many curés had received any university degrees. The late eighteenth-century visits for forty parishes in Auxerre reveal that seven curés (17.5 percent) had spent some time at a university; two reported that they held a doctorate, one was *licencié,* and four had a bachelor's degree. But this sample is probably not representative since the forty parishes visited were among the largest in the diocese, and thus more likely to attract university-educated priests. Certainly the percentage for the diocese as a whole would have been much smaller, since the closest universities to Auxerre were in Paris and Orléans.

23. AD Marne, 2 G 284, folder 13.

24. Some curés failed to fill out the *enquête* completely and gave no personal information about themselves; it is possible, then, that an even higher percentage of curés served as assistant priests than is indicated here.

25. In the seventeenth and eighteenth centuries Catholic Reformation bishops used the synod—a general meeting of diocesan clergy—as a tool to gauge the level of discipline and dedication of their curés and to issue any necessary admonitions. See Hayden and Greenshields, *Six Hundred Years of Reform,* for a thorough examination of diocesan synods and pastoral visits in medieval and early modern France. The authors argue that since the synods and the pastoral visits took place regularly for several hundred years in France, they can be used to gauge the progress of reform. They show that in the seventeenth and early eighteenth centuries, both synods and visitations occurred with more frequency and in more dioceses than they had in the past.

26. In large dioceses bishops created a hierarchy of curés to assist with the administration of the diocese. Dioceses were divided into deaneries, or *doyennés,* and one curé in each was chosen as rural dean, or *doyen.* The rural dean at times carried out visitations and inspections and reported back to the bishop. In Châlons rural deans met each year to hear the concerns of the bishop and then were responsible for relaying the information to the other curés in the deanery. Synodal ordinances are found in AD Marne, G 91–92. These synods were called by three different bishops: Gaston de Noailles, Saulx-Tavannes, and Choiseul-Beaupré.

27. Although the visitation records for Châlons are not as detailed on the behavior of curés as those from Reims and Auxerre, the information that is available makes it clear that the majority of curés did comply with this rule, and visitors rarely noted any scandals associated with young servants. For example, in a visit made to fifty-eight parishes in the deanery of Joinville, the visitor noted that twelve curés had servants aged fifty or older. One had a forty-six-year-old servant, but she was noted as "a widow of good example." Eighteen curés had family members living with them, usually a mother or a sister. Two of those curés had only a single niece as a servant; the curé of Thonnance had permission for this but the curé of Vecqueville did not. The other twenty-seven curés either had no female servants or the secretary failed to note them in the record. Many of these curés are listed as having "bonnes moeurs," however. AD Marne, G 112.

28. AD Marne, G 91, p. 4.

29. Boulanger, *Réforme et visites pastorales,* 58–60, also emphasizes that curés in Châlons generally maintained ecclesiastical standards in the eighteenth century. Using visitation records, he notes that the problems bishops cited most frequently concerned dress, hunting, and residence, but these were minor issues. He also notes that most mid-eighteenth-century visitation records indicated whether the curé had a female servant but did not include the servant's age. Boulanger believes this demonstrates that bishops no longer had to worry about young servants, since curés maintained strict celibacy no matter what their servant's age.

30. Bishops were the only members of the clergy with permission to perform this sacrament; thus, if a bishop had not visited recently there were usually dozens if not over a hundred children and young people waiting to receive confirmation. In the deanery of Coole in Châlons-sur-Marne, for example, the bishop confirmed nearly fourteen hundred individuals during a 1747 visit—an average of sixty-six per parish. See AD Marne, G 110.

31. For more on the fabric, see Goujard, *Un catholicisme bien tempéré,* 99–115, 283–335.

32. AD Yonne, G 1617, p. 253. The record is written in the third person; I have taken the liberty of changing it to the first person for the sake of clarity.

33. AD Yonne, G 1617, pp. 137–38.

34. AD Yonne, G 1617, pp. 44–49. Delabarre insisted that he could not live in his own parish because there was no *presbytère* there. Housing for the curé was usually provided by the laity, and it is possible that they were too poor to build a new house or repair an existing one. Disputes over repairs to the *presbytère* were very common in rural parishes, but since Delabarre had been serving in his parish for twenty years, he had adequate time to resolve the dispute. This certainly would have been a sign to Bishop Colbert that Delabarre was not fulfilling his duties properly.

35. AD Yonne, G 1617, p. 266.

36. Visits from 1705 to 1712 are found in AD Yonne, G 1618.

37. Visits from 1733 to 1736 are found in AD Yonne, 1 J 183. This is the last set of comprehensive *procès verbaux* for the diocese of Auxerre. There are records for forty visits done between 1767 and 1786 (found in AD Yonne, 1 J 183), but these give almost no information about the behavior of the curés. This could very well be because curés were behaving in accordance with the bishop's regulations. Instead, most of the bishop's ordinances concentrated on the laity, reminding them to perform their duties as Catholics. No legal action was taken against any of the curés visited, and none of them were asked to spend time at the seminary.

38. In 1716, the deaneries of Saint-Germainmont, Charleville, Braux, Rumigny, and Mézières were visited. AD Marne, 2 G 259, 263.

39. AD Marne, 2 G 259, folder 1, piece 7.

40. AD Marne, 2 G 263, folder 1, piece 7.

41. Visits to Gespunsart and Tarzy are both found in AD Marne 2 G 263, folder 1, piece 7.

42. Goujard, *Un catholicisme bien tempéré*, 48–51, makes a similar argument for the diocese of Rouen, although he suggests that because curés were chosen primarily based on their moral behavior, their intellectual formation was often neglected and parishes were left with curés who were not as educated as they could have been.

43. AD Marne, G 92, p. 50.

44. AD Yonne, G 1617, p. 316.

45. AD Yonne, G 1617, p. 120.

46. Bergin makes this point as well and notes further that seventeenth-century curés were usually happy to limit their instructions to *prônes*. See his *Church, Society and Religious Change*, 296–305.

47. AD Yonne, G 1618. Bishop Caylus emphasized that curés should alternate catechism and *prône* primarily in the ordinances given at the end of this series of visits; nearly every one of the thirty *procès verbaux* from 1711 and the twenty-two from 1712 has this ordinance: "The curé is ordered to review the catechism every two weeks as part of the *prône* during the parish Mass."

48. The records of these visits are in AD Yonne 1 J 183. Only ninety-eight of the *procès verbaux* for this visit contain any information on instruction.

49. Records of visits between 1767 and 1786 are found in AD Yonne, 1 J 184.

50. For records dealing with the deanery of Le Châtelet, see AD Marne, 2 G 279; the deanery was split at some point in the eighteenth century; records for what would become the deanery of La Vallage are in AD Marne, 2 G 280.

51. Very few visitation records from the middle part of the eighteenth century survive for the diocese of Reims, and those that do exist rarely mention anything about the state of parish instruction. Fortunately, the 1774 questionnaire provides many details on education.

52. AD Marne, 2 G 269, folder 2; 2 G 270, folder 4.

53. They visited the deaneries of Dun, Varennes, Buzancy, Cernay-en-Dormois, and Bétheniville. Records for these visits can be found in AD Marne, 2 G 272–78, 283–84.

54. There were three distinct forms used for visits in Châlons; the one used in 1697–1698 had one line for visitors to report on "instructions." This section was often left blank, and it is impossible to tell if the common but vague response of "il les fait les dimanches et les festes" means that curés taught catechism or only gave *prônes* after Mass. In some cases, it is clear that curés did teach catechism, but as in Auxerre and Reims at the end of the seventeenth century, classes were held most often during Lent and Advent and not according to any sort of regular schedule. The *procès verbaux* form used in the 1724–1732 visits did not include a section about catechism or instructions. Any information about religious education from this set of visits comes from the questionnaires that curés filled out just before the bishop arrived; curés often used this questionnaire to report on the regularity with which the children in their diocese attended catechism. Châlons' visits from all three periods are found in AD Marne, G 105–27.

55. AD Marne, 2 G 265, folder 11. The archbishop gave the residents of Champigneul and Mondigny permission to hire a vicaire for their villages, but they had to pay for 100 livres of his 250-livre salary themselves. Paté paid the remainder.

56. AD Marne, 2 G 278, folder 7.

57. For Montmort, see AD Marne, G 124, p. 81. For Thonnance, see AD Marne G 114, pp. 148–49. Curés in Saint-Livières (1730, G 117), Blesme (1732, G 126), Tilloy (1727, G 105), Marolles (1749, G 118), Pringy (1747, G 110), and Fère-Champenoise (1746, G 124) complained specifically about gambling and *cabarets* interrupting services and instructions; general complaints about *cabarets* were nearly universal in both periods.

58. AD Marne, G 121, p. 114; G 117, p. 140.

59. AD Marne, G 120, p. 45; G 110, p. 36; G 105, p. 15.

60. AD Yonne, 1 J 184, p. 412.

61. AD Marne, 2 G 283, folder 9; 2 G 283, folder 12.

62. AD Marne, 2 G 270, folder 7; 2 G 253, folder 17.

Chapter 4. **The Village Schoolmaster**

1. Letters of permission were referred to as *lettres,* and some visitation records note whether or not the village schoolmaster had been approved by the *écolâtre*; it was routine for both schoolmasters and schoolmistresses to teach without having been approved. For example, out of the thirty-eight schoolmasters working in the deanery of Rethel-Mazarin in 1745, we know that ten had their *lettres* and thirteen did not. No information is given for the remaining fifteen schoolmasters, but even if they all had their *lettres,* at least one-third were teaching without approbation. See AD Marne, 2 G 267–68. In the dioceses of Châlons-sur-Marne and Auxerre, no office of *écolâtre* existed; approvals for schoolteachers were given only by bishops. Unofficial or unapproved schoolmasters and schoolmistresses were common in all three dioceses throughout the seventeenth and eighteenth centuries.

2. The archbishops involved were François de Mailly (1710–1721) and Armand-Jules de Rohan Guémené (1721–1762). Judgments for both cases can be found in AD Marne, 2 G 398.

3. Hoffman, *Church and Community,* 98–138.

4. Throughout this chapter and those that follow, I have used the term "schoolteachers" to refer to both male and female teachers. However, in situations where the material applies to only male or only female teachers, I use "schoolmaster" or "schoolmistress."

5. See especially Chartier, Julia, and Compère, *L'Éducation en France;* Grosperrin, *Les petites écoles;* Viguerie, *L'institution des enfants;* Allain, *L'instruction primaire;* and Huppert, *Public Schools in Renaissance France.* Maynes, *Schooling in Western Europe,* 20, on the other hand, argues that church supervision of most local schools in western Europe was "theoretical, spasmodic, superficial."

6. Isambert, *Recueil général des anciennes lois françaises,* 20:317.

7. Vialart de Herse, "Reglemens sur plusieurs points de la discipline ecclesiastique," 40.

8. Vialart published a highly detailed regulation for schoolmasters in 1666: "Reglemens pour les maitres d'école du diocèse de Chaalons," 377–80. Bishop Noailles published a regulation for schoolmistresses in 1685: "Reglemens pour la conduite des maitresses d'école du diocèse de Chaalons," 381–89. Both were reissued with some minor changes in 1770 by Bishop Antoine-Éléonor-Léon Le Clerc de Juigné, "Reglement pour les maitres d'école," 124–41, and "Reglement pour les soeurs d'école," 142–62. In addition, records of clerical synods held in Châlons are full of exhortations to curés, urging them to make more of an effort to ensure that their parishes had acceptable schoolmasters. See AD Marne, G 91–92. Archbishops of Reims published similar (although less detailed) regulations for schoolmasters in 1647 and again in 1788. See d'Estampes de Valançay, "Ordonnances et réglemens," 150–51; and Talleyrand-Périgord, "Synode de Reims," 810–12. Bishop André Colbert of Auxerre issued an *ordonnance* in 1695 dealing with schools; he insisted that curés had the right to regulate schoolteachers and noted that all teachers should be humble, simple, modest, and temperate and avoid gambling, *cabarets,* and hunting. See Quantin, "Histoire de l'instruction primaire," 77–78.

9. In the introductory material to the printed catechisms in most of the dioceses, bishops conform with the twice weekly pattern of catechetical instruction; however, Archbishop Léonor d'Estampes de Valançay of Reims recommended in 1647 that catechism be taught only on Saturdays, but no other lessons were to be given that day in either the morning or the afternoon. See his "Ordonnances et réglemens," 151.

10. See *mandements* in *Catéchisme du diocèse d'Amiens* (1777) (*mandement* dated 1707); *Premier et second catéchismes du diocèse de Nantes*; and *Catéchisme du diocèse de Saint-Claude.*

11. Vialart de Herse, "Reglemens pour les maitres d'école du diocèse de Chaalons," 379.

12. Vialart de Herse, "Reglemens pour les maitres d'école du diocèse de Chaalons," 379. Schoolmistresses were to inspire a similar horror for sin in their students and to emphasize especially the dangers of immodesty; see Noailles, "Reglemens pour la conduite des maitresses d'école du diocèse de Chaalons," 385.

13. AD Yonne, 1 J 184, p. 372.

14. AD Yonne, 1 J 183, p. 358.

15. There are dozens of examples of ordinances prohibiting schoolteachers from teaching boys and girls together. For example, the 1733 ordinances for the parish of Migé (Auxerre) included the following: "We approve

Edme Berdin as schoolmaster for the said Parish at the usual wages and remu-
nerations. We forbid him to teach the girls at the same time as the boys." AD
Yonne, 1 J 183, p. 45. The exception is the visitation records for Châlons-sur-
Marne; unfortunately, visitors in this diocese rarely reported anything more
than simply the presence of schoolteachers. But the *règlements* do insist on sex
segregation, and there is no reason to believe that the situation was much
different in Châlons than it was in Auxerre or Reims.

16. The formula for deans' visits can be found in the Reims *rituel,* or instruction book for the clergy of the diocese. Le Tellier, *Rituel de la province de
Reims,* 328.

17. Talleyrand-Périgord, "Synode de Reims," 810–11.

18. Vialart de Herse, "Reglemens pour les maitres d'école du diocèse de
Chaalons," 380. Schoolmistresses were told in 1685 to make similar visits to
the families of their pupils; see Noailles, "Reglemens pour la conduite des
maitresses d'école du diocèse de Chaalons," 387.

19. Vialart de Herse, "Reglemens pour les maitres d'école du diocèse de
Chaalons," 377–78.

20. Talleyrand-Périgord, "Synode de Reims," 811.

21. d'Estampes de Valançay, "Ordonnances et réglemens," 151; Talleyrand-Périgord, "Synode de Reims," 811; Le Clerc de Juigné, "Reglement pour
les maitres d'école," 128.

22. Vialart de Herse, "Reglemens pour les maitres d'école du diocèse de
Chaalons," 377. Schoolmistresses in Châlons, like women in the female religious orders, were told by Bishop Noailles, in 1685, and by Bishop Le Clerc, in
1770, to go to confession and take communion every two weeks. See Noailles,
"Reglemens pour la conduite des maitresses d'école du diocèse de Chaalons,"
388; and Le Clerc de Juigné, "Reglement pour les soeurs d'école," 143.

23. AD Marne, G 14, piece 103. The records of the synods from the
early eighteenth century show that some schoolmasters did meet with their
colleagues and their deans at some point during the year, and another bishop
mentioned the retreat at a 1728 synod for curés as well. AD Marne, G 92, p. 21.

24. Noailles, "Reglemens pour la conduite des maitresses d'école du diocèse de Chaalons," 387.

25. Noailles, "Reglemens pour la conduite des maitresses d'école du diocèse de Chaalons," 381–89; Le Clerc de Juigné, "Reglement pour les soeurs
d'école," 142–62.

26. Noailles, "Reglemens pour la conduite des maitresses d'école du
diocèse de Chaalons," 385.

27. The letter is found in AD Marne, 2 G 258, folder 18.

28. Vialart de Herse, "Ordonnances Synodales," 58. See similar state-
ments in Bishop Le Clerc's 1770 ordinances, in *Abregé des statuts du diocése de*

Chaalons, 54; and in Talleyrand-Périgord, "Synode de Reims," 812. For Auxerre, I have found no similar ordinance, but it is clear from visitation records that bishops there also expected curés to visit the *petites écoles* and to apprise themselves of the schoolmasters' behavior.

29. Vialart de Herse, "Reglemens pour les maitres d'école du diocèse de Chaalons," 378.

30. See also Barnard, *Girls at School,* 16, who emphasizes the fact that local communities had a great deal of control over the *petites écoles* and over the choice of schoolmaster.

31. AD Marne, 2 G 257, folder 20.

32. In contrast, James Van Horn Melton demonstrates that eighteenth-century schoolmasters and clergy in Prussia did dispute with one another quite frequently. The difference may be due to the fact that in Protestant Prussia schoolmasters were always hoping for a position as pastor, which came with more money and prestige, and they often resented the parish pastor as a result. In Catholic France, where curés and schoolmasters never competed for jobs, conflicts were fewer. See his *Absolutism and the Eighteenth-Century Origins of Compulsory Schooling,* 20–22.

33. AD Marne, 2 G 259, folder 16.

34. AD Marne, 2 G 258, folder 17; 2 G 277, folder 5; 2 G 284, folder 14.

35. AD Yonne, G 1653, folder 16, piece 169 (1680); G 1662, folder 7 (1683).

36. Tackett, *Priest and Parish,* 178–79, argues that curés and schoolmasters were not engaged in any major rivalries in the diocese of Gap largely because the latter spent only a few months of the year in the parish (school was held only in the winter). This does not seem to have been the case in either Reims or Châlons, where schoolmasters usually resided year-round. Tackett does not indicate that schoolmasters played any sort of liturgical role in Gap or in the region of the Dauphiné, but they clearly did in Reims, Châlons, and Auxerre.

37. AD Marne, G 91–92; see especially the report for the synod of 1714, G 91, p. 128.

38. AD Marne, 2 G 272, folder 9.

39. AD Yonne, G 1658, folder 2.

40. AD Marne, G 92, p. 58.

41. AD Marne, 2 G 268, folder 1; 2 G 276, folder 16; 2 G 285, folder 4.

42. The information about Lebon comes from a summary of his life as a schoolmaster, including several extensive sections of his memoir, published in *Champagne Généalogie* ("Maître d'école au bon vieux temps," 54–55).

43. The process of choosing a schoolmaster is also described by Puiseux, *L'Instruction primaire,* 25.

44. "Maître d'école au bon vieux temps," 54.

45. Lebon received two bushels of grain from each *laboureur* who owned two plows, one bushel from each *laboureur* who owned one plow, three francs from each *manouvrier,* and one and a half francs from each household headed by a widow. The community treasury paid him an additional seventy-five francs each year.

46. The exception to this was if a foundation for a school had been set up by a wealthy patron—in those cases the patron or his or her heirs had the right to choose the schoolmaster or schoolmistress. Ferté, *La vie religieuse dans les campagnes parisiennes,* 241–51, notes that such foundations were common in the diocese of Paris, but they were much more rare outside of the capital. Furthermore, if and when the initial foundation money ran out, if the villagers chose to keep the schoolmaster and pay him themselves the right to hire and fire would then revert to the community. See also Maynes, *Schooling in Western Europe,* 24.

47. Allain, *L'instruction primaire,* 133, maintains that competition for schoolmaster positions was fierce in many cases; he notes that in 1674 in Bourbourg (Nord), fourteen candidates presented themselves for one job, and in Lucy-le-Bois (Yonne), there were eight candidates for one job in 1732. But these were most likely rare cases. Visitation records show that curés often had to seek out schoolmasters; if they simply waited for schoolmasters to knock on their doors, the position would be left vacant for years at a time.

48. Puiseux, "La condition des maîtres d'école," 141–60. Allain, *L'instruction primaire,* 133–40, and Grosperrin, *Les petites écoles,* 45–46, also argue that schoolmasters tended to hold their positions for most of their adult lives and then pass the job on to their sons.

49. AD Marne, 2 G 257, folder 13; AD Yonne, G 1619, piece 5, p. 6; AD Marne, 2 G 280, folder 8.

50. AD Marne, 2 G 277, folder 1, piece 15; 2 G 285, folder 1, piece 1. These particular visitation records are quite unique—most visitation records say almost nothing about how long a particular schoolmaster had been working in a village, and this information is rarely found in schoolmasters' contracts either.

51. This figure does not include schools run by religious orders.

52. Maynes, *Schooling for the People,* 43–44, demonstrates that this was a common practice in both France and Germany.

53. AD Marne, 2 G 263, folder 1, piece 7; AD Yonne, G 1649; AD Marne, 2 G 262, folder 7.

54. AD Marne, 2 G 268, folder 14. Sorbon was a parish of 260 communicants in 1774, and there were sixty students in the school. Maynes, *Schooling for the People,* 34–35, describes a similar system of pay for schoolmasters in

the Vaucluse. See also Chartier, Julia, and Compère, *L'Éducation en France,* 26–31, for more information and statistics about schoolmasters' pay.

55. AD Marne, 2 G 264, folder 9. Prez had 155 communicants in 1774. See also Puiseux, *L'Instruction primaire,* 26.

56. Chartier, Julia, and Compère, *L'Éducation en France,* 30–31, note that in some areas of Provence and Languedoc there were schoolmasters who were paid out of the *taille,* but this was never the case in northern France. They also claim that it was more common in eastern France for schoolmasters to be paid from tithes, but at least according to the 1774 *enquête,* this was not true for Reims. See also Maynes, *Schooling in Western Europe,* 23.

57. Huppert, *Public Schools in Renaissance France,* argues that most *collèges* founded in the sixteenth century by laymen ran out of money by the mid-seventeenth century and had to be placed under the jurisdiction of the Jesuits or other religious orders in order to stay open.

58. AD Marne, 2 G 401, pp. 32–119.

59. AD Yonne, D 39. Robert was also entitled to fifty livres from the parish fabric, sixteen livres from confraternities for help at their services, the monthly fees from his students, and the *casuel* from his service at weddings, funerals, and processions.

60. If the week included a feast day, that was considered the vacation day. The contract did not specify how many hours each day the school would be open; most likely Robert would have taught for two to three hours in the morning and two to three more in the afternoon.

61. AD Marne, 2 G 269, folder 8; AD Marne 2 G 260, folder 3.

62. AD Yonne, G 1649.

63. From the contract between Edme Desfoux and the village of Fontenoy in Auxerre. AD Yonne, G 1649.

Chapter 5. *Boys and Girls at School*

1. Isambert, *Recueil général des anciennes lois françaises,* 20:317.

2. Isambert, *Recueil général des anciennes lois françaises,* 21:263–64. Louis himself was only fourteen at the time this edict was issued.

3. Some of the standard works on nineteenth-century education include Anderson, *Education in France*; Moody, *French Education Since Napoleon*; Gildea, *Education in Provincial France*; Gontard, *L'enseignement primaire*; and Prost, *Histoire de l'enseignement.*

4. This was largely due to the influence of Charles Démia, a Lyonnais priest who founded a number of primary schools in the city. Curtis mentions

Démia, but his schools do not substantially influence her overall analysis. For a general treatment of Démia, see Gilbert, *Charles Démia.*

5. Curtis, *Educating the Faithful,* 5–7, 19–23. For two general studies that emphasize gains in nineteenth-century education at the expense of the eighteenth-century *petites écoles,* see Grew and Harrigan, *School, State, and Society,* and Weber, *Peasants into Frenchmen.* For more on girls' education in the nineteenth century, see Bricard, *Saintes ou pouliches,* and Rogers, *From the Salon to the Schoolroom.*

6. See especially Chartier, Julia, and Compère, *L'Éducation en France;* Grosperrin, *Les petites écoles;* Viguerie, *L'institution des enfants;* and Allain, *L'instruction primaire.* Barnard, *Girls at School,* does acknowledge that the ordinances pertaining to the separation of boys and girls in the *petites écoles* were often ignored, although the majority of his work deals with the education of noble girls.

7. See Sonnet, *L'éducation des filles,* who surveys girls' schools in Paris in the eighteenth century. Rapley, *The Dévotes,* and Fiévet, *L'invention de l'école des filles,* deal with the various teaching congregations. Lux-Sterritt, *Redefining Female Religious Life,* provides a good survey of the Ursulines in the seventeenth century.

8. Jo Ann Hoeppner Moran Cruz ran into a similar problem in her study of medieval schools in England; she used wills to find information about schools, demonstrating that even though most schools did not leave official records, a great number of them did exist in the two centuries before the Reformation. See her *The Growth of English Schooling.*

9. AD Marne, 2 G 400–401.

10. Châlons does not seem to have had an *écolâtre* after the fourteenth century, and there are no records of appointments of schoolmasters. Between 1626 and 1629 Bishop Henri-Cosme Clausse de Marchaumont visited 110 parishes and annexes in the deaneries of Joinville and Perthes, and 78 of the surviving records contain information about schools. Fifty-four of the communities had schoolmasters and 24 did not. If we take the 78 parishes in these two deaneries as representative of the diocese as a whole, then about 70 percent of the parishes had regular schoolmasters. Even if we assume that there actually were no schools in the other 32 communities, then at least half of the parishes had schools. AD Marne, G 111. Puiseux, *L'Instruction primaire,* 10, also insists that schoolmasters were commonplace in Châlons in the seventeenth century; he notes that the parish registers, which indicated the professions of individuals in the register after 1667, are full of schoolmasters, although their numbers have not been systematically counted.

11. Deans' visits for the twenty-three rural deaneries of Reims can be found in AD Marne, 2 G 254–86.

12. AD Marne, G 108, 112, 116, 119, 125.

13. It is unclear from the record whether or not the parish of Saint-Denis had a house of *petits frères* of its own or just sent the children to an institution in a neighboring parish. But the parishes of Saint-Hilaire, Saint-Julien, Saint-Jacques, Saint-Martin, and Saint-Timothée all seem to have established their own houses. For the girls, the parish of Saint-André employed the Soeurs du Saint-Enfant-Jésus, and the Orphelines operated in Saint-Hilaire. Saint-Julien, Saint-Jacques, and Saint-Martin had established female religious teachers in their parishes, but none of the curés mention the specific order in their questionnaires.

14. The diocese of Paris was also well stocked with schools at the end of the seventeenth century; Ferté, *La vie religieuse dans les campagnes parisiennes,* 241, notes that there were enough foundations in the diocese in the seventeenth century for every parish to have a school. Most of the schools in Reims and Châlons were funded by local communities rather than foundations, however. See also Chartier, Julia, and Compère, *L'Éducation en France,* 19–21, who provide approximations of the numbers of *petites écoles* for a number of dioceses in the seventeenth and eighteenth centuries.

15. The responses to the questionnaire are found in AD Yonne, G 1649.

16. Clamecy, Cravant, Donzy, and Saint-Bris had members of the religious orders teaching the girls, and Chevannes, Toucy, Varzy, and Vermenton had secular mistresses. These parishes were among the largest in the diocese; each had between seven hundred and twelve hundred communicants. Auxerre itself had both religious and lay schoolmasters and mistresses.

17. AD Yonne, G 1651–68. Auxerre had 202 parishes at the end of the seventeenth century (not including the urban parishes of Auxerre itself), and at least one of Bishop Colbert's reports, or *états,* survives for 188 of those parishes. The *états* are dated from 1673 to 1684. Like the rural deans in Reims, the curés were given a list of things on which to report dealing with both the temporal and the spiritual aspects of parish life: the revenue of the curé, superstitions and scandals, heretics, the capabilities of the parish midwife, and, most importantly, the presence of a schoolmaster. See also Quantin, "Histoire de l'instruction primaire." Quantin's research shows that schoolmasters did exist in the diocese in the early part of the seventeenth century, although they were few and far between: only 26 of the 99 parishes that Quantin studied had schoolmasters at some point before 1670. For the final quarter of the seventeenth century, Quantin's work fills in some of the gaps in the reports; these two sources, combined with the 1699 questionnaire, provide a much more complete assessment of primary education than the questionnaire alone.

18. Chartier, Julia, and Compère, *L'Éducation en France,* 21, give an even lower percentage, claiming that only 31 percent of the parishes in the diocese of Auxerre had schools in 1699.

19. AD Yonne, G 1651, folder 2, piece 6.

20. See AD Yonne, G 1649 for the questionnaires; for Escolives see also G 1658, folder 10, and Quantin, "Histoire de l'instruction primaire," 131; for Saint-Sauveur, see also G 1619, piece 15, p. 7; for Leugny, see also G 1618, p. 626, and Quantin, "Histoire de l'instruction primaire," 138.

21. AD Yonne, 1 J 183, G 1618.

22. AD Yonne, 1 J 184, G 1619; see also Quantin, "Histoire de l'instruction primaire."

23. Fénelon, *De l'éducation des filles,* 1–2, 65–79.

24. Prévot, *La première institutrice de France,* surveys the life and work of Madame de Maintenon and includes a number of her letters; see a larger collection of those letters in Lavallée, *Entretiens sur l'éducation des filles.*

25. Fleury, *Traité du choix et de la méthode des études,* 264–70.

26. Choudhury surveys these writings in chapter 5 of her *Convents and Nuns.*

27. For more on the popular reception of *Émile,* see Bloch, *Rousseauism and Education,* 21–29.

28. Rousseau, *Emile,* 364.

29. Julia, *Les trois couleurs de tableau noir,* 310–31. For a sampling of eighteenth-century writings on national education, see de la Fontainerie, *French Liberalism and Education.*

30. Rousseau, *Emile,* 396–97.

31. Chisick, *The Limits of Reform in the Enlightenment,* 77–91. See also Barnard, *Girls at School,* 72–73.

32. For information about girls' schools in Reims, see the records of the deanery of La Chrétienté, AD Marne, 2 G 253. Information about the schools in Châlons is found in Puiseux, *L'Instruction primaire,* 44–48. For Auxerre, see AD Yonne, G 1652.

33. Rapley, "Fénelon Revisited," 299–318. For more on the teaching congregations, see Dubois, "The Education of Women," 1–19; Lux-Sterritt, *Redefining Female Religious Life*; Chartier, Julia, and Compère, *L'Éducation en France,* 231–47; and Rapley, *The Dévotes.* Each of these authors sees the schools of the teaching congregations as the only schools available for non-noble girls.

34. AD Marne, 2 G 253, folders 1 and 2.

35. Rapley, *The Dévotes,* 8, states that the "vast majority of schoolgirls of the Old Regime" were educated by members of the religious orders or by the teaching congregations. While this may have been true in large towns and cities, most schoolgirls in France lived in rural areas, where they were taught in the *petites écoles* by lay schoolmasters and mistresses.

36. See the important articles on women's work by Davis, "Women in the Crafts in Sixteenth-Century Lyon," and Collins, "The Economic Role of

Women in Seventeenth-Century France." See also Wiesner, *Women and Gender in Early Modern Europe,* 102–40.

37. AD Yonne, D 38.

38. AD Marne, 2 G 258, folder 1, piece 5, p. 16; AD Yonne, 1 J 184, p. 46; AD Yonne, G 1655, folder 3.

39. AD Marne, 2 G 255, folder 5; AD Marne, 2 G 282, folder 18; AD Yonne, G 1616; AD Yonne, G 1618.

40. Puiseux, *L'Instruction primaire,* 40–41, takes the bishops' ordinances at face value and assumes that they were followed; evidence from visitation records contradicts this. See also Boulanger, *Réforme et visites pastorales,* 134. Barnard, *Girls at School,* shows that both sexes were routinely taught together in the seventeenth century.

41. AD Marne, 2 G 278, folder 14.

42. AD Marne, 2 G 276, folder 9; AD Marne, 2 G 286, folder 1, piece 18; AD Marne, 2 G 261, folder 5.

43. AD Marne, 2 G 270, folder 6. Interestingly enough, the king indicated in his 1698 edict that schoolmistresses should receive at least one hundred livres a year in compensation.

44. AD Yonne, G 1617, p. 182; AD Yonne, 1 J 184, p. 296. A husband and wife team was also teaching in 1736; see AD Yonne, 1 J 183, p. 463.

45. AD Marne, 2 G 284, folder 2.

46. AD Marne, 2 G 254, folder 7; 2 G 256, folder 4.

47. AD Yonne, G 1649; 1 J 183, pp. 270, 383.

48. AD Marne, G 114, p. 263; G 117, p. 161; G 118, p. 94.

49. AD Marne, 2 G 267, folder 7; 2 G 271, folder 10; 2 G 256, folder 14.

50. AD Marne, 2 G 269, folder 10; 2 G 270, folder 7.

51. AD Yonne, 1 J 183, p. 198; 1 J 184, p. 145.

Chapter 6. **Learning to Read, Write, and Recite**

1. See especially Houston, *Literacy in Early Modern Europe;* Furet and Ozouf, *Reading and Writing;* and Ferguson, *Dido's Daughters.*

2. The number of women who signed their marriage record in the department of the Marne, which included parts of the dioceses of Châlons-sur-Marne and Reims, increased by 169.72 percent between 1686 and 1820. The percentage increase in signature rates for women in France as a whole is 148.68 percent, and for men 87.03 percent.

3. Because this study deals primarily with literacy rather than numeracy, I discuss only reading and writing in this section and omit arithmetic. In addition, it is unlikely that schoolmasters taught most children anything more

than how to recognize numerals. For a brief treatment of how students were taught basic math, see Grosperrin, *Les petites écoles,* 97–98; and Chartier, Julia, and Compère, *L'Éducation en France,* 135–36.

4. Ferguson, *Dido's Daughters,* 67–68; Chartier, Julia, and Compère, *L'Éducation en France,* 117–18; Grosperrin, *Les petites écoles,* 75.

5. La Salle, *Conduite des Écoles chrétiennes,* 42.

6. Grosperrin, *Les petites écoles,* 80–82; Chartier, Julia, and Compère, *L'Éducation en France,* 126–28.

7. La Salle, *Conduite des Écoles chrétiennes,* 16–40. See also Grosperrin, *Les petites écoles,* 83–85, for more on the issue of teaching children to read in French rather than Latin.

8. Furet and Ozouf, *Reading and Writing,* 76. See also Grosperrin, *Les petites écoles,* 93–96; Chartier, Julia, and Compère, *L'Éducation en France,* 132–35; and Thomas, "The Meaning of Literacy," 100.

9. La Salle, *Conduite des Écoles chrétiennes,* 49.

10. The thirty-two contracts that exist for the diocese of Auxerre can be found in AD Yonne, D 39; G 1642, 1647, 1649, 1662. See also Grosperrin, *Les petites écoles,* 54.

11. The results of the Maggiolo report, in a simplified form, were published by the Ministère de l'Instruction Publique et des Beaux-Arts in *Statistique de l'enseignement primaire,* 2:clxvi–clxxiii. This report does not include the statistics from 1872 to 1876, and as my focus is on the eighteenth century, I have not felt the need to use them here. For more on Maggiolo and his work, see Furet and Ozouf, *Reading and Writing,* 5–47.

12. The following departments had higher literacy rates according to the Maggiolo report: Calvados (82.51 percent) and Manche (82 percent) in Normandy; Doubs (80.71 percent) and Jura (88.88 percent) in the Franche-Comté, bordering Switzerland; and Meurthe (88.2 percent), Moselle (84.81 percent), Meuse (90.64 percent), and Vosges (92.18 percent) in Lorraine, the region that borders Champagne to the east.

13. Fleury and Valmary, "Les progrès de l'instruction élémentaire," 71–92.

14. Furet and Ozouf, *Reading and Writing,* 34–47; Chartier, Julia, and Compère, *L'Éducation en France,* 92–105.

15. Furet and Ozouf, *Reading and Writing,* 34–35.

16. A recent study of signature rates in Champagne shows that Maggiolo's data is very reliable for that region, although it does conceal some geographical variations. Nahoum, "En Champagne: signatures au mariage," demonstrates that the areas of the province involved in viticulture had the highest signature rates, while heavily forested areas had the lowest.

17. Desan, *Reclaiming the Sacred,* 34.

18. Furet and Ozouf, *Reading and Writing*, 11–23. Cressy, *Literacy and the Social Order*, defends the use of signatures to calculate literacy, as does Maynes, *Schooling in Western Europe*. See also Wiesner-Hanks, *Gender in History*, 188–200; Ferguson, *Dido's Daughters*, 61–82; and Thomas, "The Meaning of Literacy," 102–3, for critiques of the methods traditionally used to calculate early modern literacy.

19. Grosperrin, *Les petites écoles*, 93.

20. Grosperrin, *Les petites écoles*, 140–42, explains women's low signature rates by arguing that girls did not attend the *petites écoles* as often as boys, and that if they did attend, they spent fewer months in school. Yet he does not provide any convincing evidence for this fact. Since bishops repeatedly had to issue ordinances against boys and girls attending school together, and since the attendance figures in table 6.4 show at the very least equal numbers of both sexes in schools, it seems more likely that they spent just as much if not more time in school, although perhaps that time was devoted to reading rather than writing. Barnard, *Girls at School*, 3, also insists that girls did not attend school with as much regularity as their brothers did, despite the fact that he shows that coeducational schools were normal for the period.

21. Houston, *Literacy in Early Modern Europe*, 4. See also Thomas, "The Meaning of Literacy," 97–100; and Graff, *The Labyrinths of Literacy*.

22. AD Marne, 2 G 273, folder 2 (1779).

23. AD Yonne, G 1640, folder 7.

24. AD Marne, 2 G 286, folder 1, piece 18, p. 12 (1672).

25. See Rapley, *The Dévotes*, 163, who emphasizes that any girl from any social class would have learned some sort of handwork, needlework, or sewing in seventeenth- and eighteenth-century schools. This certainly would have been true in schools run by the religious teaching congregations; schoolmasters' wives who helped their husbands in the schoolroom may have focused on teaching girls practical skills as well, although there is no direct evidence for this in any of the visitation records or contracts.

26. Houston, *Literacy in Early Modern Europe*, 99–104. See also Maynes, *Schooling in Western Europe*, 7–20.

27. Johansson, *The History of Literacy in Sweden*, 63–64.

28. Isambert, *Recueil général des anciennes lois françaises*, 20:317.

29. Ferguson, *Dido's Daughters*, 61–82, offers a convincing critique of the methods that historians and others have used to calculate literacy in the medieval and early modern periods; she argues that concrete evidence that could lead to any sort of statistical certainty about literacy rates simply does not exist. Instead, we should look at literacy as an unstable, ambiguous, and culturally determined concept that meant different things for men and women

and for members of different social orders. She suggests that instead of trying to compile statistics about literacy, we should examine it as a way to understand culture and gender. Rather than using signatures as the most important source about literacy, she argues that other types of sources be used, including wills, book production, book ownership, school curricula, letters, literary works, inventories, and court records. To this list I would add church documents, such as visitation records, clerical correspondence, catechisms, and ordinances and regulations issued by bishops.

30. Weber, *Peasants into Frenchmen,* 304–5.

31. Nadaud, "Memoirs of Léonard, a Former Mason's Assistant," 185–89.

32. McManners, *Church and Society,* 2:98, argues that most ordinary people considered Mass attendance necessary every Sunday, despite the fact that the Clergy of France actually required a lesser standard: in 1645, they decreed that only individuals who had missed more than one Sunday Mass out of three could be prosecuted for nonattendance.

33. These records, for visits between 1767 and 1786, are found in AD Yonne, 1 J 184.

34. The Easter duty consisted of several steps. During Lent, each individual was required to confess his sins to his own parish priest. The priest would then issue the appropriate penance. The priest had to be informed that the penance had been completed before the individual was allowed to approach the altar. This could be done during any number of Sunday Masses during the Easter season—the Easter duty did not actually have to be completed on Easter Sunday itself. In addition, some individuals preferred to take communion at a church other than their own parish church. In this case, the individual would still have to confess to his own priest, but the priest could issue a ticket indicating that the penance had been completed, which would then be shown to the officiating priest at any other church.

35. AD Yonne, 1 J 184, pp. 433–34; 1 J 184, p. 383; 1 J 184, p. 229. See also McManners, *Church and Society,* 2:94–95, who notes that Easter communion was nearly universal in the villages and small towns; only in the largest towns were large portions of the population failing to comply with the church's requirement of yearly confession and communion.

36. AD Marne, G 105, p. 56.

37. AD Marne, G 118, pp. 161, 163.

38. McManners insists that incidents of large numbers of people confessing but not taking communion were rare exceptions rather than the rule; he argues that cases like these were probably the result of disputes over tithes or the suppression of a confraternity. The noncommunicants are thus indications of a power struggle between the curé and the laity, rather than of de-

creased desire for religious conformity. McManners, *Church and Society,* 2:95. Boulanger, *Réforme et visites pastorales,* 88, also downplays the few cases in which large numbers of people failed to complete their Easter duty and argues that for the most part, Easter confession and communion were universal.

39. Sabean, *Power in the Blood,* 37–60, describes similar circumstances in a Protestant community in Germany in the sixteenth century.

40. AD Marne, 2 G 258, folder 14; 2 G 263, folder 4.

41. AD Marne, 2 G 274, folder 8; 2 G 273, folder 2; 2 G 287, folder 19.

42. AD Marne, 2 G 270, folder 7; 2 G 281, folder 13.

43. AD Marne, 2 G 278, folder 7.

44. AD Marne, 2 G 257, folder 20; 2 G 255, folder 16; 2 G 255, folder 18; 2 G 267, folder 6.

45. AD Marne, 2 G 255, folder 18; 2 G 265, folder 11; 2 G 261, folder 3.

46. AD Marne, 2 G 263, folder 4; 2 G 254, folder 13.

47. Hoffman, *Church and Community,* 167–70.

48. AD Marne, 2 G 256, folder 4. In his work on curés in the diocese of Gap, Timothy Tackett emphasizes that, by the eighteenth century, curés had begun to see themselves as particular advocates for the poor in their parishes. In addition to doling out church funds, they often contributed their own money to poor relief and even offered small loans to their parishioners, with the full knowledge that they would probably never be repaid. See his *Priest and Parish,* 157–59.

49. AD Marne, 2 G 256, folder 18; 2 G 268, folder 9; 2 G 278, folder 14; 2 G 286, folder 2.

50. Goujard, *Un catholicisme bien tempéré,* 67–68, shows that requests for a greater clerical presence were frequent in the diocese of Rouen as well.

51. AD Marne, 2 G 265, folder 13; 2 G 266, folder 9.

52. AD Marne, 2 G 273, folder 3.

53. AD Yonne, G 1651, folder 10; G 1657, folder 2; G 1653, folder 4. Apparently, the inhabitants of Beaumont were still unable to procure enough funds: the village remained dependent on Chemilly throughout the eighteenth century.

54. For a comprehensive treatment of the *cahiers,* see Shapiro and Markoff, *Revolutionary Demands.*

55. Laurent, *Reims et la région rémoise,* 695. For Châlons' *cahiers,* see Laurent, *Département de la Marne, Cahiers de doléances.* The general *cahier* of the Third Estate of the Baillage of Auxerre is found in AD Yonne, L 169, piece 1.

56. The *portion congrue*—the salary that curés received from the primary tithe-holder—was set at three hundred livres a year until 1768, when it was raised to five hundred livres. In 1786, it was set at seven hundred livres due to the rising price of grain in France as a whole. Curés who were themselves the

primary tithe-holders could theoretically earn more than the *portion congrue,* but this was rarely the case. See McManners, *Church and Society,* 1:335, 344. See also Tackett, *Priest and Parish,* 124.

57. AD Marne, 2 G 267, folder 7.

Conclusion

1. Jamerey-Duval, *Mémoires,* 112.
2. Desan, *Reclaiming the Sacred,* 93–104.
3. Tackett, *Religion, Revolution, and Regional Culture,* 341, 363.

Bibliography

Archival Sources

Archives Départementales de l'Yonne
    Series D, numbers 1–41
    Series G, numbers 1600, 1602, 1608–12, 1617–19, 1622, 1636, 1638,
        1640–43, 1647, 1649, 1651–68, 1690
    Series 1 J, numbers 183–84
    Series L, number 169
Archives Départementales de la Marne
    Series G, numbers 14, 91–92, 98, 105–27, 134
    Series 2 G, numbers 250–51, 253–87, 398–401

Printed Primary Sources: Catechisms

Included in this list are catechisms found in a microfiche collection, *The Catholic Reformation, including French Diocesan Catechisms, 1615–1900* (Leiden: Inter Documentation Co., 1987), and those mentioned by Pierre-Modeste Hézard in his *Histoire du catéchisme depuis la naissance de l'église jusqu'à nos jours* (Paris: Victor-Retaux, 1900). Catechisms are organized by diocese.

Agde
Catéchisme ou abrégé de la doctrine chrétienne. Béziers: Et. Barbat, 1733.
    Bishop Claude-Louis de la Chatre (1726–1740).

Agen

Les devoirs du chrestien dressez en forme de catéchisme. 6th ed. Paris: Pierre Le Petit, 1677.

> First edition published in 1665; 14th edition published in 1751. Bishop Claude Joly (1664–1678). Includes a small and a large catechism.

Aire

Catéchisme ou abrégé de la foi et des vérités chrétiennes. Bayonne: Aluseau, n.d.
Bishop Plaicart de Raigecourt (1757–1783).

Aix

Catéchisme de la doctrine chrétienne. 1713.

> Archbishop Charles-Gaspar-Guillaume de Vintimille du Luc (1708–1729).

Catéchisme, ou abrégé de la doctrine chrétienne composé par Mgr Jean-Baptiste Antoine de Brancas, Archevêque d'Aix, pour l'usage de son diocèse. Aix: Veuve d'Augustin Adibert, 1737.

> Introduction dated January 6, 1737. Archbishop Jean-Baptiste-Antoine de Brancas (1729–1770). A small and an ordinary catechism.

Grand catéchisme par demandes et par réponses, composé par Mgr Jean-Baptiste Antoine de Brancas, Archevêque d'Aix, à l'usage de son diocèse. 2 vols. Aix: René Adibert, 1738.

> Introduction dated January 6, 1737. Archbishop Jean-Baptiste-Antoine de Brancas (1729–1770). Large catechism only.

Amiens

Catéchisme fait par le commandement de Mgr. l'Illustrissime et Révérendissime Evêque d'Amiens. Amiens: Veuve Robert Hubart, 1685.

> Introduction dated November 8, 1673. Bishop François Faure (1653–1687).

Catéchisme du diocèse d'Amiens. Amiens: Nic. Caron Hubault, 1701.

> Introduction dated October 7, 1699. Bishop Henri Feydeau de Brou (1687–1706). Ordinary catechism only.

Catéchisme du diocèse d'Amiens. Amiens: Louis-Charles Caron, 1777.

> Introduction dated July 25, 1707. Bishop Pierre de Sabatier (1706–1733). Small catechism only.

Angers

Catéchisme ou doctrine chestienne. 2nd ed. Paris: Antoine Dezallier, 1679.

> "Catechism of the Three Henris." First edition printed in 1676. Bishop Henri Arnauld (1650–1692). Another edition, with a new small catechism, published in 1684.

Catéchisme du diocèse d'Angers, par ordre de Mgr. Pelletier. 1697.
Bishop Michel le Peletier (1692–1706).

Catéchisme à l'usage du diocèse d'Angers. 1719.
Introduction dated December 1, 1719. Bishop Michel Poncet de la Rivière (1706–1730). Reprinted in 1734 and 1738 by Bishop Jean de Vaugirault (1730–1758).

Catéchisme à l'usage du diocèse d'Angers. Angers: Pierre-Louis Dubé, 1762.
Introduction dated September 18, 1761. Bishop Jacques de Grasse (1758–1782). Ordinary catechism only. Reprinted in 1790 and 1800.

Explication et développement de la première partie du catéchisme du diocèse d'Angers. Angers: Citoyens Mame, Père et Fils aîné, 1801.

Explication du catéchisme, sur les sacrements. Angers: Veuve Pavie, 1802.

Explication du catéchisme, sur la loi de Dieu, Ou sur les commandements de Dieu et de l'église, 1803.

Arras

Catéchisme du diocèse de Nantes à l'usage du diocèse d'Arras. Arras: Urbain César Duchamp, 1719.
Introduction dated March 27, 1719. Bishop Guy de Sève de Rochechouart (1670–1721).

Catéchisme imprimé par ordonnance de Monseigneur François de Baglion de La Salle. Douay: J. F. Willerval, 1745.
Bishop François de Baglion de La Salle (1725–1752). Small, ordinary, and large catechisms. Small and ordinary versions reprinted in 1766.

Auch

Catéchisme pour le diocèse d'Auch avec l'exercice du chrétien par Mgr de Montillet. 2nd ed. Auch: J. Destadens, 1764.
Includes two introductions from the same archbishop, Jean-François de Chastellard de Montillet de Grenaud (1742–1776), dated 1743 and 1764. Small and ordinary catechisms.

Autun

Catéchisme ou abrégé de la foi et des vérités chrétiennes. Moulins: Denis Vernoy, 1693.
Bishop Gabriel de Roquette (1666–1702). Reprinted in 1779. Small and ordinary catechisms.

Auxerre

Catéchisme ou instruction sur les principales vérités de la Religion Catholique. Auxerre: François Fournier, 1751.
Introduction dated September 22, 1734. Bishop Charles de Caylus (1704–1754). Ordinary catechism only.

Catéchisme ou instruction sur les principales vérités de la Religion Catholique. Auxerre:
L. Fournier, 1821.
First edition published in 1720. The 1821 edition includes an introduction
dated 1725 and written by Bishop Charles de Caylus (1704–1754),
and a second introduction dated 1755 and written by Bishop Jacques-
Marie de Caritat de Condorcet (1754–1761).

Avignon
*Catéchisme imprimé par l'ordre du dernier concile provincial d'Avignon, pour être seul en-
seigné dans les diocèses de la province.* Avignon: Alexandre Giroud, 1763.
First published in 1725. Archbishop François-Maurice Gonterio
(1705–1742). Reprinted at least twice before 1800, in 1774 and 1790.
Small and ordinary catechisms. Also used in Digne.

Bayeux
Catéchisme du diocèse de Bayeux. 1700.
Bishop François de Nesmond (1662–1715).
Catéchisme ou abrégé de la doctrine chrétienne. Bayeux: Gabriel Briard, 1753.
Introduction dated November 8, 1745. Bishop Paul d'Albert de Luynes
(1728–1753). Based on the Rouen 1730 catechism. At least two more
editions were published, in 1778 and 1790. Small and ordinary cate-
chisms.

Bayonne
Catéchisme à l'usage des jeunes enfants. 1731.
Bishop Pierre-Guillaume de la Vieuxville (1728–1734). Small and ordi-
nary catechisms.

Bazas
Catéchisme imprimé par le commandement de Mgr l'Évêque de Bazas. Bordeaux, 1677.
Bishop Guillaume de Boissonnade d'Orty (1667–1682).
Catéchisme imprimé par ordre de Monseigneur l'Évêque de Bazas. Bordeaux: Michel
Racle, 1786.
Introduction dated October 11, 1773. Bishop Jean-Baptiste-Amédée de
Grégoire de Saint-Sauveur (1746–1792). Small and ordinary cate-
chisms.

Beauvais
Catéchisme à l'usage du diocèse de Beauvais. Beauvais: Ach. Desjardins, 1827.
Introduction dated July 16, 1680. Bishop Toussaint, Cardinal de Forbin
Janson (1679–1713). Small catechism only.

Belley

Catéchisme du diocèse de Belley. Lyon: Aimé de la Roche, 1787.
> Introduction dated August 15, 1763. Bishop Gabriel Cortois de Quincey
> (1751–1791). Small and ordinary catechisms.

Besançon

Le catéchisme ou instruction de la doctrine chrétienne, où l'on apprend à devenir bon chrétien et à bien faire son salut. 4th ed. Grenoble: Franç. Provençal, 1673.
> Archbishop Antoine-Pierre de Grammont (1662–1698). Large catechism
> only.

Catéchisme nouveau, dressé en faveur de la jeunesse du diocèse de Besançon pour la faciliter à apprendre les vérités du christianisme divisé en quatre parties. Besançon: Fr. Louis Rigoine, 1687.
> Archbishop Antoine-Pierre de Grammont (1662–1698). Ordinary catechism only.

Catéchisme en faveur de la jeunesse du diocèse de Besançon. Besançon: Cl. Jos. Daclin, 1762.
> Introduction dated December 14, 1756. Archbishop Antoine-Cleriadus,
> Cardinal de Choiseul-Beaupré (1754–1774). Reprinted in 1776,
> 1779, and 1787. Small and ordinary catechisms.

Béziers

Catéchisme contenant en abrégé tout ce qu'il faut savoir sur les vérités de la religion, à l'usage du diocèse de Béziers. 1696.
> Bishop Jean-Armand de Rotundis de Biscaras (1670–1702).

Catéchisme du diocèse de Béziers. Béziers: Fr. Barbut, 1749.
> Introduction dated August 22, 1749. Bishop Joseph Bruno de Bausset-
> Roquefort (1746–1771). New edition published in 1775. Small and
> ordinary catechisms.

Blois

Catéchisme imprimé par l'ordre de Mgr l'Evêque de Blois. Blois: P. J. Masson, 1776.
> Introduction dated July 6, 1728. Bishop Jean-François-Paul le Fèvre de
> Caumartin (1719–1733).

Premier catéchisme à l'usage du diocèse de Blois. Blois: M. Lefebvre, 1789.
> Bishop Alexandre-François-Amédée-Adonis-Louis-Joseph de Lauzières
> de Thémines (1776–1791). Ordinary catechism only.

Bordeaux

Catéchisme, ou abrégé de la doctrine chrétienne. Bordeaux: R. N. Lafargue, n.d.
> Introduction dated April 8, 1704. Archbishop Jean-Baptiste-Armand
> Bazin de Besons (1698–1719). Reprint edition, authorized by

Jérome-Marie Champion de Cicé (1781–1802). Small and ordinary catechisms. This catechism was reprinted throughout the eighteenth century.

Boulogne

Catéchisme du diocèse de Boulogne. 1707.
Bishop Pierre de Langle (1698–1724).
Catéchisme du diocèse de Boulogne. Boulogne: P. Battut, 1726.
Bishop Jean-Marie Henriau (1724–1738). Reprinted in 1730. Small and ordinary catechisms.
Autre catéchisme du diocèse de Boulogne. 4th ed. Boulogne: Charles Battut, 1771.
Bishop François-Joseph-Gaston de Partz de Pressy (1742–1789).

Bourges

Catéchisme ou abrégé de la doctrine chrétienne. Bourges: François Toubeau, 1688.
Introduction dated May 5, 1688. Archbishop Michel Phélypeaux de la Vrillière (1678–1694). Reprinted in 1690 and 1693. Ordinary catechism only.
Catéchismes ou abrégés de la doctrine chrétienne. Bourges: François Tobeau, 1699.
Introduction dated April 16, 1699. Archbishop Léon Potier (1694–1729). Large catechism only.
Catéchismes ou abrégés de la doctrine chrétienne. Bourges: François Toubeau, 1701.
Archbishop Léon Potier (1694–1729). Ordinary version of the 1699 large catechism.
Catéchismes, ou abrégéz de la doctrine chrétienne, cy-devant intitulez, Catéchisme de Bourges. Paris: Raymond Mazieres, 1707.
Archbishop Léon Potier (1694–1729). Reprinted with small changes in 1716 and 1736. Small and ordinary catechisms.

Cahors

Catéchisme nouveau imprimé par l'ordre de Mgr Henri de Briqueville de La Luzerne. Cahors: Fran. Richard, 1738.
Bishop Henri de Briqueville de La Luzerne (1693–1741).
Catéchisme imprimé par ordre de Mgr du Guesclin. Cahors, 1747.
Bishop Bertrand-Jean-Baptiste-René du Guesclin (1741–1766).
Catéchisme réimprimé par ordre de Monseigneur Louis-Marie de Nicolay. 1781.
Introduction dated February 4, 1781. Bishop Louis-Marie de Nicolay (1776–1791). Small and ordinary catechisms.

Cambrai

Catéchisme ou sommaire de la doctrine chrétienne. Cambrai: Samuel Berthoud, 1758.
Introduction by Archbishop Charles de Saint-Albin (1723–1764) dated February 20, 1726; second introduction dated February 28, 1758.

Grand catéchisme pour servir de suite au petit catéchisme, qui est en usage dans les diocèses de Cambrai, de Liège et de Namur. Maestricht: P. L. Lekens, 1788.
Introduction dated June 9, 1788. Archbishop Ferdinand-Maximilien-Mériadec de Rohan-Guémené (1781–1801).

Castres
Doctrine chrétienne ou catéchisme du diocèse de Castres. 5th ed. Castres: F. Gausy, n.d.
Bishop François de Lastic de Saint-Jal (1736–1752). First edition published in 1747. Ordinary catechism only.

Châlons-sur-Marne
L'escole chrestienne, ou l'on apprend a devenir bon chrestien, & à faire son salut. Châlons: H. et I. Seneuze, 1660.
Bishop Félix Vialart de Herse (1642–1680). Reprinted in 1664 and 1670. Small and large catechisms.
Catéchisme du diocèse de Châlons. Châlons: Seneuze, 1727.
Introduction dated March 29, 1727. Bishop Nicolas-Charles de Saulx-Tavannes (1721–1733). Reprinted in 1781. Small and ordinary catechisms.
Catéchisme à l'usage des enfans. Châlons: Veuve Bouchard, 1759.
Introduction dated November 12, 1709. Bishop Gaston-Jean-Baptiste-Louis de Noailles (1695–1720). Reprinted by Bishop Claude-Antoine de Choiseul-Beaupré (1733–1763).

Châlon-sur-Saône
Catéchisme imprimé par l'ordre de Mgr l'Evêque et comte de Châlon-sur-Saône pour l'instruction des peuples de son diocèse, revu, corrigé et augmenté. Châlon-sur-Saône: Claude de Saint, 1735.
Bishop François de Madot (1711–1753).

Chartres
Catéchismes du diocèse de Chartres. Chartres: Claude Peigné, 1707.
Introduction dated November 16, 1698. Bishop Paul Godet des Marais (1690–1709).
Gros catéchisme du diocèse de Chartres. Chartres: Étienne Cormier, 1766.
Bishop Pierre-Augustin-Bernardin de Rosset de Rocozel de Fleury (1746–1780). Reprinted in 1779. Ordinary catechism only.
Abrégé du catéchisme du diocèse de Chartres, avec les prières du matin, du soir et de la messe. Chartres: Fr. Labalte, 1788.
Bishop Joseph-Baptiste-Joseph de Lubersac (1780–1801). Small catechism only.

Clermont

Catéchisme de la foi et des moeurs chrétiennes. Clermont: Nicolas Jacquard, 1674.
Bishop Gilbert de Vény d'Arbouze (1664–1682).

Abrégé du catéchisme du diocèse de Clermont. Clermont Ferrand: P. Boutaudon, 1731.
Bishop Jean-Baptiste Massillon (1717–1742). Reprinted in 1735, 1758, and 1772. Ordinary catechism only; 1758 and 1772 editions include a short small version.

Catéchisme à l'usage du diocèse de Clermont. Clermont Ferrand: Antoine Delcros, 1789.
Introduction dated January 27, 1789. Bishop François de Bonal (1775–1800). Ordinary catechism only.

Comminges

Catéchisme imprimé par ordre de Mgr l'illustrissime et révérendissime Père en Dieu, Messire Gabriel Olivier de Lubière de Bouchet, évêque de Cominges. Toulouse: Aug. Henault, n.d.
Bishop Olivier-Gabriel de Lubières du Bouchet (1710–1739).

Coutances

Catéchisme avec les instructions, pour les dispositions à la 1er Communion et pour les principales fêtes et solennités de l'année. Caen: Guillaume Richard Poisson, n.d.
Bishop Charles-François de Loménie de Brienne (1666–1720).

Dax

Catéchisme ou abrégé de la foi et des vérités chrétiennes. 1740.
Bishop Louis-Marie de Suarès d'Aulan (1736–1771). Reprinted at least once, by Charles-Auguste le Quien de la Neufville (1771–1801). Small and ordinary catechisms.

Die

Petit catéchisme ou abrégé de la doctrine chrétienne imprimé par ordre de Mgr l'Evêque et comte de Die. Grenoble: André Faure, 1736.
Introduction dated December 27, 1735. Bishop Daniel-Joseph de Cosnac (1734–1741).

Dijon

Catéchisme imprimé par l'ordre de Mgr l'Evêque de Dijon pour l'instruction des fidèles de son diocèse. Dijon: Jean-Baptiste Augé, 1736.
Introduction dated July 6, 1736. Bishop Jean-Jacques Bouhier de Lantenay (1731–1743). Small and ordinary catechisms.

Catéchisme du diocèse de Dijon. Dijon: L. N. Frantin, 1770.
> Introduction dated November 3, 1761. Bishop Claude-Marc-Antoine
> d'Apchon (1755–1776). Reprinted in 1796. Ordinary catechism only.

Catéchisme ou abrégé de la foi. Dijon: Jean-Baptiste Capel, 1785.
> Bishop Jacques-Joseph-François de Vogué (1776–1786).

Evreux

Catéchisme imprimé par ordre de Mgr Jacques Potier de Novion, évêque d'Evreux.
> Evreux: Veuve De La Lande, 1708.
> Bishop Jacques Potier de Novion (1681–1709).

Fréjus

Catéchisme du diocèse de Fréjus. Paris: Cl. Simon, 1779.
> Introduction dated January 2, 1779. Bishop Emmanuel-François de Baus-
> set de Roquefort (1766–1801).

Gap

Catéchisme à l'usage du diocèse de Gap. Paris: Raymond Mazière, 1707.
> Bishop François Berger de Malissoles (1706–1738).

Grasse

La doctrine chrétienne . . . par Mgr de Mesgrigny, évêque de Grasse. Lyon, 1713.
> Bishop Joseph-Ignace-Jean-Baptiste de Mesgrigny (1711–1726).

Catéchisme pour être seul enseigné dans le diocèse de Grasse. Aix: Jos. David, 1733.
> Bishop Claude-Léonce-Octavien d'Antelmy (1726–1752). Based on Jean-
> Joseph Languet de Gergy's catechism, first published for Sens in
> 1716.

Grenoble

Catéchisme de la doctrine chrétienne, avec l'explication des mystères, commandements,
> *sacrements, prières et devoirs particuliers de chacun, avec les citations aux marges, de*
> *l'Ecriture Sainte et des Conciles.* Lyon: Laurent Aubin, 1685.
> Bishop Etienne, Cardinal Le Camus (1671–1707).

Catéchisme où les principales vérités de la doctrine chrétienne sont expliquées. Grenoble:
> François Champ, 1712.
> Introduction dated January 2, 1712. Bishop Ennemond Alleman de Mont-
> martin (1707–1719). Small and large catechisms.

Catéchisme du diocèse de Grenoble. Grenoble: Veuve Giroud et Fils, 1786.
> Bishop Jean de Cairol de Madaillan (1771–1779). Small and ordinary cate-
> chisms.

Langres

Le grand catéchisme de Langres, pour toutes sortes de personnes qui ont charge d'âmes, ou qui auront dessein de s'instruire des mystères de la religion catholique et des principales cérémonies paroissiales. Dijon: Pierre Paillot, 1664.

Bishop Louis Barbier de la Rivière (1655–1670).

Catéchisme de Langres publié par M. de Clermont Tonnerre, 1698.

Bishop François-Louis de Clermont-Tonnerre (1695–1724).

Instruction générale par demandes et par réponses sur la foi, l'espérance et la charité, les sacrements, les devoirs du chrétien, et sur plusieurs pratiques de piété. Langres: Charles Personnet, n.d.

Introduction dated December 22, 1731. Bishop Pierre de Pardaillan de Gondrin d'Antin (1724–1733). Small, ordinary, and large catechisms. New edition published in 1734, with a catechism for confirmation.

Catéchisme ou abrégé de la doctrine chrétienne. Langres: Pierre Defay, 1792.

Bishop César-Guillaume de la Luzerne (1770–1801). Ordinary catechism only.

Laon

Catéchisme à l'usage du diocèse de Laon. Laon: A. Rennesson, 1698.

Introduction dated April 10, 1698. Bishop Louis-Annet de Clermont de Chaste de Roussillon (1695–1721). Small, ordinary, and large catechisms.

La Rochelle

Catéchisme ou doctrine chrétienne, imprimé par ordre de Messeigneurs les Évêques d'Angers, de La Rochelle et de Luçon, pour l'usage de leurs diocèses. Lyon: Veuve Fleury Martin, 1685.

"Catechism of the Three Henris," first published in 1676. Bishop Henri-Marie de Laval-Boisdaupin (1661–1693). Small, ordinary, and large catechisms.

Catéchisme ou Abbrégé des véritéz, et des devoirs de la religion chrestienne. La Rochelle: François Courson, 1717.

Introduction dated December 2, 1716. Bishop Étienne de Champflour (1702–1724). Ordinary catechism only. Reprinted in 1741.

Lectoure

Abrégé de la doctrine chrétienne. 1688.

Bishop Hugues de Bar (1671–1691). Ordinary catechism only; a small version published in 1690.

Le Mans

Catéchisme ou abrégé de la foy, et des véritez chrétiennes. Le Mans: Ambrose Ysam-
bar, 1695.
   Bishop Louis de La Vergne-Montenard de Tressan (1671–1712). Ordi-
   nary catechism only.
Catéchisme ou abrégé de la foy et des vérités chrétiennes. Le Mans: Jacques Guillaume
Ysambart, 1763.
   Bishop Charles-Louis de Froullay de Tessé (1723–1767).
Catéchisme ou abrégé de la foy, et des véritez chrétiennes. Le Mans: Ambrose Ysam-
bar, n.d.
   Bishop Pierre-Rogier du Crévy (1712–1723).

Le Puy

*Catéchisme de la foi, et des moeurs chrétiennes, dressé particuliérement pour l'usage du
diocèse du Puy.* Vol. 1. Le Puy: P. et G. F. Delagarde, 1684.
   First published in 1674. Introduction dated September 27, 1684. Bishop
   Armand de Béthune (1661–1703). Large catechism only.
Catéchisme du diocèse du Puy. Le Puy, 1749.
   Introduction dated April 22, 1749. Bishop Jean-George le Franc de
   Pompignan (1742–1774). Small and ordinary catechisms. Reprinted
   in 1772 and 1776.

Limoges

Catéchisme ou instruction de la doctrine chrétienne. Limoges: Jean Barbou, 1718.
   Introduction dated October 1, 1708. Bishop Antoine Charpin de Gen-
   netines (1706–1729). Small and ordinary catechisms.
Catéchisme ou instruction de la doctrine chrétienne. Limoges: Dalesme, 1786.
   Bishop Louis-Charles du Plessis d'Argentré (1758–1801).

Lisieux

Instruction chrétienne ou catéchisme. 1719.
   Bishop Henri-Ignace de Brancas (1714–1760).

Luçon

*Catéchisme ou doctrine chrétienne, imprimé par ordre de Messeigneurs les évêques d'Angers,
de La Rochelle et de Luçon, pour l'usage de leurs diocèses.* Lyon: Veuve Martin,
1685.
   "Catechism of the Three Henris." First published in 1676. Bishop Henri
   de Barillon (1671–1699). Small, ordinary, and large catechisms.

Catéchisme ou doctrine chrétienne, imprimé par ordre de Messeigneurs les Évêques d'Angers, de La Rochelle, & de Luçon. 4th ed. Paris: Veuve Lottin, et J. H. Butard, 1756.
> Reprint of the "Catechism of the Three Henris." Bishop Samuel-Guillaume de Verthamon de Chavagnac (1737–1758). Small, ordinary, and large catechisms.

Lyon

Catéchisme du diocèse de Lyon pour l'instruction de la jeunesse. Lyon: Antoine Jullieron, 1665.
> Introduction dated March 15, 1665. Archbishop Camille de Neufville de Villeroy (1653–1693). Ordinary catechism only.

Catéchisme du diocèse de Lyon. Lyon: Pierre Valfray, 1715.
> Introduction dated December 4, 1700. Archbishop Claude de Saint-Georges (1693–1714). Small and ordinary catechisms.

Catéchisme pour les écoles du diocèse de Lyon. Lyon: Placide Jacquenod, 1730.
> Archbishop François-Paul de Neufville de Villeroy (1714–1731). Ordinary catechism only.

Catéchisme du diocèse de Lyon. Lyon: Aimé de la Roche, 1767.
> Introduction dated August 28, 1767. Archbishop Antoine Malvin de Montazet (1758–1788). Ordinary catechism only. Reprinted in 1772.

Catéchisme du diocèse de Lyon. Lyon: Aimé de la Roche, 1785.
> Archbishop Antoine Malvin de Montazet (1758–1788).

Mâcon

Catéchisme du diocèse de Mâcon. Paris: Bordelet, 1744.
> Introduction dated February 17, 1744. Bishop Henri-Constance de Lort de Sérignan de Valras (1732–1763).

Catéchisme du diocèse de Mâcon. Mâcon: J. P. Goery, 1765.
> Introduction dated February 26, 1765. Bishop Gabriel-François Moreau (1763–1801). Small and ordinary catechisms.

Marseille

Le nouveau catéchisme ou instruction de la doctrine chrétienne. 5th ed. Marseille: Garcin, 1675.
> Bishop Jean-Baptiste d'Estampes (1679–1684). Based on a Besançon catechism issued by Archbishop Grammont.

Catéchisme ou instruction familière, sur les principaux points de la Religion Chrétienne. 17th ed. Marseille: Veuve de J. P. Brebion, n.d.
> Introduction dated September 10, 1712. Bishop Henry-François-Xavier de Belsunce de Castelmoron (1709–1755). Ordinary catechism only.

Meaux

Catéchisme du diocèse de Meaux. 1652.

> Introduction dated September 1, 1652. Bishop Dominique de Ligny (1659–1681).

Catéchisme du diocèse de Meaux. Paris: Sebastien Mabre-Cramoist, 1687.

> Introduction dated October 6, 1686. Bishop Jacques Bénigne Bossuet (1681–1704). Small and ordinary catechisms. Reprinted at least six times, in 1691, 1698, 1707, 1723, 1764, and 1781, as well as several nineteenth-century editions.

Mende

Catéchisme ou abrégé de la doctrine chrétienne. 1684.

> Bishop François-Placide de Baudry de Piancourt (1677–1707).

Catéchisme du diocèse de Mende, ou abrégé de la doctrine chrétienne. Avignon: François Chambeau, 1825.

> Introduction dated January 23, 1770. Bishop Jean Arnaud de Castellane (1767–1792). Small and ordinary catechisms.

Metz

Catéchisme du diocèse de Metz. Metz: Brice Antoine, 1701.

> Introduction dated October 21, 1700. Bishop Henri-Charles du Camboust de Coislin (1697–1732). Small and ordinary catechisms.

Catéchisme du diocèse de Metz. Metz: Veuve Brice Antoine, 1737.

> Bishop Claude de Rouvroy de Saint-Simon (1733–1760). German edition published in the same year.

Mirepoix

Catéchisme de Mirepoix par le commandement de Mgr l'illustrissime et révérendissime Pierre De La Broue, évêque de Mirepoix. Toulouse: J. Deladoure, 1699.

> Bishop Pierre De La Broue (1679–1720).

Montauban

Catéchisme pour le diocèse de Montauban. 1765.

> Bishop Anne-François-Victor le Tonnelier de Breteuil (1762–1794).

Montpellier

Catéchisme du diocèse de Montpellier, contenant les IV parties de la doctrine chrétienne, par l'ordre de Mgr l'évêque de Montpellier. Montpellier: Pierre et Daniel Perronnet, 1687.

> Bishop Charles de Pradel (1675–1696). Small and ordinary catechisms.

Catéchismes du diocèse de Montpellier. Lyon: Leonard Plaignard, 1705.
>   Introduction dated June 2, 1701. Bishop Charles-Joachim Colbert de Croissy (1696–1738). Small and ordinary catechisms.

Catéchisme du diocèse de Montpellier avec un abrégé pour les petits enfants. Montpellier, 1750.
>   Bishop Louis Renaud de Villeneuve (1748–1766). Small and ordinary catechisms.

Nancy

Catéchisme du diocèse de Nancy. Nancy: H. Haner, 1785.
>   Introduction dated September 4, 1785. Bishop François de Fontanges (1783–1788). Small and ordinary catechisms. First catechism published for the diocese of Nancy, created out of Toul in 1777.

Nantes

Catéchisme du diocèse de Nantes. 4th ed. Nantes: Michel Mareschal, 1718.
>   Introduction dated September 7, 1689. Published again in 1723 and 1726. Bishop Gilles-Jean-François de Beauvau (1677–1717). Small, ordinary, and large catechisms.

Premier et second catéchismes du diocèse de Nantes, pour les plus jeunes enfants & pour ceux qu'on prépare à la première communion. Nantes: Despilly, 1783.
>   Introduction dated January 15, 1781. Bishop Jean-Auguste de Frétat de Sarra (1775–1783). Small and ordinary catechisms.

Nevers

Catéchisme du diocèse de Nevers. 1734.
>   Introduction dated February 8, 1734. Bishop Charles Fontaine des Montées (1719–1740). Reprinted at least once, in 1745.

Nîmes

Catéchisme ou abrégé de la doctrine chrétienne. Nîmes: Gaspard Fernel, 1798.
>   Introduction dated April 16, 1698. Bishop Esprit Fléchier (1692–1710). Small and ordinary catechisms.

Noyon

Catéchisme composé par Mgr l'évêque, comte de Noyon, en faveur des fideles de son diocèse. S. Quentin: Le Queux, 1691.
>   Bishop François de Clermont-Tonnerre (1660–1701). Small and ordinary catechisms. Reprinted at least twice, in 1738 and 1743.

Oloron

Catéchisme à l'usage du diocèse d'Oloron. Oloron: Jean Poux, 1727.
>   Introduction dated September 13, 1706. Bishop Joseph de Révol
>   (1705–1735). Printed in French, Béarnais, and Basque.

Orléans

Catéchisme du diocèse d'Orléans. Orléans: Félix Borde, 1709.
>   Bishop Louis-Gaston Fleuriau d'Armenonville (1706–1733).
Catéchisme du diocèse d'Orléans. Orléans: Rouzeau Montant, 1822.
>   Introduction dated July 4, 1762. Bishop Louis-Sextius de Jarente de la
>   Bruyère (1758–1788). Small and ordinary catechisms.

Pamiers

Catéchisme pour l'usage du diocèse de Pamiers. Toulouse: Bosc, 1672.
>   Bishop François-Étienne de Caulet (1645–1680).
Catéchisme dressé par ordre de Mgr de Verthamon, évêque de Pamiers. 1718.
>   Bishop Jean-Baptiste de Verthamon (1693–1735). Reprinted at least
>   once by François-Barthélemi de Salignac de La Mothe Fénelon
>   (1735–1741).
Catéchisme du diocèse de Pamiers. 1765.
>   Introduction dated April 4, 1765. Includes a catechism for confirmation
>   and communion. Bishop Henri-Gaston de Lévis-Leran (1741–1786).

Paris

Instruction de la doctrine chrétienne, ou catéchisme. Paris: Muguet, 1670.
>   Introduction dated November 18, 1664. Archbishop Hardouin de Beau-
>   mont de Péréfixe (1662–1670). Small, ordinary, and large catechisms.
Catéchisme ou abrégé de la foi & des véritez chrestiennes. Paris: Veuve François Muguet, 1714.
>   Introduction dated October 31, 1687. Archbishop François de Harlay de
>   Champvallon (1670–1695). Ordinary catechism only. Reprinted in
>   1730 and 1742 by Archbishop Charles-Gaspard-Guillaume de Vin-
>   timille du Luc (1729–1746), who added a catechism for confession
>   and communion, and in 1747 by Archbishop Christophe de Beau-
>   mont de Repayre (1746–1781).

Périgueux

Formulaire d'instruction ou méthode facile pour instruire le peuple de la campagne. 1676.
>   Bishop Guillaume Le Boux (1666–1693). Same catechism published in
>   Saintes in the same year.

Catéchisme imprimé par ordre de Mgr l'Illustrissime et Révérendissime J. Ch. de Prémeau, évêque de Périgueux, à l'usage de son diocèse. Périgueux: P. Daloy, 1750.

> Introduction dated May 24, 1750. Bishop Jean-Chrétien de Macheco de Prémeaux (1731–1771). Small and ordinary catechisms.

Poitiers

Catéchisme du diocèse de Poitiers. Poitiers: Faulcon, 1780.

> Introduction dated January 30, 1737. Bishop Jérôme-Louis de Foudras de Courcenay (1732–1748). Includes "Méthode pour bien faire le Catéchisme," dated 1715 and written by Bishop Jean-Claude de La Poype de Vertrieu (1702–1732). Ordinary catechism only.

Quimper

Catéchisme français-breton dressé en faveur des enfants. Quimper: Perrier, 1717.

> Introduction dated October 26, 1711. Bishop François-Hyacinthe de Ploeuc du Timeur (1707–1739).

Reims

Sommaire de la doctrine chrétienne. Reims: Nicolas Hécard, 1621.

> Archbishop Louis de Lorraine, Cardinal de Guise (1605–1621).

Catéchisme ou abrégé de la doctrine chrétienne imprimé par ordre de Mgr l'archevêque de Reims. Reims: Nicolas Pottier, 1684.

> Archbishop Charles-Maurice Le Tellier (1671–1710).

Catéchisme ou doctrine chrétienne. Paris: Antoine Dezallier, 1692.

> Reprint of the "Catechism of the Three Henris." Introduction dated May 25, 1692. Archbishop Charles-Maurice Le Tellier (1671–1710). Small, ordinary, and large catechisms.

Troisième catéchisme ou abrégé de la doctrine chrétienne imprimé par ordre de Mgr l'archevêque de Reims. Reims: Barthélemi Multeau, 1716.

> Introduction dated December 12, 1715. Archbishop François, Cardinal de Mailly (1710–1721).

Catéchisme imprimé par ordre de son Altesse Monseigneur le Prince de Rohan, Archevêque, Duc de Reims, Premier Pair de France, etc. Reims: Barthelemi Multeau, 1746.

> Introduction dated June 12, 1746. Archbishop Armand-Jules de Rohan-Guémené (1721–1762). Ordinary catechism only.

Rennes

Catéchisme ou doctrine chrétienne. Rennes: Jules Front, 1769.

> Bishop François Bareau de Girac (1769–1801).

Riez
Catéchisme du diocèse de Riez. 1773.
> Introduction dated October 1, 1773. Bishop François de Clugny
> (1772–1801).

Rodez
La doctrine chrétienne en forme d'instruction familière. 2nd ed. 1677.
> Bishop Gabriel de Voyer de Paulmy d'Argenson (1666–1682).
Catéchisme à l'usage du diocèse de Rodez. 1721.
> Bishop Jean-Armand de La Vove de Tourouvre (1716–1733).

Rouen
Catéchisme ou abrégé de la doctrine chrétienne. Rouen: Besogne, 1720.
> Introduction dated May 22, 1720. Archbishop Jean-Baptiste-Armand
> Bazin de Besons (1719–1721). Catechism first published by Bazin
> de Besons in 1704, when he was the archbishop of Bordeaux.
Catéchisme ou abrégé de la foy et de la doctrine chrétienne. Rouen: Jacques Joseph Le
Boullenger, 1730.
> Introduction dated April 11, 1730. Archbishop Louis de La Vergne-
> Montenard de Tressan (1723–1733). Ordinary catechism only.
Catéchisme ou abrégé de la foy et de la doctrine chrétienne. Rouen: Jacques Joseph Le
Boullenger, 1769.
> Archbishop Dominique, Cardinal de La Rochefoucauld (1759–1800).

Saint-Claude
Catéchisme du diocèse de Saint-Claude. Lons-le-Saunier: C. Delhorme, 1765.
> Introduction dated June 25, 1765. Bishop Jean-Baptiste-Joseph Méallet
> de Fargues (1741–1785). Small and ordinary catechisms.

Saint-Dié
1787. [Title page missing.]
> Introduction dated September 24, 1787. Bishop Barthélemy-Louis de
> Chaumont de la Galaisière (1774–1801). Small catechism only.

Saintes
Formulaire d'instruction, ou méthode facile pour instruire le peuple de la campagne.
1676.
> Bishop Louis de Bassompierre (1649–1677). Same catechism published
> in Périgueux in the same year. Reprinted at least once, in 1724.

Saint-Flour

Catéchisme du diocèse de Saint-Flour, divisé en deux, proportionné à l'état des personnes que l'on doit instruire. Saint-Flour: Lallement, 1801.
> Introduction dated October 2, 1748. Bishop Paul de Ribeyre (1742–1776). Small and ordinary catechism.

Saint-Malo

Catéchismes pour les petits enfants et pour les enfants, à l'usage du diocèse de Saint-Malo. 2 vols. Saint-Malo: L. Hovius, 1764.
> Bishop Jean-Joseph de Fogasses d'Entrechaux de la Bastie (1739–1767). Small, ordinary, and large catechisms.

Premier et second catéchismes, imprimés par l'ordre de Monseigneur l'Évêque de Saint-Malo, pour être enseignés dans son diocèse. Saint-Malo: Julien Valias, 1778.
> Introduction dated December 17, 1770. Bishop Antoine-Joseph des Laurents (1767–1785). Small and ordinary catechisms.

Saint-Omer

Catéchisme du diocèse de Saint-Omer. 1729.
> Introduction dated April 19, 1729. Bishop Joseph-Alphonse de Valbelle de Tourves (1727–1754). Reprinted at least once, in 1764.

Saint-Papoul

Catéchisme du diocèse de Saint Papoul. Catelnaudarry: Matthieu Domenc, 1738.
> Introduction dated August 15, 1738. Bishop Georges-Lazare Berger de Charancy (1735–1738).

Saint-Paul-Trois-Châteaux

Catéchisme du diocèse de Saint-Paul-Trois-Châteaux. n.d.
> Introduction dated September 8, 1747. Bishop Pierre-François-Xavier de Reboul de Lambert (1743–1791).

Saint-Pons-de Tomières

Catéchisme pour instruire les enfants des obligations du baptême et pour les préparer au sacrement de confirmation et à la première communion. Béziers: Barbut, 1702.
> Bishop Pierre-Jean-François Percin de Montgaillard (1665–1713).

Séez

Grand catéchisme de la doctrine chrétienne. 1694.
> Bishop Mathurin Savary (1682–1698).

La doctrine chétienne rédigée en forme de catéchisme par Mgr l'Evêque de Séez, pour servir d'instruction aux fidèles de son diocèse. Séez: Jean-Baptiste Briard, 1731.
>   Bishop Jacques-Charles-Alexandre Lallemant (1728–1740). Small, ordinary, and large catechisms. Reprinted in 1789 by Bishop Jean-Baptiste du Plessis d'Argentré (1775–1801).

Senlis
Catéchisme à l'usage du diocèse de Senlis. 1709.
>   Bishop Jean-François de Chamillart (1702–1714).
Catéchisme du diocèse de Senlis, avec des prières pour le matin, pour le soir, et pendant la Messe. Senlis: René Caron, 1723.
>   Bishop François-Firmin Trudaine (1714–1754).

Sens
Catéchisme ou Instruction chrétienne pour le diocèse de Sens. Sens: Loüis Prussurot, 1669.
>   Introduction dated June 18, 1669. Archbishop Louis Henri de Pardaillon de Gondrin (1646–1674). Ordinary catechism only.
Catéchisme du diocèse de Sens. Sens: André Jannot, 1737.
>   Introduction dated September 8, 1731. Archbishop Jean-Joseph Languet de Gergy (1730–1753). Small and ordinary catechisms.
Catéchisme ou abrégé de la foy et de la doctrine chrétienne. Sens: André Jannot, 1754.
>   Introduction dated October 1, 1754. Archbishop Paul d'Albert, Cardinal de Luynes (1753–1788). Small and ordinary catechisms.

Soissons
Catéchisme ou doctrine chrétienne, imprimé par l'ordre de Mgr l'Evêque de Soissons, pour l'usage de son diocèse. Soissons: J. de Levy, 1708.
>   Introduction dated April 18, 1696. Bishop Fabio Brulart de Sillery (1692–1714).
Catéchisme du diocèse de Soissons. Soissons: Charles Courtois, 1730.
>   Introduction dated October 14, 1716. Bishop Jean-Joseph Languet de Gergy (1715–1730). Small and ordinary catechisms. Reprinted at least once, in 1740.
Catéchisme, ou Exposition de la doctrine chrétienne. Soissons: Ponce Courtois, 1756.
>   Introduction dated February 11, 1756. Bishop François de Fitz-James (1738–1764). Ordinary catechism only.
Prières et instructions chrétiennes. Soissons: Charles-Pierre Berton, Libraire, 1782.
>   Bishop Henri-Joseph-Claude de Bourdeilles (1764–1791).
Abrégé de la doctrine chrétienne. Soissons: L. F. Waroquier, 1785.
>   Bishop Henri-Joseph-Claude de Bourdeilles (1764–1791).

Strasbourg

Catéchisme, ou abrégé des vérités chrétiennes. Strasbourg: Jean François le Roux, 1700.

> Bishop Guillaume-Egon, Cardinal de Furstenberg (1682–1704); introduction written by the *grand-vicaire* François de Camily and dated August 28, 1700. Ordinary catechism only.

Tarbes

Catéchisme ou abrégé de la foi et des vérités chrétiennes. Tarbes: Paul Roquemaurel, n.d.

> Introduction dated November 30, 1726. Bishop Anne-François-Guillaume du Camboust-Beçay (1719–1729).

Toul

Catéchisme du diocèse de Toul. Toul: Alexis Laurent, 1703.

> Bishop Henri-Pons Thyard de Bissy (1687–1704).

Catéchisme du diocèse de Toul. Toul: Loüis et Étienne Rolin, 1736.

> Introduction dated July 12, 1732. Bishop Scipion Jérôme Bégon (1721–1753). Small and large catechisms. Reprinted in 1752, 1754, 1785, and 1787.

Toulon

Instructions familières par demandes et par réponses sur les quatre principales parties de la doctrine chrétienne. 1712.

> Bishop Armand-Louis Bonnin de Chalucet (1684–1712).

Catéchisme ou instruction familière sur les principaux points de la religion chrétienne. Toulon: Duplessis Ollivault, 1827.

> Reprint edition of a catechism published by Bishop Elléon de Castellane-Mazangues (1786–1801).

Toulouse

Catéchisme réimprimé par l'ordre de Monseigneur l'Illustrissime & Reverendissime, Père en Dieu, Messire Jean-Baptiste Michel Colbert, Archevêque de Toulouse. 16th ed. Toulouse: Claude-Gilles Lecamus, 1710.

> Introduction dated March 24, 1685. Archbishop Jean-Baptiste-Michel Colbert de Saint-Pouange (1687–1710). Ordinary catechism only.

Tours

Catéchisme ou doctrine chrétienne. Tours: Jac. Poinsot, 1681.

> Introduction dated February 6, 1681. Archbishop Michel Amelot de Gournay (1672–1687).

Catéchisme ou abrégé des vérités chrétiennes, divisé en cinq parties. n.d.

> Introduction dated June 26, 1723. Archbishop François Blouet de Camilly (1721–1723). Reprinted at least once, in 1726, with a catechism for confession and communion.

Catéchisme ou abrégé des vérités chrétiennes divisé en quatre parties, publié par feu Mgr de Vaugirault, Evêque d'Angers. Tours: L. M. F. Ligier, 1781.

> Introduction dated November 3, 1781. Archbishop Joachim-François-Mamert de Conzié (1774–1795). Jean de Vaugirault was bishop of Angers from 1730 to 1758.

Tréguier

Catéchisme en breton par Mgr Frétat de Sarra, évêque de Tréguier. Montroullez: Pierre Guyon, 1775.

> Introduction dated December 9, 1774. Bishop Jean-Augustin Frétat de Sarra (1773–1775). A French translation was issued in 1783.

Troyes

Catéchisme du diocèse de Troyes. 2nd ed. Troyes: Charles Briden, 1715.

> Introduction dated April 15, 1705. Bishop Denis François Le Bouthillier de Chavigny (1697–1716). Small and ordinary catechisms. Reprinted in 1772 and 1792.

Catéchisme de Troyes. Troyes: J. B. F. Bouillerat, 1744.

> Bishop Mathias Poncet de la Rivière (1742–1758).

Valence

Catéchisme du diocèse de Valence, Qui explique tous les Mystères de la Religion, ses Dogmes, etc. Valence: J. J. Viret, 1773.

> Introduction dated June 24, 1773. Bishop François-Fiacre de Grave (1771–1787). Small and ordinary catechisms.

Vannes

Catechim eitchervige d'er ré e ra profession ag er religion catholiq, apostoliq ha romaen. 1859.

> First published in 1750. Bishop Charles-Jean Bertin (1746–1774). In Breton.

Verdun

Grand catéchisme de Verdun. Verdun: Jean Jacquet, 1685.

> Introduction dated August 31, 1684. Bishop Hippolyte de Béthune (1681–1720). Small and ordinary catechisms.

Vienne

Catéchisme à l'usage du diocèse de Vienne. Grenoble: Baratier frères, 1817.
   Introduction dated January 21, 1767. Archbishop Guillaume d'Hugues
      de La Motte (1751–1774).

Viviers

Catéchisme du diocèse de Viviers. Avignon: Claude Delorde, 1743.
   Introduction dated October 15, 1740. Bishop François-Renaud de Ville-
      neuve (1724–1748). Small and ordinary catechisms.

Other Printed Primary Sources

de la Fontainerie, François, ed. and trans. *French Liberalism and Education in the
   Eighteenth Century: The Writings of La Chalotais, Turgot, Diderot, and Condorcet on National Education.* New York: McGraw-Hill, 1932.
d'Estampes de Valançay, Léonor. "Ordonnances et réglemens pour estre
   gardez par tout le diocèse de Reims." In *Les actes de la province ecclésiastique de
   Reims: Ou canons et décrets des conciles, constitutions, statuts, et lettres des évêques des
   différents diocèses qui dépendent ou qui dépendaient autrefois de la métropole de Reims,*
   edited by Thomas-Marie Gousset, 4:138–160. Reims: L. Jacquet, 1844.
Erasmus, Desiderius. "De pueris statim ac liberaliter instituendis libellus." In
   Desiderius Erasmus: Concerning the Aim and Method of Education, edited and
   translated by William Harrison Woodward, 180–222. Cambridge: Cambridge University Press, 1904.
———. "De ratione studii." In *Desiderius Erasmus: Concerning the Aim and
   Method of Education,* edited and translated by William Harrison Woodward, 162–78. Cambridge: Cambridge University Press, 1904.
Farrell, Allan P., ed. and trans. *The Jesuit Ratio Studiorum of 1599.* Washington, DC: Conference of Major Superiors of Jesuits, 1970.
Fénelon, François de Salignac de la Mothe. *De l'éducation des filles.* Paris: Bas-
   sompiere, 1771; reprint, Plan de la Tour, France: Éditions d'aujourd'hui,
   1983.
Fleury, Claude. *Traité du choix et de la méthode des études.* 1686; reprint, Paris,
   1724.
Gousset, Thomas-Marie, ed. *Les actes de la province ecclésiastique de Reims: Ou
   canons et décrets des conciles, constitutions, statuts, et lettres des évêques des différents
   diocèses qui dépendent ou qui dépendaient autrefois de la métropole de Reims.* Vol. 4.
   Reims: L. Jacquet, 1844.
Isambert, François, ed. *Recueil général des anciennes lois françaises depuis l'an 420
   jusqu'à la Révolution de 1789.* 29 vols. Paris: Belin-Le-Prieur, 1821–1833.

Jamerey-Duval, Valentin. *Mémoires: Enfance et éducation d'un paysan au XVIIIe siècle,* edited by Jean Goulemot. Paris: Sycomore, 1981.

La Chalotais, Louis-René de Caradeuc de. "Essay on National Education." In *French Liberalism and Education in the Eighteenth Century: The Writings of La Chalotais, Turgot, Diderot, and Condorcet on National Education.* Translated and edited by François de la Fontainerie, 27–169. New York: Mc-Graw-Hill, 1932.

La Salle, Jean-Baptiste de. *Conduite des Écoles chrétiennes.* Rome: Maison Saint Jean-Baptiste de La Salle, 1965.

Laurent, Gustave, ed. *Collection de documents inédits sur l'histoire économique de la Révolution Française.* Vol. 1, *Département de la Marne, Cahiers de doléances pour les États Généraux de 1789, Bailliage de Châlons-sur-Marne.* Épernay: Imprimerie Henri Villers, 1906.

———. *Collection de documents inédits sur l'histoire economique de la Révolution Française.* Vol. 4, *Reims et la région rémoise à la veille de la Révolution. Introduction aux cahiers de doléances du bailliage de Reims.* Reims: Imprimerie Matot-Braine, 1930.

Lavallée, Théophile, ed. *Entretiens sur l'éducation des filles.* Paris: Charpentier, 1854.

Le Clerc de Juigné, Antoine-Éléonor-Léon. "Reglement pour les maitres d'école." In *Abregé des statuts du diocése de Chaalons,* edited by Antoine-Éléonor-Léon Le Clerc de Juigné, 124–41. Châlons: Seneuze, 1770.

———. "Reglement pour les soeurs d'école." In *Abregé des statuts du diocése de Chaalons,* edited by Antoine-Éléonor-Léon Le Clerc de Juigné, 142–62. Châlons: Seneuze, 1770.

Le Clerc de Juigné, Antoine-Éléonor-Léon, ed. *Abregé des statuts du diocése de Chaalons.* Châlons: Seneuze, 1770.

Le Tellier, Charles Maurice. *Rituel de la province de Reims, renouvelé et augmenté.* Paris: Frederic Leonard, 1677.

Locke, John. *Some Thoughts Concerning Education.* Edited by John W. and Jean S. Yolton. Oxford: Clarendon Press, 1989.

"Maître d'école au bon vieux temps." In *Champagne Généalogie,* no. 102 (2004): 54–55.

McHugh, John A., and Charles J. Callan, eds. and trans. *Catechism of the Council of Trent for Parish Priests Issued by Order of Pope Pius V.* New York: Joseph F. Wagner, Inc., 1923.

Ministère de l'Instruction Publique et des Beaux-Arts. *Statistique de l'enseignement primaire.* Vol. 2, *Statistique comparée de l'enseignement primaire (1829–1877).* Paris: Imprimerie Nationale, 1880.

Nadaud, Martin. "Memoirs of Léonard, a Former Mason's Assistant." In *The French Worker: Autobiographies from the Early Industrial Era,* edited and translated by Mark Traugott, 183–249. Berkeley: University of California Press, 1993.

Noailles, Louis-Antoine de. "Reglemens pour la conduite des maitresses d'école du diocèse de Chaalons." In *Statuts, ordonnances, mandemens, reglemens, et lettres pastorales,* edited by Louis-Antoine de Noailles, 381–89. Châlons: Jacques Seneuze, 1693.

Noailles, Louis-Antoine de, ed. *Statuts, ordonnances, mandemens, reglemens, et lettres pastorales.* Châlons: Jacques Seneuze, 1693.

Quintilian. *The Orator's Education.* Edited and translated by Donald A. Russell. 5 vols. Cambridge, MA: Harvard University Press, 2001.

Rousseau, Jean-Jacques. *Emile, or On Education.* Translated by Allan Bloom. New York: Basic Books, 1979.

Schroeder, Henry Joseph, ed. and trans. *Canons and Decrees of the Council of Trent.* St. Louis, MO: B. Herder Book Company, 1941.

Talleyrand-Périgord, Alexandre-Angélique de. "Synode de Reims." In *Les actes de la province ecclésiastique de Reims: Ou canons et décrets des conciles, constitutions, statuts, et lettres des évêques des différents diocèses qui dépendent ou qui dépendaient autrefois de la métropole de Reims,* edited by Thomas-Marie Gousset, 4:773–812. Reims: L. Jacquet, 1844.

Traugott, Mark, ed. and trans. *The French Worker: Autobiographies from the Early Industrial Era.* Berkeley: University of California Press, 1993.

Vialart de Herse, Félix. "Ordonnances Synodales." In *Statuts, ordonnances, mandemens, reglemens, et lettres pastorales,* edited by Louis-Antoine de Noailles, 55–70. Châlons: Jacques Seneuze, 1693.

―――. "Reglemens pour les maitres d'école du diocèse de Chaalons." In *Statuts, ordonnances, mandemens, reglemens, et lettres pastorales,* edited by Louis-Antoine de Noailles, 377–80. Châlons: Jacques Seneuze, 1693.

―――. "Reglemens sur plusieurs points de la discipline ecclesiastique, faits en l'Assemblée des Archidiacres, Doiens et Promoteurs Ruraux, tenuë les 7 et 8 Novembre 1662." In *Statuts, ordonnances, mandemens, reglemens, et lettres pastorales,* edited by Louis-Antoine de Noailles, 32–47. Châlons: Jacques Seneuze, 1693.

Woodward, William Harrison, ed. and trans. *Desiderius Erasmus: Concerning the Aim and Method of Education.* Cambridge: Cambridge University Press, 1904.

Secondary Sources

Adam, Paul. *La vie paroissiale en France au XIVe siècle.* Histoire et sociologie de l'Église, directed by G. Le Bras and J. Gaudemet. Paris: Sirey, 1964.

Allain, Ernest. *L'instruction primaire en France avant la Révolution*. Paris, 1881; reprint, Geneva: Slatkine Reprints, 1970.

Anderson, R. D. *Education in France, 1848–1870*. Oxford: Clarendon Press, 1975.

Andriès, Lise. *La bibliothèque bleu au dix-huitième siècle: une tradition éditoriale*. Studies on Voltaire and the Eighteenth Century, no. 270. Oxford: Voltaire Foundation, 1989.

Ariès, Philippe. *Centuries of Childhood: A Social History of Family Life*. Translated by Robert Baldick. New York: Vintage Books, 1965.

Armogathe, Jean-Robert. "Les catéchismes et l'enseignement populaire en France au dix-huitième siècle." In *Images du peuple au dix-huitième siècle: Colloque d'Aix-en-Provence 25 et 26 Octobre 1969*, 103–21. Paris: A. Colin, 1973.

Armstrong, Megan C. *The Politics of Piety: Franciscan Preachers During the Wars of Religion, 1560–1600*. Rochester, NY: University of Rochester Press, 2004.

Arnold, John H. *Belief and Unbelief in Medieval Europe*. London: Hodder Arnold, 2005.

Aston, Nigel. *The End of an Élite: The French Bishops and the Coming of the Revolution 1786–1790*. Oxford: Clarendon Press, 1992.

———. *Religion and Revolution in France, 1780–1804*. Washington, DC: Catholic University of America Press, 2000.

Aulagne, Joseph. *La réforme catholique du dix-septième siècle dans le diocèse de Limoges*. Paris: Honoré Champion, 1908.

Baccrabère, Georges. *Les paroisses rurales du diocèse de Toulouse aux 16e–17e siècles*. Strasbourg: Muh-Le Roux, 1968.

Baker, Donald N., and Patrick J. Harrigan. *The Making of Frenchmen: Current Directions in the History of Education in France, 1679–1979*. Waterloo, Ontario: Historical Reflections Press, 1980.

Barnard, H. C. *The French Tradition in Education: Ramus to Mme Necker de Saussure*. 1922; reprint, Cambridge: Cambridge University Press, 1970.

———. *Girls at School under the Ancien Régime*. London: Burns and Oates, 1954.

Barnes, Andrew E. *The Social Dimension of Piety: Associative Life and Devotional Change in the Penitent Confraternities of Marseilles (1499–1892)*. New York: Paulist Press, 1994.

Bast, Robert James. *Honor Your Fathers: Catechisms and the Emergence of a Patriarchal Ideology in Germany 1400–1600*. Studies in Medieval and Reformation Thought, vol. 63. Leiden: Brill, 1997.

Beam, Sara. *Laughing Matters: Farce and the Making of Absolutism in France*. Ithaca, NY: Cornell University Press, 2007.

Bedouelle, Guy. "L'influence des catéchismes de Canisius en France." In *Aux origines du catéchisme en France*, edited by Pierre Colin et al., 67–86. Paris: Desclée, 1989.

Beik, William. *Absolutism and Society in Seventeenth-Century France: State Power and Provincial Aristocracy in Languedoc.* Cambridge: Cambridge University Press, 1985.

Benedict, Philip. "Confessionalization in France? Critical Reflections and New Evidence." In *Society and Culture in the Huguenot World, 1559–1685,* edited by Raymond A. Mentzer and Andrew Spicer, 44–61. Cambridge: Cambridge University Press, 2002.

———. *The Huguenot Population of France, 1600–1685: The Demographic Fate and Customs of a Religious Minority.* Philadelphia: American Philosophical Society, 1991.

———. *Rouen during the Wars of Religion.* Cambridge: Cambridge University Press, 1981.

Bergin, Joseph. *Church, Society and Religious Change in France, 1580–1730.* New Haven, CT: Yale University Press, 2009.

———. *Crown, Church and Episcopate under Louis XIV.* New Haven, CT: Yale University Press, 2004.

———. *The Making of the French Episcopate, 1589–1661.* New Haven, CT: Yale University Press, 1996.

Berthelot du Chesnay, Charles. *Les Prêtres séculiers en Haute-Bretagne au XVIIIe siècle.* Rennes: Presses universitaires de Rennes, 1974.

Bloch, Jean. *Rousseauism and Education in Eighteenth-Century France.* Studies on Voltaire and the Eighteenth Century, no. 325. Oxford: Voltaire Foundation, 1995.

Bossy, John. *Christianity in the West, 1400–1700.* Oxford: Oxford University Press, 1985.

Boulanger, Jean-François. "Deux siècles de réforme catholique (1640–1789)." In *Le diocèse de Châlons,* edited by Georges Clause, 83–119. Paris: Beauchesne, 1989.

———. *Réforme et visites pastorales dans le diocèse de Châlons-sur-Marne (1642–1752).* Mémoire de maîtrise, Université de Reims, 1971.

Brady, Thomas A., et al. *Handbook of European History, 1400–1600: Late Middle Ages, Renaissance and Reformation.* 2 vols. Leiden: E. J. Brill, 1994–1995.

Bricard, Isabelle. *Saintes ou pouliches: L'Éducation des jeunes filles au XIXe siècle.* Paris: Albin Michel, 1985.

Brown, Peter. *The Cult of the Saints: Its Rise and Function in Latin Christianity.* Chicago: University of Chicago Press, 1981.

Cabantous, Alain, and Jean Delumeau, eds. *La première Communion: Quatre siècles d'histoire.* Paris: Desclée de Brouwer, 1987.

Carrière, Victor. *Introduction aux études d'histoire ecclésiastique locale.* 3 vols. Paris: Letouzey et Ané, 1934–1940.

Carroll, Michael P. *Veiled Threats: The Logic of Popular Catholicism in Italy.* Baltimore, MD: Johns Hopkins University Press, 1996.

Carruthers, Mary. *The Book of Memory: A Study of Memory in Medieval Culture.* Cambridge: Cambridge University Press, 1990.

Carter, Karen E. "'Les garçons et les filles sont pêle-mêle dans l'école': Gender and Primary Education in Early Modern France." *French Historical Studies* 31, no. 3 (Summer 2008): 417–43.

———. "The Science of Salvation: French Diocesan Catechisms and Catholic Reform (1650–1800)." *Catholic Historical Review* 96 (2010): 234–61.

Chaline, Nadine Josette, ed. *Le diocèse de Rouen-Le Havre.* Histoire des diocèses de France, no. 5. Paris: Beauchesne, 1976.

Charlton, Kenneth. *Women, Religion and Education in Early Modern England.* London: Routledge, 1999.

Chartier, Roger. *The Cultural Uses of Print in Early Modern France.* Translated by Lydia G. Cochrane. Princeton, NJ: Princeton University Press, 1987.

———. *The Cultural Origins of the French Revolution.* Translated by Lydia G. Cochrane. Durham, NC: Duke University Press, 1991.

———. *The Order of Books: Readers, Authors, and Libraries in Europe between the Fourteenth and Eighteenth Centuries.* Translated by Lydia G. Cochrane. Stanford: Stanford University Press, 1994.

Chartier, Roger, Dominique Julia, and Marie-Madeleine Compère. *L'Éducation en France du XVIe au XVIIIe siècle.* Paris: Société d'Édition d'Enseignement Supérieur, 1976.

Châtellier, Louis. *L'Europe des dévots.* Paris: Flammarion, 1987.

———. *The Religion of the Poor: Rural Missions in Europe and the Formation of Modern Catholicism, c. 1500–c. 1800.* Translated by Brian Pearce. Cambridge: Cambridge University Press, 1997.

———. *Tradition chrétienne et renouveau catholique: dans le cadre de l'ancien diocèse de Strasbourg (1650–1770).* Paris: Ophrys, 1981.

Chisick, Harvey. *The Limits of Reform in the Enlightenment: Attitudes toward the Education of the Lower Classes in Eighteenth-Century France.* Princeton, NJ: Princeton University Press, 1981.

Cholvy, Gérard, ed. *Le diocèse de Montpellier.* Histoire des diocèses de France, no. 4. Paris: Beauchesne, 1976.

Chomel, Vital, ed. *Le diocèse de Grenoble.* Histoire des diocèses de France, no. 12. Paris: Beauchesne, 1979.

Choudhury, Mita. *Convents and Nuns in Eighteenth-Century French Politics and Culture.* Ithaca, NY: Cornell University Press, 2004.

Christian, William A., Jr. *Local Religion in Sixteenth-Century Spain.* Princeton, NJ: Princeton University Press, 1981.

Clause, Georges, ed. *Le diocèse de Châlons.* Histoire des diocèses de France, no. 23. Paris: Beauchesne, 1989.

Colin, Pierre et al., eds. *Aux origines du catéchisme en France.* Paris: Desclée, 1989.

Collins, James B. "The Economic Role of Women in Seventeenth-Century France." *French Historical Studies* 16 (1989): 436–70.

———. *The Fiscal Limits of Absolutism: Direct Taxation in Early Seventeenth-Century France.* Berkeley: University of California Press, 1988.

———. *The State in Early Modern France.* 2nd ed. Cambridge: Cambridge University Press, 2009.

Comerford, Kathleen M. "Clerical Education, Catechesis, and Catholic Confessionalism: Teaching Religion in the Sixteenth and Seventeenth Centuries." In *Early Modern Catholicism: Essays in Honour of John W. O'Malley, S.J.,* edited by Kathleen M. Comerford and Hilmar M. Pabel, 241–65. Toronto: University of Toronto Press, 2001.

Compère, Marie-Madeleine, and Dominique Julia. *Les collèges français, 16e–18e siècles.* 2 vols. Paris: Institut national de recherche pédagogique, 1984–1988.

Cramer, Peter. *Baptism and Change in the Early Middle Ages, c. 200–c. 1150.* Cambridge: Cambridge University Press, 1993.

Cressy, David. *Literacy and the Social Order: Reading and Writing in Tudor and Stuart England.* Cambridge: Cambridge University Press, 1980.

Cunningham, Hugh. *Children and Childhood in Western Society since 1500.* 2nd ed. London: Longman, 2005.

Curtis, Sarah A. *Educating the Faithful: Religion, Schooling, and Society in Nineteenth-Century France.* DeKalb: Northern Illinois University Press, 2000.

Dainville, François de. *L'Éducation des jésuites: XVIe–XVIIIe siècles.* Paris: Éditions de Minuit, 1978.

Darricau, Raymond. "Les catéchismes, au XVIIIe siècle, dans les diocèses de l'Ouest." *Annales de Bretagne* 81 (1974): 599–614.

Davis, Natalie Zemon. *Society and Culture in Early Modern France.* Stanford: Stanford University Press, 1975.

———. "Women in the Crafts in Sixteenth-Century Lyon." *Feminist Studies* 8 (1982): 46–80.

de Boer, Wietse. *The Conquest of the Soul: Confession, Discipline, and Public Order in Counter-Reformation Milan.* Leiden: Brill, 2001.

———. "Social Discipline in Italy: Peregrinations of a Historical Paradigm." *Archive for Reformation History* 94 (2003): 294–307.

Degert, A. *Histoire des séminaires français jusqu'à la Révolution.* 2 vols. Paris: Beauchesne, 1912.

Delumeau, Jean. *Catholicism between Luther and Voltaire: A New View of the Counter-Reformation.* Translated by Jeremy Moiser. London: Burns and Oates, 1977.

————. *Le péché et la peur: la culpabilisation en Occident, XIIIe–XVIIIe siècles.* Paris: Fayard, 1983.

Delumeau, Jean, ed. *Le diocèse de Rennes.* Histoire des diocèses de France, no. 10. Paris: Beauchesne, 1979.

Deregnaucourt, Gilles. *De Fénelon à la Révolution: Le clergé paroissial de l'archevêché de Cambrai.* Lille: Presses Universitaires de Lille, 1991.

Desan, Suzanne. *Reclaiming the Sacred: Lay Religion and Popular Politics in Revolutionary France.* Ithaca, NY: Cornell University Press, 1990.

Desportes, Pierre. *Diocèse de Reims.* Fasti ecclesiae Gallicanae, no. 3. Turnhout: Brepols, 1998.

Devailly, Guy, ed. *Le diocèse de Bourges.* Histoire des diocèses de France. Paris: Letouzey et Ané, 1973.

Dhotel, Jean-Claude. *Les origines du Catéchisme moderne d'après les premiers manuels imprimés en France.* Paris: Éditions Montaigne, 1967.

Diefendorf, Barbara B. *From Penitence to Charity: Pious Women and the Catholic Reformation in Paris.* Oxford: Oxford University Press, 2004.

Dompnier, Bernard. *Le venin de l'hérésie: Image du protestantisme et combat catholique au XVIIe siècle.* Paris: Le Centurion, 1985.

Doyle, William. *Jansenism: Catholic Resistance to Authority from the Reformation to the French Revolution.* New York: St. Martin's Press, 2000.

Dubois, Elfrieda T. "The Education of Women in Seventeenth-Century France." *French Studies* 32 (1978): 1–19.

Durand, Yves, ed. *Le diocèse de Nantes.* Histoire des diocèses de France, no. 18. Paris: Beauchesne, 1985.

Elias, Norbert. *The Civilizing Process: Sociogenetic and Psychogenetic Investigations.* Translated by Edmund Jephcott. Oxford: Blackwell, 2000.

Enright, Amy. "The Politics of Education: Municipal *Collèges* and Political Culture in Early Modern Champagne." Ph.D. diss., Emory University, 2004.

Farr, James R. "Confessionalization and Social Discipline in France, 1530–1685." *Archive for Reformation History* 94 (2003): 276–93.

Farrell, Allan P. *The Jesuit Code of Liberal Education: Development and Scope of the Ratio Studiorum.* Milwaukee: Bruce, 1938.

Favreau, Robert, ed. *The diocèse de Poitiers.* Histoire des diocèses de France, no. 22. Paris: Beauchesne, 1988.

Ferguson, Margaret W. *Dido's Daughters: Literacy, Gender, and Empire in Early Modern England and France.* Chicago: University of Chicago Press, 2003.

Ferté, Jeanne. *La vie religieuse dans les campagnes parisiennes (1622–1695).* Paris: Librairie Philosophique J. Vrin, 1962.

Fiévet, Michel. *L'invention de l'école des filles: Des Amazones de Dieu aux XVIIe et XVIIIe siècles.* Paris: Imago, 2006.

Fletcher, Anthony. *Growing Up in England: The Experience of Childhood, 1600–1914*. New Haven, CT: Yale University Press, 2008.

Fleury, Michel, and Pierre Valmary. "Les progrès de l'instruction élémentaire de Louis XIV à Napoléon III d'après l'enquête de L. Maggiolo (1877–79)." *Population* 12 (January–March 1957): 71–92.

Forrestal, Alison. *Fathers, Pastors and Kings: Visions of Episcopacy in Seventeenth-Century France*. Manchester: Manchester University Press, 2004.

Forster, Marc. *Catholic Revival in the Age of the Baroque: Religious Identity in Southwest Germany, 1550–1750*. Cambridge: Cambridge University Press, 2001.

Foucault, Michel. *Histoire de la folie à l'âge classique*. Paris: Gallimard, 1972.

———. *Histoire de la sexualité*. 3 vols. Paris: Gallimard, 1976–1984.

———. *Surveiller et punir: Naissance de la prison*. Paris: Gallimard, 1975.

Frijhoff, Willem, and Dominique Julia. *École et société dans la France d'Ancien Régime: Quatre exemples, Auch, Avallon, Condom et Gisors*. Paris: A. Colin, 1975.

Froeschlé-Chopard, Marie-Hélène. *La religion populaire en Provence orientale au XVIIIe siècle*. Paris: Éditions Beauchesne, 1980.

Furet, François, and Jacques Ozouf. *Reading and Writing: Literacy in France from Calvin to Jules Ferry*. Cambridge: Cambridge University Press, 1982.

Gadille, Jacques, ed. *Le diocèse de Lyon*. Histoire des diocèses de France, no. 16. Paris: Beauchesne, 1983.

Galpern, A. N. *The Religions of the People in Sixteenth-Century Champagne*. Cambridge, MA: Harvard University Press, 1976.

Germain, Elisabeth. *Jésus Christ dans les catéchismes: Étude historique*. Paris: Desclée, 1986.

———. *Langages de la foi à travers l'histoire*. Paris: Fayard-Mame, 1972.

———. *Parler du salut? Aux origines d'une mentalité religieuse*. Paris: Beauchesne et ses fils, 1968.

———. *2000 ans d'éducation de la foi*. Paris: Desclée, 1983.

Gilbert, Roger. *Charles Démia (1637–1689): Fondateur Lyonnais des petites écoles des pauvres*. Lyon: E. Robert, 1989.

Gildea, Robert. *Education in Provincial France, 1800–1914: A Study of Three Departments*. Oxford: Clarendon Press, 1983.

Gontard, Maurice. *L'enseignement primaire en France de la Révolution de 1789 à la loi Guizot, 1789–1833: Des petites écoles de la monarchie d'ancien régime aux écoles primaires de la monarchie bourgeoise*. Paris: Belles Lettres, 1959.

Gorski, Philip S. *The Disciplinary Revolution: Calvinism and the Rise of the State in Early Modern Europe*. Chicago: University of Chicago Press, 2003.

Goubet-Mahé, Maryvonne. "Le premier rituel de la première Communion XVIe–XVIIe siècle." In *La première Communion: Quatre siècles d'histoire*, edited by Alain Cabantous and Jean Delumeau, 51–76. Paris: Desclée de Brouwer, 1987.

Goujard, Philippe. *Un catholicisme bien tempéré: La vie religieuse dans les paroisses rurales de Haute-Normandie 1680–1789*. Paris: Éditions du C.T.H.S., 1996.

Graff, Harvey J. *The Labyrinths of Literacy: Reflections on Literacy Past and Present*. Rev. Ed. Pittsburgh: University of Pittsburgh Press, 1995.

———. *The Legacies of Literacy: Continuities and Contradictions in Western Culture and Society*. Bloomington: Indiana University Press, 1987.

Grandière, Marcel. *L'Idéal pédagogique en France au dix-huitième siècle*. Studies on Voltaire and the Eighteenth Century, no. 361. Oxford: Voltaire Foundation, 1998.

Green, I. M. *The Christian's ABC: Catechisms and Catechizing in England, c. 1530–1740*. New York: Clarendon Press, 1996.

Grendler, Paul F. *Books and Schools in the Italian Renaissance*. Aldershot: Variorum, 1995.

———. "Schools, Seminaries, and Catechetical Instruction." In *Catholicism in Early Modern History: A Guide to Research,* edited by John O'Malley, 315–30. St. Louis: Center for Reformation Research, 1988.

Grew, Raymond, and Patrick J. Harrigan. *School, State, and Society: The Growth of Elementary Schooling in Nineteenth-Century France: A Quantitative Analysis*. Ann Arbor: University of Michigan Press, 1991.

Grosperrin, Bernard. *Les petites écoles sous l'Ancien Régime*. Rennes: Ouest France, 1984.

Guillemain, Bernard, ed. *Le diocèse de Bordeaux*. Histoire des diocèses de France, no. 2. Paris: Beauchesne, 1974.

Hanlon, Gregory. *Confession and Community in Seventeenth-Century France: Catholic and Protestant Coexistence in Aquitaine*. Philadelphia: University of Pennsylvania Press, 1993.

Harline, Craig. *The Burdens of Sister Margaret: Inside a Seventeenth-Century Convent*. Abr. ed. New Haven, CT: Yale University Press, 2000.

Harline, Craig, and Eddy Put. *A Bishop's Tale: Mathias Hovius Among His Flock in Seventeenth-Century Flanders*. New Haven, CT: Yale University Press, 2000.

Hayden, J. Michael, and Malcolm R. Greenshields. *Six Hundred Years of Reform: Bishops and the French Church, 1190–1789*. Montreal: McGill-Queen's University Press, 2005.

Heywood, Colin. *Growing Up in France: From the Ancien Régime to the Third Republic*. Cambridge: Cambridge University Press, 2007.

Hézard, Pierre-Modeste. *Histoire du catéchisme depuis la naissance de l'église jusqu'à nos jours*. Paris: Victor-Retaux, 1900.

Hildesheimer, Françoise, ed. *Les diocèses de Nice et Monaco*. Histoire des diocèses de France, no. 17. Paris: Beauchesne, 1984.

Hoffman, Philip T. *Church and Community in the Diocese of Lyon, 1500–1789*. New Haven, CT: Yale University Press, 1984.

Houston, R. A. *Literacy in Early Modern Europe: Culture and Education, 1500–1800.* 2nd ed. New York: Longman, 2002.

Hsia, R. Po-chia. *Social Discipline in the Reformation: Central Europe, 1550–1750.* London: Routledge, 1989.

Huppert, George. *Public Schools in Renaissance France.* Urbana: University of Illinois Press, 1984.

Jean, Armand. *Les Évêques et les Archevêques de France depuis 1682 jusqu'à 1801.* Paris: Alphonse Picard, 1891.

Jedin, Hubert. "Catholic Reformation or Counter-Reformation?" In *The Counter-Reformation: The Essential Readings,* edited by David M. Luebke, 21–45. Malden, MA: Blackwell, 1999.

Johansson, Egil. *The History of Literacy in Sweden in Comparison with Some Other Countries.* Education Reports Umeå, no. 12, 1977.

Julg, Jean. *Les évêques dans l'histoire de la France: Des origines à nos jours.* Paris: Téqui, 2004.

Julia, Dominique. "Le clergé paroissial dans le diocèse de Reims à la fin du XVIIIe siècle." *Revue d'histoire moderne et contemporaine* 13 (1966): 195–216.

———. "L'Enseignement primaire dans le diocèse de Reims à la fin de l'Ancien Régime." *Annales Historiques de la Révolution Française* 2 (1970): 233–86.

———. "La leçon de catéchisme dans *L'Escole Paroissiale* (1654)." In *Aux origines du catéchisme en France,* edited by Pierre Colin et al., 160–83. Paris: Desclée, 1989.

———. "Les pèlerinages de Pierre Bernard, maître d'école Amiénois (1730–1764). In *Foi, fidelité, amitié en Europe à la période moderne: Mélanges offerts à Robert Sauzet,* edited by Brigitte Maillard, 2:355–73. Tours: Publication de l'Université de Tours, 1995.

———. "Les petites écoles rurales dans le diocèse de Reims dans la second moitié du XVIIe siècle." *Travaux de l'Académie Nationale de Reims* 161 (1982): 23–48.

———. "Le prêtre au XVIIIe siècle: La théologie et les institutions." *Recherches de science religieuse* 58 (1970): 521–34.

———. *Les trois couleurs de tableau noir: La Révolution.* Paris: Belin, 1981.

Kaplan, Benjamin J. *Calvinists and Libertines: Confession and Community in Utrecht, 1578–1620.* Oxford: Clarendon Press, 1995.

Kselman, Thomas, ed. *Belief in History: Innovative Approaches to European and American Religion.* Notre Dame, IN: University of Notre Dame Press, 1991.

Laffon, Jean-Baptiste, ed. *Le diocèse de Tarbes et Lourdes.* Histoire des diocèses de France. Paris: Letouzey et Ané, 1971.

Le Bras, Gabriel. *L'Église et le village.* Paris: Flammarion, 1976.

———. *Études de sociologie religieuse.* 2 vols. Paris: Presses Universitaires de France, 1955–1956.

————. *Introduction à l'histoire de la pratique religieuse en France*. 2 vols. Paris: Presses Universitaires de France, 1942–1945.

————, ed. *Répertoire des visites pastorales de la France*. Series 1, Anciens diocèses jusqu'en 1790. Paris: Éditions du C. N. R. S., 1977–1985.

Lebrun, François, ed. *Le diocèse d'Angers*. Histoire des diocèses de France, no. 13. Paris: Beauchesne, 1981.

Lemaitre, Nicole. "Avant la Communion solennelle." In *La première Communion: Quatre siècles d'histoire*, edited by Alain Cabantous and Jean Delumeau, 15–32. Paris: Desclée de Brouwer, 1987.

————. "Le catéchisme avant les catéchismes, dans les rituels." In *Aux origines du catéchisme en France*, edited by Pierre Colin et al., 28–41. Paris: Desclée, 1989.

Leonard, Amy. *Nails in the Wall: Catholic Nuns in Reformation Germany*. Chicago: University of Chicago Press, 2005.

Lotz-Heumann, Ute. "Social Control and Church Discipline in Ireland in the Sixteenth and Early Seventeenth Centuries." In *Institutions, Instruments, and Agents of Social Control and Discipline in Early Modern Europe*, edited by Heinz Schilling and Lars Behrisch, 275–304. Frankfurt: Vittorio Klostermann, 1999.

Luria, Keith P. *Sacred Boundaries: Religious Coexistence and Conflict in Early-Modern France*. Washington, DC: Catholic University of America Press, 2005.

————. *Territories of Grace: Cultural Change in the Seventeenth-Century Diocese of Grenoble*. Berkeley: University of California Press, 1991.

Lux-Sterritt, Laurence. *Redefining Female Religious Life: French Ursulines and English Ladies in Seventeenth-Century Catholicism*. Burlington, VT: Ashgate, 2005.

Maillard, Brigitte. "De la visite pastorale à l'enquête administrative: les méthodes d'investigation des archevêques de Tours au temps des lumières." In *Foi, fidelité, amitié en Europe à la période moderne: Mélanges offerts à Robert Sauzet*, edited by Brigitte Maillard, 1:67–76. Tours: Publication de l'Université de Tours, 1995.

Maillard, Brigitte, ed. *Foi, fidelité, amitié en Europe à la période moderne: Mélanges offerts à Robert Sauzet*. 2 vols. Tours: Publication de l'Université de Tours, 1995.

Maillard, Jacques. "Le livre religieux dans la boutique d'un libraire Angevin en 1777." In *Foi, fidelité, amitié en Europe à la période moderne: Mélanges offerts à Robert Sauzet*, edited by Brigitte Maillard, 2:383–90. Tours: Publication de l'Université de Tours, 1995.

Marthaler, Berard L. *The Catechism Yesterday and Today: The Evolution of a Genre*. Collegeville, MN: Liturgical Press, 1995.

Martin, Henri-Jean. *The History and Power of Writing*. Translated by Lydia G. Cochrane. Chicago: University of Chicago Press, 1994.

Martin, Henri-Jean, and Roger Chartier. *Histoire de l'édition française*. 4 vols. Paris: Promodis, 1983–1986.

Martin, Marie de Saint John. *Ursuline Method of Education*. Rahway, NJ: Quinn and Boden, 1946.

Martin, Philippe. *Une religion des livres (1640–1850)*. Paris: Les Éditions du Cerf, 2003.

Maynes, Mary Jo. *Schooling for the People: Comparative Local Studies of Schooling History in France and Germany, 1750–1850*. New York: Holmes and Meier, 1985.

———. *Schooling in Western Europe: A Social History*. Albany: State University of New York Press, 1985.

McGuire, Brian Patrick. *Jean Gerson and the Last Medieval Reformation*. University Park: Pennsylvania State University Press, 2005.

McManners, John. *Church and Society in Eighteenth-Century France*. 2 vols. Oxford: Oxford University Press, 1998.

Melton, James Van Horn. *Absolutism and the Eighteenth-Century Origins of Compulsory Schooling in Prussia and Austria*. Cambridge: Cambridge University Press, 1988.

Miller, C. Ronald. "The French Seminary in the Eighteenth Century." Ph.D. diss., Catholic University of America, 1988.

Millet, Olivier. "Rendre raison de la foi: Le Catéchisme de Calvin (1542)." In *Aux origines du catéchisme en France*, edited by Pierre Colin et al., 188–203. Paris: Desclée, 1989.

Minois, Georges. *La Bretagne des prêtres en Trégor d'Ancien Régime*. Beltan, 1987.

Moody, Joseph N. *French Education Since Napoleon*. Syracuse: Syracuse University Press, 1978.

Moran Cruz, Jo Ann Hoeppner. *The Growth of English Schooling, 1340–1548: Learning, Literacy and Laicization in Pre-Reformation York Diocese*. Princeton, NJ: Princeton University Press, 1985.

Nahoum, V. "En Champagne: signatures au mariage (XVIIe–XVIIIe siècles)." In *Lire et écrire: l'alphabétisation des Français de Calvin à Jules Ferry*, edited by François Furet and Jacques Ozouf, 2:187–216. Paris: Les Éditions de Minuit, 1977.

Nalle, Sara T. *God in La Mancha: Religious Reform and the People of Cuenca, 1500–1650*. Baltimore, MD: Johns Hopkins University Press, 1992.

Nelson, Eric. *The Jesuits and the Monarchy: Catholic Reform and Political Authority in France (1590–1615)*. Burlington, VT: Ashgate, 2005.

O'Malley, John. *The First Jesuits*. Cambridge, MA: Harvard University Press, 1993.

———. *Trent and All That: Renaming Catholicism in the Early Modern Era*. Cambridge, MA: Harvard University Press, 2000.

Ong, Walter J. "Writing Is a Technology that Restructures Thought." In *The Written Word: Literacy in Transition,* edited by Gerd Baumann, 23–50. Oxford: Clarendon Press, 1986.

Orme, Nicholas. *Education and Society in Medieval and Renaissance England.* London: Hambledon Press, 1989.

————. *Medieval Children.* New Haven, CT: Yale University Press, 2001.

————. *Medieval Schools: From Roman Britain to Renaissance England.* New Haven, CT: Yale University Press, 2006.

Ozouf, Mona. *L'École, l'Église et la République, 1871–1914.* Paris: A. Colin, 1963.

Palanque, Jean-Rémy, ed. *Le diocèse d'Aix-en-Provence.* Histoire des diocèses de France, no. 3. Paris: Beauchesne, 1975.

————. *Le diocèse de Marseilles.* Histoire des diocèses de France. Paris: Letouzey et Ané, 1967.

Parker, Charles H. *Faith on the Margins: Catholics and Catholicism in the Dutch Golden Age.* Cambridge, MA: Harvard University Press, 2008.

Parsons, Jotham. *The Church in the Republic: Gallicanism and Political Ideology in Renaissance France.* Washington, DC: Catholic University of America Press, 2004.

Peronnet, M. C. *Les Évêques de l'ancienne France.* 2 vols. Paris: Diffusion H. Champion, 1977.

Pérouas, Louis. *Le diocèse de La Rochelle de 1648 à 1724: Sociologie et pastorale.* Paris: S.E.V.P.E.N., 1964.

Pettegree, Andrew, Paul Nelles, and Philip Conner, eds. *The Sixteenth-Century French Religious Book.* Burlington, VT: Ashgate, 2001.

Phillips, Henry. *Church and Culture in Seventeenth-Century France.* Cambridge: Cambridge University Press, 1997.

Pierrard, Pierre, ed. *Les diocèses de Cambrai et de Lille.* Histoire des diocèses de France, no. 8. Paris: Beauchesne, 1978.

Plongeron, Bernard, ed. *Le diocèse de Paris.* Histoire des diocèses de France, no. 20. Paris: Beauchesne, 1987.

Plongeron, Bernard, and Robert Pannet, eds. *Le Christianisme populaire: Les dossiers de l'histoire.* Paris: Le Centurion, 1976.

Poitrineau, Abel, ed. *Le diocèse de Clermont.* Histoire des diocèses de France, no. 9. Paris: Beauchesne, 1979.

Poska, Allyson M. *Regulating the People: The Catholic Reformation in Seventeenth-Century Spain.* Leiden: Brill, 1998.

————. "Confessionalization and Social Discipline in the Iberian World." *Archive for Reformation History* 94 (2003): 308–18.

Prévot, Jacques. *La première institutrice de France: Madame de Maintenon.* Paris: Belin, 1981.

Prost, Antoine. *Histoire de l'enseignement en France, 1800–1967.* Paris: A. Colin, 1968.

Puiseux, Jules-Ernest. "La condition des maîtres d'école au XVIIe et XVIIIe siècle." *Mémoires de la société d'agriculture, commerce, sciences et arts du département de la Marne* (1881–1882): 141–60.

————. *L'Instruction primaire dans le diocèse ancien de Châlons-sur-Marne avant 1789.* Châlons-sur-Marne: T. Martin, 1881.

Put, Eddy. *De Cleijne Schoolen: Het volksonderwijs in het hertogdom Brabant tussen Katholieke Reformatie en Verlichting (eind 16de eeuw–1795).* Leuven: Universitaire Pers Leuven, 1990.

Py, Gilbert. *Rousseau et les éducateurs: Étude sur la fortune des idées pédagogiques de Jean Jacques Rousseau en France et en Europe au XVIIIe siècle.* Studies on Voltaire and the Eighteenth Century, no. 356. Oxford: Voltaire Foundation, 1997.

Quantin, Max. "Histoire de l'instruction primaire avant 1790 dans les pays qui forment le département de l'Yonne." *Annuaire historique du Département de l'Yonne* 14 (1875): 50–190.

Rapley, Elizabeth. *The Dévotes: Women and Church in Seventeenth-Century France.* Montreal: McGill-Queen's University Press, 1990.

————. "Fénelon Revisited: A Review of Girls' Education in Seventeenth Century France." *Social History* 20 (1987): 299–318.

Rapp, Francis, ed. *Le diocèse de Strasbourg.* Histoire des diocèses de France, no. 14. Paris: Beauchesne, 1982.

Reinhard, Wolfgang. "Gegenreformation als Modernisierung? Prolegomena zu einer Theorie des konfessionellen Zeitalters." *Archive for Reformation History* 68 (1977): 226–52.

————. "Reformation, Counter-Reformation, and the Early Modern State: A Reassessment." *Catholic Historical Review* 75 (1989): 383–404.

Rey, Maurice, ed. *Les diocèses de Besançon et de Saint-Claude.* Histoire des diocèses de France, no. 6. Paris: Beauchesne, 1977.

Rigogne, Thierry. *Between State and Market: Printing and Bookselling in Eighteenth-Century France.* Oxford: Voltaire Foundation, 2007.

Robert, Odile. "Fonctionnement et enjeux d'une institution chrétienne au XVIIIe siècle." In *La première Communion: Quatre siècles d'histoire,* edited by Alain Cabantous and Jean Delumeau, 77–113. Paris: Desclée de Brouwer, 1987.

Rogers, Rebecca. *From the Salon to the Schoolroom: Educating Bourgeois Girls in Nineteenth-Century France.* University Park: Pennsylvania State University Press, 2005.

Ross, Sydney. "Scientist: The Story of a Word." *Annals of Science* 18 (1962): 65–85.

Sabean, David. *Power in the Blood: Popular Culture and Village Discourse in Early Modern Germany*. Cambridge: Cambridge University Press, 1984.

Sauzet, Robert. "Aux origines." In *La première Communion: Quatre siècles d'histoire*, edited by Jean Delumeau, 33–50. Paris: Desclée de Brouwer, 1987.

———. *Contre-réforme et réforme catholique en bas-Languedoc: Le diocèse de Nîmes au XVIIe siècle*. Brussels: Éditions Nauwelaerts, 1979.

———. *Les visites pastorales dans le diocèse de Chartres pendant la première moitié du XVIIe siècle*. Rome: Edizioni di Storia e Letteratura, 1975.

Schilling, Heinz. "'Konfessionsbildung' und 'Konfessionalisierung.'" *Geschichte in Wissenschaft und Unterricht* 42 (1991): 447–63.

———. "Confessional Europe." In *Handbook of European History, 1400–1600: Late Middle Ages, Renaissance and Reformation*, vol. 2, *Visions, Programs, Outcomes*, edited by Thomas A. Brady et al., 641–81. Leiden: E. J. Brill, 1995.

———. "Confessionalization in the Empire: Religious and Societal Change in Germany between 1555 and 1620." In *Religion, Political Culture and the Emergence of Early Modern Society: Essays in German and Dutch History*, 205–45. Leiden: Brill, 1992.

Sedgwick, Alexander. *Jansenism in Seventeenth-Century France: Voices from the Wilderness*. Charlottesville: University Press of Virginia, 1977.

Selwyn, Jennifer D. *A Paradise Inhabited by Devils: The Jesuits' Civilizing Mission in Early Modern Naples*. Burlington, VT: Ashgate, 2004.

Shahar, Shulamith. *Childhood in the Middle Ages*. London: Routledge, 1990.

Shapiro, Gilbert, and John Markoff. *Revolutionary Demands: A Content Analysis of the Cahiers de Doléances of 1789*. Stanford: Stanford University Press, 1998.

Singer, Barnett. *Village Notables in Nineteenth-Century France: Priests, Mayors, Schoolmasters*. Albany: State University of New York Press, 1983.

Sommerville, C. John. *The Discovery of Childhood in Puritan England*. Athens: University of Georgia Press, 1992.

Sonnet, Martine. *L'éducation des filles au temps des Lumières*. Paris: Cerf, 1987.

Spence, Jonathan D. *The Memory Palace of Matteo Ricci*. New York: Viking Penguin, 1984.

Strauss, Gerald. *Luther's House of Learning: Indoctrination of the Young in the German Reformation*. Baltimore, MD: Johns Hopkins University Press, 1978.

Tackett, Timothy. *Priest and Parish in Eighteenth-Century France: A Social and Political Study of the Curés in a Diocese of Dauphiné, 1750–1791*. Princeton, NJ: Princeton University Press, 1977.

———. *Religion, Revolution, and Regional Culture in Eighteenth-Century France: The Ecclesiastical Oath of 1791*. Princeton, NJ: Princeton University Press, 1986.

Tallon, Alain. *La France et le Concile de Trente, 1518–1563*. Rome: École française de Rome, 1997.

Thomas, Keith. "The Meaning of Literacy in Early Modern England." In *The Written Word: Literacy in Transition,* edited by Gerd Baumann, 97–131. Oxford: Clarendon Press, 1986.

Trénard, Louis. *Le diocèse de Belley.* Histoire des diocèses de France, no. 7. Paris: Beauchesne, 1978.

Van Kley, Dale. *The Jansenists and the Expulsion of the Jesuits from France, 1757–1765.* New Haven, CT: Yale University Press, 1975.

———. *The Religious Origins of the French Revolution: From Calvin to the Civil Constitution, 1560–1791.* New Haven, CT: Yale University Press, 1996.

Venard, Marc. "Les visites pastorales françaises du XVIe au XVIIIe siècle." In *Le catholicisme à l'épreuve dans la France du XVIe siècle,* 27–63. Paris: Cerf, 2000.

Viguerie, Jean de. *L'institution des enfants: L'éducation en France, XVIe–XVIIIe siècle.* Paris: Calmann-Lévy, 1978.

———. *Une oeuvre d'éducation sous l'ancien régime: Les Pères de la doctrine chrétienne en France et en Italie 1592–1792.* Paris: Éditions de la Nouvelle Aurore, 1976.

Weber, Eugen. *Peasants into Frenchmen: The Modernization of Rural France, 1870–1914.* Stanford: Stanford University Press, 1976.

Weber, Max. *The Protestant Ethic and the Spirit of Capitalism.* Translated by Talcott Parsons. London: Routledge, 2001.

Whaley, Joachim. *Religious Toleration and Social Change in Hamburg, 1529–1819.* Cambridge: Cambridge University Press, 1985.

Wiesner, Merry E. *Women and Gender in Early Modern Europe.* 2nd ed. Cambridge: Cambridge University Press, 2000.

Wiesner-Hanks, Merry E. *Gender in History.* Oxford: Oxford University Press, 2001.

Wolff, Philippe, ed. *Le diocèse de Toulouse.* Histoire des diocèses de France, no. 15. Paris: Beauchesne, 1983.

Wood, Diana, ed. *The Church and Childhood.* Cambridge: Blackwell, 1994.

Yates, Frances A. *The Art of Memory.* Chicago: University of Chicago Press, 1966.

Zeeden, Ernst Walter. "Grundlagen und Wege der Konfessionsbildung in Deutschland im Zeitalter der Glaubenskämpfe." *Historische Zeitschrift* 185 (1958): 249–99.

Index

Alleman de Montmartin, Ennemond (bishop of Grenoble), 75–77
Apostles' Creed, 4, 30–34, 41–44, 80
Aquinas, Thomas, 67
archbishops. *See* bishops
Ariès, Philippe, 62–63, 68, 245n3
Auger, Edmund, 30–31
Auxerre, diocese of, 9, 97, 103, 174, 205, 235n16

baptism, sacrament of, 2, 27, 93, 110, 129, 134, 223, 225; as a catechism topic, 35; and midwives, 117; and schoolmasters, 146
Barberin, Antoine (archbishop of Reims), 10
Bégon, Scipion Jérôme (bishop of Toul), 23, 61
Bellarmine, Robert, 31–32, 34
bishops, 104, 250n5; and catechetical education, 18, 25–26, 36–37, 69–77, 80, 86–93; and publication of catechisms, 8, 32–33, 239n4, 240n25; and reform, 9, 11, 17, 24, 58–59, 140, 250n7; relationship with schoolmasters,

3, 139–48; relationship with the laity, 8–11, 14, 17, 37, 115–17. *See also* pastoral visits
Bonal, François de (bishop of Clermont), 74
Borromeo, Charles, 25, 29, 248n78
Bossuet, Jacques Bénigne (bishop of Meaux), 41, 56, 76, 160

cahiers de doléances, 224–25
Calvin, John, 29–30
Canisius, Peter, 30–31, 35, 41, 240n23
casuel, 166, 225
catechism, 2–6, 25, 228, 234n10, 239n7, 241n26; content and organization, 4–5, 18, 33–37, 40–44; emphasis on behavior, 5, 26, 44–57, 60, 135, 228–29; gender distinctions, 7–8, 91–92; length of, 29, 31, 35–37, 241n31, 242n33; origins of, 26–33; and orthodoxy, 3, 7–8, 18, 19, 59, 71, 75; and pedagogy, 38–40, 45, 59–61, 69, 86–93; topical, 39–40, 49. *See also* education, religious; educational theory

Karen E. Carter

is assistant professor of history at Brigham Young University.